SUBURBIA

ITS PEOPLE AND THEIR POLITICS

SUBURBIA

ITS PEOPLE AND THEIR POLITICS

by Robert C. Wood

The Riverside Press Cambridge

HOUGHTON MIFFLIN COMPANY BOSTON

1959

To Peg, Franny, Mother, and Marg
who each, in her own way, provided
the incentives for writing

Preface

THIS IS another book about the American suburb and another criticism of the suburban character. It is, however, a different kind of book with a different kind of criticism.

Other studies have stressed the social aspects of the modern suburb, usually relying on an intensive investigation of a limited number of suburbs to support their conclusions. This investigation emphasizes suburban political ideology, its history, values and consequences, and so far as historical and statistical evidence allows, goes beyond the examination of the better-than-average dormitory town to consider other types of suburban communities.

A different interpretation results from this difference in emphasis and method. While earlier reports indicate that the suburb epitomizes modern culture, I have been more impressed by the suburban resistance to twentieth century ideals and values and by how consistently suburbanites look to the past for guidance. The longer the suburbs were studied, the more closely they seemed to me to represent long-established American traditions, although not necessarily the best of these traditions.

Although I have presented factual evidence for my major

conclusions, my colleagues in the field will recognize the incompleteness of data on which some of them are based. The lack of detailed information is especially evident as far as the patterns of suburban political behavior are concerned, and a fairly systematic effort to bring together the existing intelligence in the field, to include previously unpublished material and to undertake new research on a limited scale has not corrected this situation.

Incompleteness of data is an old story in the social sciences, of course, and meantime judgments must be rendered and decisions made in political and social life. Important judgments and decisions are being made about metropolitan areas and the governments in those areas today in the United States and by and large they are being made on the basis of a limited number of assumptions about what metropolitan life and politics represent. Because the available facts suggest another set of assumptions, it seems useful to bring them forward for consideration even though all the returns are not yet in.

Since the major aim is to indicate a new perspective by which the current problems of metropolitan regions can be seen, readability has seemed, at least to the editors, an important consideration. Therefore, notes and references for each chapter have been set aside in a separate section at the end of the book. The professional student may wish to refer to these before reading a chapter to see the basis for my general arguments.

To the extent that this limited foray is a success, the credit belongs to those who have contributed to its writing. Robert G. McCloskey of Harvard University and Alan K. Campbell of Hofstra College have, from the beginning, provided counsel, stimulation and encouragement. To them and to Dean Chester A. Hanford I am indebted for assistance which was quite beyond the normal bounds of friendship. Norton

A. Long of Northwestern University, Wallace Sayre of Columbia and Herbert Kaufman of Yale gave lucid and constructive criticism to each chapter. Lawrence Fuchs of Brandeis University, Abram Chayes of the Harvard Law School, Ernest May of Harvard University, Antonia Chayes and Alex Morin brought the insights of their special fields to bear with effective results. V. O. Key of Harvard and Daniel Lerner of the Massachusetts Institute of Technology were kind enough to review the chapters dealing with politics and sociology respectively and to save me from serious errors in fact and judgment. And although he was probably never aware of the fact, Raymond Vernon provided a continuous stream of provocative insights and suggestions throughout the time of writing. While none of my associates is responsible for the deficiencies of the book, they all worked strenuously to make it a better one.

Mrs. Gerta Kennedy made valiant efforts to provide a modicum of clarity and coherence in the manuscript, and Mrs. Samuel P. Huntington and Mrs. Walter C. Wood undertook its actual preparation. I did not always accept their comments and criticisms, but I always profited by them, and the final product was improved tremendously by their efforts.

I am also grateful for the encouragement of my parents, Thomas Frank and Mary Bradshaw Wood, who permitted a holiday to be marred so that the manuscript might begin. The greatest credit belongs to my wife, Margaret Byers Wood, who, throughout a year of increasingly unsettled home life, encouraged, criticized, soothed and insisted, as the need arose, with an almost uncanny sense of the appropriate moment.

A final word is due my friends and neighbors in my suburb, Lincoln. On balance, the judgment of the book is not favorable to suburbia and they may wonder why I choose to live in a place I criticize so strongly. The answer is simply

that my professional opinion should never be confused with
my personal tastes, and the fact that I recommend a general
philosophy and outlook as desirable does not mean that I
have succeeded in living by it. Lincoln is undoubtedly an
anachronism and it is probably obstructive to the larger purposes of the Boston region. But it is a very pleasant and hos-
pitable anachronism, and while it exists, I am quite happy
to indict myself.

ROBERT C. WOOD

Lincoln, Massachusetts

Contents

Part II

Part III

7. THE MINIATURE RE-EXAMINED

PART I

CHAPTER 1

The Image of Suburbia

Suburbia as Looking Glass

Strictly speaking, suburbs are places and suburbanites are people. Even more strictly speaking, suburbs are places in the country immediately outside a city and suburbanites are the inhabitants of that country. Suburbs depend upon the special technological advances of the age: the automobile and rapid transit line, asphalt pavement, delivery trucks, septic tanks, water mains, and motor-driven pumps. Suburbanites have habits which distinguish them more or less sharply from other Americans: they are commuters, they tend to own their own homes, which have at least some access to open space, and they have more children than the average American family. These definitions and characteristics indicate in concrete ways what suburbs and suburbanites are.

They do not, however, explain *why* suburbs exist, or, aside from simple progress, what accounts for the extraordinary explosion of our large cities into the countryside. To understand the underlying motives and aspirations which gave momentum to the massive shift of population another definition is necessary. We have to explain an abstraction, a concept of the mind, with elusive and subtle connotations. We have to explain "suburbia."

The most fashionable definition of suburbia today is that it is a looking glass in which the character, behavior, and culture of middle class America is displayed. When we look at suburbs we see our homes; when we look at suburbanites we see ourselves. Suburbia, according to this interpretation, reflects with fidelity modern man, his way of living, his institutions and beliefs, his family and his social associations. Because forty-seven million of us live in suburbs — more than in the cities or in isolated towns or on the farms — the suburbanite is, by statistical definition, the average American. Because over twelve million of us have moved to the suburbs in the last ten years — marking the greatest migration in the shortest time of the nation's history — the suburban trend should typify our contemporary way of life.

Many of the specialists who have looked carefully into the mirror find a man who is not appealing. The old images of national life seem to them to have disappeared; the stern Puritan, the sturdy yeoman, the hard-working capitalist are gone. In their place is a prototype whom it is difficult to idealize: a man without direction or ambition except for his desire for a certain portion of material security, a man so conscious of his fellows that he has no convictions of his own. Lacking the stern code of conduct of the "inner directed" man of the nineteenth century, separated from the Protestant ethic that maintained individuality fifty years ago, the suburbanite seeks direction from a passing parade of "experts" who, in the rapid succession of changing fashions, dictate the design of his house, the education of his children, the choice of his friends, and the use of his income. He willingly turns the direction of community affairs over to others. But since his neighbors are just as uncertain as he is, few real individualists appear to guide civic destinies. In the suburbs, in the opinion of its prominent investigators, the modern American exchanges individuality, privacy, the certain satisfactions of pride of craftsmanship and work well done, for something obscurely defined as the social ethic, being a good fellow, and group cooperation.

In this context, the suburb is the home of the modern man, the big organization on his doorstep. Suburban culture and the pattern of suburban life are designed to intensify the pressures on the individual. They encourage conformity, and subtly rearrange the use of space and time, the relations of the family, the activities of social and political organizations for the higher purpose of "the group." Each characteristic and institution of suburban life bears witness to the fact that David Riesman's lonely crowd is everywhere.

Thus, John Seeley and his associates point out that the suburbanite lives not in a house that expresses his individuality or that blends landscape and architecture to emphasize man's oneness with nature. Instead, he builds a house which expresses values of real estate experts but never his own, or he settles in a big development constructed on too little land. In either case, except for trivial detail, he builds his house as much like his neighbor's as possible. He whistles up the bulldozers, in John Keats' words, "to knock down all the trees, bat the lumps off the terrain, and level the ensuing desolation." He becomes lost in "squads and platoons" of little boxes on concrete slabs each surrounded by "a patch of bilious sod and two rusty dwarf cedars struggling for life beside each identical doorstep." If income permits, the houses are larger, though their lots are proportionately the same, and crammed with mechanical conveniences that testify to a preoccupation with consumption. They are arranged to "stage" elaborate displays of entertainment, built to encourage family and neighborhood sociability, erected as symbols of ma-

terial well-being. The disappearance of clean styles of architecture, the rise of the modified Cape Cod–ranch-type Colonials, their uniform reproduction row on row, the violence
done to the natural terrain — all these are taken to document "togetherness," the new social ethic in practice.

The use of time in the suburbs is described as a further
indication of the new America. Most observers find an im-
placable array of schedules which seem to testify to the suburbanite's inability to live as an individual and as he chooses.
The commuter schedule for the husband, the nursery and
social schedule for the wife, the school day for the growing
child, these govern suburban life relentlessly. There are no
longer any options, but instead unbreakable patterns for the
day, the week, the year, and the generation. Time spent going to and from work, time spent in hauling children, time
spent in class, the weekday for work, the weekend for "career
maneuvering" or "improving" social status, all are by the
clock. To the reporters of Crestwood Heights, one of the
suburbs most meticulously observed, time is apparently the
master of each and every inhabitant. Endlessly active, constantly harassed, the suburbanite hurries everywhere, caught
up in a chain of events never of his own making but from
which he cannot withdraw. He is plunged into a "hotbed of
participation," an endless circle of meetings, appointments,
arrivals, departures, and consultations.

Suburban institutions provide further ammunition for the
looking-glass theory. They are shown as monuments of a
society in which each member is attuned to the others but
never to himself. The school emerges as the all-important
focus of existence, and from the school, to children and parents alike, comes the constant message of "life adjustment."
As "opinion leaders," teachers strive to inculcate cooperation, belongingness, togetherness. Courses aim at "social-
izing" the child through a process by which he learns specific

skills at the same time that he is taught to use them only in an overtly friendly manner. Competition is subdued; so is individuality; the cry is for a common outlook, and discipline is achieved by indirect measures of ostracism. The generalization has even been made that by the time he gets to college, a suburban student chooses his career in business administration or science, where there are human relations to be cultivated or where there are facts, but where there are never values.

The aim of learning to get along with others, of advancing oneself only as a member of the group, infects, it is said, family life and leisure hours. The commuter father is no longer the figure of authority; stern measures of discipline are not countenanced, and even if they were, the father is not home enough to use them in the proper time and place. Although family life is "important," and love and constant association are expected, the means for holding the family together are obscure. It is left to the mother and the schools, and the experts on whom both rely, to rear the child and run the suburb. Educated women, wanting motherhood but expecting something more, anxious to put their talents to use beyond the family circle, are in charge. Skipping from one meeting to another, indulging or wanting to indulge in extramarital affairs, ceaselessly expunging their feelings of guilt by overprotecting their children, they rule suburbia. So the desires and demands of children — space for their play, their training, their future careers, their happiness — become the predominant force in suburbia.

The decline of individuality is also found, according to most reports, in adult associations and activities. Suburban friendships are determined, by and large, by the physical layout of the neighborhoods in which they take place, or dictated by career maneuvering necessary in big-organization office politics. In the politics of public life, suburbanites are passive consumers of the national issues of the day or "inside-dopesters" on what the issues really are. On the local scene their political activity is frenzied but ineffective, for suburbanites are always ultimately manipulated by the shrewd, calculating developer, the old residents, or the school superintendent.

From this pattern of character, space, time, and the interaction of these institutions and beliefs, most observers go on to say, has come a new type of culture. Self-consciously friendly, in constant association, afraid or unable to differentiate themselves from their neighbors, the suburban residents form a classless society. Suburbia is a melting pot of executives, managers, white-collar workers, successful or unsuccessful, who may be distinguished only by subtle variations in the cars they drive, the number of bedrooms in their houses, or the tables they set. Their consumption is inconspicuous because they cannot deviate too far from the standards of their neighbors — but for the same reason it has a common quality. It is never ceasing, and for almost all suburbanites, time payments for purchases in an already overextended budget have replaced the savings account.

By this interpretation the life of suburbanites is "outgoing" in the sense that, lacking internal resources, they search for status and reassurance from the group around them, and that life is pathetic in the same sense. A fundamental transformation of American society is in full swing, and since the suburbs are seen to represent the transformation with such fidelity, they should be taken as the symbol and sign of the future.

Holdouts in Suburbia

Intriguing as the looking-glass interpretation is, it cannot be taken as a precise definition of suburbia. It is more a commentary on middle class Americans wherever they live: on the farms now equipped with central heating and television, within the city limits, in Peyton Place, Middletown updated, or the growing Southern town absorbing the second industrial revolution in the United States. As a generalization, the group-man theory is far too sweeping to take into account the suburbs which are not residential. It cannot explain the industrial suburb, where more people work than live, the slum suburb, deserted by the middle class and fallen on evil days, the racetrack suburb, the honky-tonk suburb of night clubs, amusement parks and used-car lots. It deals only with the dormitory suburb, and principally with the better type of dormitory suburb.

Even in the residential suburb, there are limitations to the theory. Against the broad wave of mass culture, mass values, and mass society, there is at least one stubborn holdout. While residential suburban living and individual suburbanites may represent modern character and behavior, their suburban governments do not. They join the other suburban political units around our large cities in clinging persistently to the independence they received when they were isolated villages and hamlets in a rustic countryside. If the suburb is a brand new development taking the place of forest or potato farm, the inhabitants insist on creating governments modeled after their older autonomous neighbors. These rural neighbors, far from acquiescing to the cult of size, turn their backs on progress and resist the influences of modernity. Though they accept the homes of the organization man, they insist on retaining the legal form and the public institutions which are relics of a bygone age.

This superimposition of provincial government on cosmopolitan people provides a strange pattern of incongruity. Within the single economic and social complex we have come to call a metropolitan area, hundreds and hundreds of local governments jostle one another about. Counties overlie school districts, which overlie municipalities, which overlie sanitary and water districts, which sometimes overlie townships and villages. Except for the special-purpose "districts," each suburban government maintains its own police force, its fire station, its health department, its library, its welfare service. Each retains its authority to enact ordinances, hold elections, zone land, raise taxes, grant building licenses, borrow money, and fix speed limits.

The spectacle of these ancient jurisdictions careening merrily on their way is often amusing and more frequently disturbing. By ordinary standards of effective, responsible public services, the mosaic of suburban principalities creates governmental havoc. Across a typical suburban terrain, twenty or thirty or fifty volunteer fire departments buy equipment and, with varying degrees of efficiency, put out fires. A welter of semi-professional police forces, usually poorly equipped and inadequately staffed, jealously compete or lackadaisically cooperate, uncertain of the limits of their jurisdiction. Independent school systems build costly plants, some crammed to capacity, others with excess space. In one municipality the water table dips perilously low; in another, foresighted or fortunate enough to have access to a reservoir, sprinklers turn all summer long. And, always, for suburban governments taken together, there is the extra and apparently unnecessary cost of doing individually what might be done collectively: the additional expense of making separate purchases without benefit of quantity discounts, of administrative and political overhead, of holding local elections and hiring city managers, of reporting, accounting, and auditing these separate activities.

The anachronisms of suburban governments have long been apparent and long decried. For almost half a century, the conditions of inefficiency, confusion, duplication, over-

lapping and waste have been under fire. For at least twenty-
five years, reform movement after reform movement has
moved against the antiquated political structures, proposing
their consolidation, advancing one scheme after another to
bring together their conflicting activities. Again and again
the call has rung out for a king-sized government to fit the
king-sized metropolitan community. Some critics emphasize
the inequities of tax burdens and public services among
the suburbs, some point to their incapacity to solve common
problems of water supply and mass transportation, some
underscore the absence of a responsible region-wide political
process and system of representation. All condemn the com-
pounding of confusion which the array of municipalities,
boroughs, and districts brings about as they play hob with
the orderly provision of municipal services and public
finance.

Yet with extraordinarily few exceptions the ranks of suburban governments hold fast. They cling to their independence, stand successfully against the demands for efficiency and
economy, and resist the lure of the big organization. More
numerous than at any time in our history, their boundaries
bursting with new inhabitants, their administrative and tax
structure apparently strained to capacity or beyond, suburban political institutions remain adamant. They reject the
prospect of consolidation with the larger society; they continue to hold out when every other influence in modern life
calls for their absorption.

Suburbia as Renaissance

The paradox which suburban government presents to suburban society sharply limits the theory of suburbia as the
looking glass and suburbanites as the advance guard of the
new America. A social order apparently built upon a com-

mitment to the virtues of large organizations, indoctrinated to the advantages of size and scale, still tolerates tiny, ineffective governments which seem almost willfully bent on producing chaos, and which are still multiplying. As political entities, suburbs represent an order unwilling to join in the change going on about them; they flout the modern ideology attributed to suburban man.

They flout this ideology, moreover, by raising an ancient and honorable standard straight out of American political folklore. The justification of suburban legal independence rests on the classic belief in grassroots democracy, our long-standing conviction that small political units represent the purest expression of popular rule, that the government closest to home is best. The defense of suburban autonomy is that no voter is a faceless member in a political rally, but an individual citizen who knows his elected officials, can judge their performance personally and hold them accountable.

In the suburb, according to the folklore, the school board is likely to be composed of neighbors or friends, or at least friends of friends or neighbors of neighbors. Its members do not come from another part of a large city; they are available and accessible. So are the mayor, the county clerk, the commissioners, the councilmen, and selectmen. So are the chief of police, the water superintendent, the plumbing inspector, and the health officers. In this way, elected officials, bureaucrats, party leaders — the entire apparatus of democratic politics — are exposed to view, recognized and approached as they never are in a great metropolis. In politics, the suburb dwellers hold fast to a conviction that the small organization, run by a group of relatively few individuals, provides the best management of public affairs that is possible.

The strength of this conviction has been powerful enough, at least to date, to blunt the edge of all the reform efforts to bring suburban governments into the twentieth century. In spite of statistics indicating that the metropolitan area in which suburbia exists is actually a single community, in spite of the obvious organizational chaos brought on by this political multiplicity, even the most ardent efficiency expert hesitates to deny the values small governments represent. Instead of recommending outright abolition of suburban jurisdictions, he presents one ingenious scheme after another — federations, special authorities, new systems of representation, new complexities of local government — designed to provide some measure of administrative rationality while still maintaining suburban autonomy. At rock bottom he accepts the value of small size and he works to preserve the suburb as a legal entity even if its powers must be reduced in the face of the realities of the modern world.

So, as yet there is little sign that this array of small municipalities merely represents a cultural lag. On the contrary, the statistics point in exactly the opposite direction, for every census report shows more — and smaller — and more self-consciously independent suburban governments than existed ten years earlier. And those which the looking-glass theory selects as the best examples of the home of modern man are also the ones which exhibit the most independent political institutions.

There are also signs that this renaissance of small-scale autonomy is not confined to suburban governments alone. Even the most confirmed advocate of the New American Character still finds signs of small town behavior throughout the suburbs he studies. So William H. Whyte, Jr., in investigating the organization man at home, discovers two sides to every coin he examines, notes something old as well as something new, remains ambivalent in his judgment of the suburb in a way which contrasts sharply with his indictment of the organizational world in general.

Whyte's residents are, of course, transients, newcomers to the town in which they live, and they are soon to move on to other, better suburbs. Nonetheless, they try to put down roots and they succeed to some degree; even though the roots are shallow. To Whyte there is something admirable in the vigor with which they respond to the advertisements that call their suburb a friendly small town, as contrasted to the lonely big city, and in the way they work to make the advertisement a reality. The suburbanite penchant for joining his neighbors to agitate against the town hall indifference and the developer may be participation for participation's sake, but it also may express citizenship of the highest sort. Small roots are better than none, civic spirit is to be preferred to apathy, and the chance to "chew on real problems" in public affairs is desirable, for it creates allegiances that have purpose.

Whyte does not scorn community affairs then. He approves of the suburbanite's self-conscious efforts to guide his town's future, even though he is only passing through and cannot stay to enjoy it. It is still an indication of older values, however sugar-coated in new jargon, and so is the classlessness of his suburbia. The melting-pot analogy is, after all, another cherished American ideal. It seems a laudable fact that the suburb often promotes better understanding among inhabitants with different ethnic origins, religions, and backgrounds, even though they are all within the middle class, that it helps prevent the emergence of classes and furthers the ideal of equality. It is to be preferred to the jarring hostility of groups wrangling among themselves in the large cities and it is a sign of small town life as it has always been known.

The pattern of inconspicuous consumption, the web of friendship, and the outgoing life that Whyte describes also have something of the flavor of a renaissance. Although "keeping down with the Joneses" may indicate group tyranny, it is still better than keeping up with them. At least it displays disapproval of overt snobbishness and obvious symptoms of city superciliousness; it harks back once again to the frontier spirit of equality. While suburbanites should probably manage their budgets more prudently than they do, at least their desire for improvement and progress is a sturdy American trait. Even suburban friendships have their admirable qualities so far as the observers are concerned. They may be largely determined by the location of play areas, the placement of driveways and lawns, and the size of the living room, and they may impose a surveillance that makes privacy clandestine and the way of the introvert hard. But here are old-time qualities of warmth, helpfulness, and service to others. While Whyte finds pressures for benevolent conformity, he also discovers brotherhood. He sees that the church may have sacrificed theology for acceptance and the school may stress adjustment at the expense of the liberal arts, but he sees also that it is good to have churches and schools. These provide a sense of community, institutions that are socially useful, and it is not surprising that in the end Whyte speaks of his suburbanites as pioneers.

Even more impressive than the fragments of small town culture still persisting in the suburb is the ideal that every analyst of suburbia seems to cherish of what suburbia ought to be. There is a special temper in the rage which the looking-glass philosopher expresses when he uncovers the organization man at home, for to him there is a special irony and incongruity in making the suburb synonymous with modern life.

John Keats sketches the idealized suburb most clearly. Following Mary and John Drone through their weary succession of inadequate, overpriced homes in suburbs inhabited by directionless people who do not know they are unhappy, he is angry not at suburbia but at what has been done to it. He objects not a whit to the popular demand for space, for relatively small neighborhoods, for private homes, for roots, however temporary. He protests only against the degradation of these aspirations by greedy, selfish contractors and by the foolish, undisciplined residents themselves. He describes developments, and he wants communities.

Keats' prescription is not to tear suburbia apart, but to build it better. He wants homes arranged so that the illusions of privacy and aesthetics can be cultivated in small space. He wants suburbanites to join together to build libraries and swimming pools, where truly useful and common purposes are served. He would encourage the flight from the city so long as it is properly done, with taste and recognition of family budgetary limits and with awareness of the public problems to be faced. He would surround with regulations and controls the builder who remains the sturdy nineteenth century individualist and is responsible for the damage suburbs do. What suburbia ought to be, for Keats, is a carefully designed constellation of small towns, each with its own community center, each self-contained, each controlling its local affairs at the local level with polite regard for the larger region to which it belongs.

The small town, the small community, this is what seems good about the suburb to most observers, what needs to be preserved, and what the large organization should not be permitted to despoil. Spontaneous collaboration, voluntary neighborliness, purposeful participation, these are the goals of real suburbanites. And all of the observers seem to cherish the hope that in the suburbs we can re-create the small

communities we have lost in our industrial sprawl since the
Civil War. The irony they find is that our suburbanites do
not discriminate between the type of association a small
town can give and that which Madison Avenue promotes.
The ambivalence of Whyte is genuine; to him suburban virtues lie in the degree to which the suburb approximates
the small town, and vices lie in deviation from this ideal.
The image of the small community shines through the condemnation of modern life. If it is faithful to this ideal, the
suburb may save us all from the artificial group without re-
establishing the unpalatable culture of the rugged individualist.

Even the harshest critic of our modern suburb is not insensitive to this appeal. Although the great organization seems
essential to contemporary society, and the pressures of mass
society appear overwhelming, no analysis counsels surrender.
For the most pessimistic there is, it seems, still a chance for
an individual to fight the organization, even if he has to
cheat. And the best way to fight is on home ground where the
suburbanite can try to fuse the political ideology of the small
government with the social mores of the small community.

Thus, while the looking-glass theory protests the onrush of
modern culture, it takes comfort in the hope that suburbia
can somehow hold out against it. It is encouraged by the possibility that the suburbs may break up the sprawling metropolitan area into discrete units distributing here an industrial area, here a low-income neighborhood, here a retail center, here an exclusive residential area, but everywhere permitting a closer communion within the small localities. It
applauds newspaper editorials which warn against making
governments and communities "so big that no one counts"
and speaks out for "the concept of people working together
in identifiable units in a community with a cohesive past

and future . . . of which the individual can feel a part and for the life of which he can feel a sense of participation and responsibility."

These hopes are imperfectly realized today, of course; modern circumstances always threaten them and frequently combine to subvert them. But the vision is powerful; it helps move the ordinary citizen to suburbia, the sociologist to protect it, and the political scientist to preserve it. The ancient symbol of the "republic in miniature" persists, and the suburb is its contemporary expression. For all our changes in culture and behavior, for all the heavy price we pay in inadequate local public services, nonexistent metropolitan services, and high taxes, the good life and the good government still come for us in small packages. Although minimum adjustments to the demands of urban life must be made, it seems the job of the suburb, either by social resistance or political compromise, to ensure the preservation of these values.

Suburbia, defined as an ideology, a faith in communities of limited size and a belief in the conditions of intimacy, is quite real. The dominance of the old values explains more about the people and the politics of the suburbs than any other interpretation. Fundamentally, it explains the nature of the American metropolis. It indicates why our large urban complexes are built as they are, why their inhabitants live the way they do, and why public programs are carried out the way they are. If these values were not dominant it would be quite possible to conceive of a single gigantic metropolitan region under one government and socially conscious of itself as one community. The new social ethic, the rise of the large organization, would lead us to expect this development as a natural one. The automobile, the subway, the telephone, the power line certainly make it technically possible; they even push us in this direction.

But the American metropolis is not constructed in such a way; it sets its face directly against modernity. Those who wish to rebuild the American city, who protest the shapeless urban sprawl, who find some value in the organizational skills of modern society must recognize the potency of the ideology. Until these beliefs have been accommodated reform will not come in the metropolitan areas nor will men buckle down to the task of directing, in a manner consonant with freedom, the great political and social organizations on which the nation's strength depends. A theory of community and a theory of local government are at odds with the prerequisites of contemporary life and, so far, theory has been the crucial force that preserves the suburb. There is no economic reason for its existence and there is no technological basis for its support. There is only the stubborn conviction of the majority of suburbanites that it ought to exist, even though it plays havoc with both the life and government of our urban age.

CHAPTER 2

Roots for the Image

The American Miniature

If a belief in small government and small society helps explain why the modern suburb exists in an age of bigness, the suburban renaissance should not be surprising. The conviction that provincial life is best has been with us for a long time and it has endured in the face of greater attacks than the ones contemporary America presents. We show our instinctive commitment to the ideology by the fact that we rarely examine its assumptions critically. We show our conscious allegiance by the oratorical homage we pay to the ideal of small neighborhoods, single homes, and political jurisdictions of limited size.

It is difficult to overestimate the vigor and pervasiveness of the belief. Three centuries stand behind the heritage — a full two hundred years of spectacular success and one hundred years of abject failure. The first period endowed the American cult of localism with its basic articles of faith: an assertion that local communities should maintain their own identity and manage their own affairs, and a justification for that assertion by the claim that the small society is the natural home of democracy. The last hundred years added endurance and stubbornness to the ideal by the very adversity which the reality of the urban world inflicted upon it. But whether made confident by success or contentious by disaster, the creed has remained to shape the American metropolis and make it what it is today.

Not the least of the reasons for the strength of the ideology is in its natural partiality to the American habitat. Grassroots life existed in fact in the United States long before the justification for its existence was ever articulated. The first settlements on the new continent were by necessity small and relatively isolated, and the characteristics usually associated with small town life developed spontaneously. Colonial conditions led to a similarity of interests, and a sharing of customs, aims and ambitions. Some degree of economic interdependence and equality, a constant recognition of a vast, unexplored land beyond the frontier outposts, close daily contact, bred early a conscious sense of community identity.

Under these social circumstances, nothing was more natural than the independence in fact, if not in legal theory, of local political institutions. Technically speaking, the first New England towns relied on grants of power from the Massachusetts Bay Company and later from the colonial legislature. Early settlements in the other colonies used the medieval corporation as the model for their authority. But in actual fact, colonial towns exercised independently the essential powers of police and taxation, and were, from the beginning, self-governing. They were independent because there was no other alternative; local authority stemmed from "the exercise of English common sense combined with the circumstance of the place."

Not only were the towns possessed with self-conscious identity, but by any standard of seventeenth century life, their political institutions seemed democratic. Small groups of people, barely sustaining themselves economically and faced with constant dangers, congregated without forethought to discuss common affairs. They elected their own officials, and these officials knew they were accountable to the citizens. In Lane Lancaster's words:

"The original government of the New England town was that of a pure democracy. We may well admit that it was inquisitive and gossipy, that it gave too liberal rein to the crank, the bore, the windbag and the troublemaker, that it put a premium upon talk, and that it was tolerant of somnolent administration. But in spite of these defects, it had the sovereign merit of bringing the rulers and the ruled together, it made easy the ventilation of grievances, it encouraged an intelligent and disinterested attitude toward public questions, and it fostered at its best a keen sense of the reality of the community."

This state of affairs usually contrasted sharply with contemporary conditions in the Old World, though the forms of local social organization and government appeared similar and scholars later sought to trace the principle of local autonomy back to the rights accorded English boroughs and before them to Teutonic and ecclesiastical sources. Yet no European locality, however consciously a community, exhibited the autonomy and democracy of its American counterpart.

Even in England the parish of the seventeenth century, that mixture of church and secular authority, could not parallel the colonial experience. Theoretically, all members of the parish had their say in civic management, but actually only the "most substantial" exercised authority. Nor was the second unit of English local organization, the manor, a truer expression of the local will. In this jurisdiction the eminent landlord of the area presided aristocratically as justice of the peace and principal officer of the countryside. At the county

level, no pretense of local autonomy or democracy was maintained: the lord lieutenant, the high sheriff, and the justice
of the peace were appointed by the king from among the
county gentry. While the American localities moved toward
increasing autonomy, comparable English governments remained oligarchies, organs of "local obligation," "thoroughly
undemocratic and thoroughly responsible."

From the middle of the seventeenth century to well into
the nineteenth, local communities in America ran their
own affairs, by and large, and ran them by a popular political process. Along the entire Atlantic seaboard, counties,
cities, towns and villages tackled energetically the problems
of land disposition, the regulation of commerce, public
health, law enforcement, fire protection, building control,
and education. The manageable size of even the largest colonial city and its relative isolation allowed the town fathers to
behave both decisively and responsibly; the New England
selectmen might seem to have "the broad finality of dictatorship in local matters," but "the spirit of their service
resembles the humblest agent . . . thoroughly and publicly checked."

Even the Revolution and the subsequent establishment
of state authority by the Constitution did not seriously affect
these prerogatives. Although the states were granted legal
control over public activities below the national level, their
authority existed mainly in the law books. The exercise of
government, in fact, depended on the town and county. It
was the local unit which, almost to the Civil War, collected
the taxes, established the schools, cared for the poor, maintained the roads — in short, which exercised the responsibility for prime community endeavors. Practice and habit
kept local democracy strong, even when legal independence
was denied.

Of course, neither perfect autonomy nor pure democracy, even of the character sanctioned by the times, was ever completely realized. So far as political institutions were concerned, the structures which were later to define suburbia were sometimes hobbled at the very start. In the case of Charlestown, for example, the colonial government interfered so continually and so closely in local affairs that genuine self-government never developed and the legacy of legislative dominance continues in South Carolina to this day. For the larger cities, the medieval corporation was everywhere an imperfect model and never provided all the powers needed properly to direct municipal growth.

So far as popular control was concerned, both formally and informally there were limitations on democracy. Almost immediately after settlement the ministry and the merchants exercised disproportionate influence, and property restrictions limited participation. In New England there was a distinction between the freeman and the inhabitant in the early town meeting, and in other colonies the voting electorate was even more narrowly defined. There was also, throughout the colonies, class conflict — accusations that social position rather than numbers was decisive in the management of town affairs. A tendency toward tight political dominance by a few, a forerunner of city machines, could be discerned in Boston, New York, Philadelphia, and Charlestown by 1700, and editors and ministers could thunder against cliques and individual misuse of public authority generations before the Constitution.

These aberrations were real enough, and not to be discounted in painting an accurate picture of colonial life in the United States. The fact remains, however, that the predominant tendency was toward autonomy and democracy, and in sufficient measure so that when men came to rationalize these institutions the characteristics they recognized were distinctively these two. The schoolboy's conception of the American miniature republic is right, by and large, when applied to our early history.

When the abstractions about localism began to appear, then, there was historical precedent and a tradition of actual practice on which to rest the case. And the eloquence and distinction of the men who chose to advance its cause added luster to the theory. Jefferson before the Revolution, Tocqueville afterward — what better advocates could be imagined to hand on the faith to coming generations?

It was Jefferson who first proclaimed the superiority of the New England town and urged the rest of the nation to follow this example. "Those wards," he wrote, "called townships in New England, are vital principles of their governments, and have proved themselves the wisest inventions ever devised by the wit of man for the perfect exercise of self-government. Each ward would be a small republic within itself and every man in the State would thus become an active member of the common government, transacting in person a great portion of its rights and duties, subordinate indeed, yet important and entirely within his competence."

No contemporary disputed Jefferson's opinion. The founding fathers found the local governments in being when they met to organize the nation. In drafting the new state constitutions, sometimes the legal authorities of the large municipalities were revised. The new doctrine of the separation of powers was occasionally extended downward, apparently stimulated as much by a desire to carry logic to its ultimate conclusion as to correct deficiencies. But the new Congress showed its approval of the basic pattern of local government in the Northwest Ordinance of 1789, when it established the township as the basic unit in the new territory and decreed its universality.

Forty years later Tocqueville found the image flourishing.

He was in error when he asserted that American political authority originated in the township and that municipal independence was a natural consequence of the sovereignty of the people. But in actual practice, he was close to the truth — close enough, at any rate, so that his generalizations sounded right to his generation and to ours. His unbounded enthusiasm reinforced and extended Jefferson's early claims. To Tocqueville, the careful deference paid to local autonomy within the federal system was the secret of American political success. On the one hand, it permitted a centralized government of sufficient power to face world problems. On the other, it required decentralized administration, which precluded usurpation.

But even more important than institutional checks and balances, this pattern of government set benign influences to work upon the people and their social life. The dissemination of power, Tocqueville was certain, created a town spirit which civilized all who felt its touch, stimulating affection rather than ambition and reason in place of emotion. To him, "the township, at the center of the ordinary relations of life, serves as a field for the desire of public esteem, the want of exciting interest, and the taste for authority and popularity; and the passions which commonly embroil society change their character, when they find a vent so near the domestic hearth and family circle." Thus "provincial" institutions became the best protection against despotism or the license of mob, for otherwise, "How can a populace, unaccustomed to freedom in small concerns, learn to use it temperately in great affairs?" In short, vigorous small governments enhanced the influence of small communities, and small communities, by their very nature, brought out the best in man, the qualities of reason and good will on which a Lockian commonwealth was based.

So the image crystallized. Small communities apparently experienced the sense of self-identity, the compactness, the self-sufficiency necessary to produce interdependence and equality and the sharing of common values and objectives. Given these circumstances, their governments should be independent, positive and aggressive, asserting their claim to all the powers and prerogatives they could possibly exercise, with a minimum of supervision and restraint.

Small towns deserved their autonomy because they were the natural home of democracy. Only in small governments could each man participate effectively, not in selfish pursuit of his own interests but with the capacity to understand the problems his community faced and thus further the common good. Independent local governments had legitimate claims to power because they were closest to home. And in the early days of the nation, the concept of home, of distinct social groupings, discrete social systems, was real and tangible. Small town life was the American way because there was, beyond the seaports, literally no other method to organize communal existence.

In this way the miniature republic was established, beginning as institution and rationalized brilliantly as a theory of how government and society actually did operate and should operate in America. Because initially it worked, and worked well, and because it was sanctioned by illustrious native philosophers and distinguished foreign observers, it has been, like all beliefs so established, a powerful force. Since its logic was simple, consisting of only two parts, easily grasped and instinctively felt by every man, its force expanded exponentially. With no other better way at hand for organizing government, the prospects for serious criticism of its propositions diminished, also exponentially. With the passing of the years, the conditions under which the working principles of

autonomy and direct democracy were first established became obscure and hardly recognized; only the principles
themselves remained in view. In this way, the image became
a legacy, and like all legacies, was accepted as something precious and therefore useful for each generation.

When men receive legacies under new conditions of society, they are more prone to try to adjust their circumstances
so that the bequest may be applied than to abandon their
inheritance. This has been done in many areas of American
government and social life; our founding fathers were so successful that they have often inhibited our own search for
success. It was true with a vengeance in the case of Jefferson's miniature republic. When alternatives for the organization of local government and local communities arose,
we could not see them. For a hundred years, we strove to
make the facts fit the beliefs, never pausing to consider the
possibility that the legacy itself was no longer precious.

The Miniature Under Pressure

Jacksonian economics provided the first crucible in which
the proposition that every locality was democratic and therefore every locality should be a thing in itself was tested. Jacksonian democracy provided the institutional modifications
that strove to keep the proposition intact. Even before the
Revolution, the larger commercial cities and towns had
found it difficult to pose as small communities and to maintain the processes of direct intercourse, political and social,
among all their citizens. Boston, in 1822, was the last to
abandon the town meeting and capitulate, with hesitation
and reluctance, to representative government. But if institutional modifications were necessary for the dozen great
settlements, they were, in so far as possible, in keeping with
the precepts of the past. If every man could not attend town

meeting, still more men were allowed to vote. If more offices than those of selectmen and justice of the peace were required, the path to office remained the same as in the old colonial community — by direct election. Deviations, down to the Jacksonian era, were few.

By the 1830's, however, intimations of urbanization were appearing, and commercial activities were taking second place to the manufacturing function of the cities. The new industrial life of the nation meant a steady increase in population of the largest municipalities. By 1840, New York counted 312,000 residents, Philadelphia, 220,000, Baltimore, 102,000, and Boston 93,000. Mill towns and industrial towns dotted the seaboard, Massachusetts leading the way with almost two thirds of the nation's textile factories operating within its borders.

City problems multiplied at an astonishing rate. The provision and maintenance of the most basic public utilities, of law and order, and the regulation of housing and commerce — all previously well within the competence of local government — now became increasingly difficult to effect. Slums appeared, as wretched as in any European city; congestion, disorder, blight, all furnished ammunition for the recitation of workingmen's grievances and their inclusion in national party and union demands. The first large-scale immigration of the poor and ignorant added to the difficulties of the cities and mill towns, with racial and religious antagonism flaring in bitter street fights and vandalism.

Not only were industrial growing pains raising awkward questions about the capacity of autonomous municipalities to protect person and property and provide essential services, but the image of the town as a neighborhood of friendly folk was itself under pressure. The melting pot was only beginning to bubble, and large portions of its mix were still

insoluble. Evidence of class conflict — merchant against
farmer, manufacturer against mechanic — grew, and the disruptive members of local society were no longer only sailors,
vagrants, bondsmen, and prostitutes. Urban life became
more and more impersonal; the moral code of the new en-
trepreneur now made its first tentative excursions into communal affairs and its first uneasy alliance with immigrant
leaders.

The substance of local politics swiftly deteriorated. In
New York Tammany Hall completed its transition from a
patriotic and fraternal society to a partisan and political one,
and perfected the most obvious tactics of election manipulation and administrative fraud. Mike Walsh personified the
new people's politician, exhibiting "on the one hand, an
honest fervor for popular rights; on the other, the methods
of an accomplished political gangster."

Even the staunchest defender of the local tradition reeled
under those blows. Charles Francis Adams could write
bleakly of the conditions of Massachusetts town government
in the 1830's.

"In the town, as in the nation, the process of absorption
and amalgamation was now to be gone through with. The
inrush of foreign elements had been too rapid. It tended to
upset everything . . . It was a change also for the worse.
The old order of things was doubtless slow, conservative,
traditional; but it was economical, simple and businesslike.
The new order of things was in all respects the reverse. The
leaders in it prided themselves on their enterprise, their lack
of reverence for tradition, their confidence in themselves;
but they were noisy, unmethodical, in reality incompetent,
and much too often intemperate."

Yet although unmistakable danger signals were flying, the
image of what American localities should be was not shat-
tered. Most local communities remained self-governing, and

by a strenuous exercise of logic they could argue that the overthrow of the old town fathers constituted the removal of aristocratic elements in local government. Jacksonian tenets of government by the common man and universal manhood suffrage were substituted as new means to the same democratic end.

The broadening of the electorate, the proclamation that any man could serve effectively in public office, resulted in the long ballot and short term in municipal governments across the land. The office of the mayor became elective, and rapidly other administrative offices were made directly responsible to the people. Independent commissions multiplied, as a direct consequence of the desire for public supervision of what could not be done by the public itself. The power of municipal councils was expanded in the cities at the expense of the executive, and a dispersion of responsibilities took place among innumerable boards, agencies, and ex-officio positions. Direct public participation might no longer be manageable, but the most radical concept of representation expressed itself forcibly in local governments. By and large, there was no institutional evidence of any distrust of the ordinary citizen as a man sincerely devoted to the best interests of his town, no formal recognition of the potential impact of spoils and parties, and no abdication of municipal powers.

Moreover, even as evidence of the divergence between image and reality mounted, observers could still argue that city life was tolerable, or could be made so. Although Charles Dickens saw New York as "low, flat and straggling . . . a city without baths or plumbing, lighted by gas and scavenged by pigs," the rudiments of public services continued. Beginnings were made in transforming the colonial constable and night watch into police forces; water supply facilities were passably adequate; public sewers began to supersede privately owned drains; oil and gas street lights appeared; streets were cleaned more frequently, sidewalks constructed, and fire protection by volunteer companies continued. The free public school system continued to expand, though too slowly to keep pace with the mounting population, and here and there even land reservations for parks and recreation appeared. Men of social vision, like Francis Lowell, strove to prove by their model factories that it was possible to maintain civilized behavior by educating the newly immigrated. The role of the better classes in communal affairs was restricted, to be sure, but it seemed at least possible that Emerson's requirement for "restless prying, conscientious criticism" could be cultivated among the masses.

The defenders of local autonomy and democracy had a final argument for the perpetuation of their principles. The rush to the cities might be larger in number than the western migration at that time, but the town and city population was well under 10 per cent of the nation's total. The United States was still rural, and farm and woodland dominated the landscape. For most of America's local governments, in the counties, towns and townships, Jackson's common man was as capable in government as his colonial predecessor, since both shared backwoods life. "The average man," Croly observed, "without any special qualification was, in the pioneer states, the useful man. In that country it was sheer waste to spend much energy upon tasks which demanded skill, prolonged experience, high technical standards, or exclusive devotion. The cheaply and easily made instrument was the effective instrument and for the service of such tools one man was likely to be as good as another." The inhabitant of the small hamlet escaped the mounting pressures of urban life because he was still a part of the legacy itself.

While by 1850 no one could deny the strain placed on larger local governments, the burdens seemed manageable. The principles of radical democracy might be increasingly dubious, but they were not disproved outright. The assumption still held that each citizen gave his best efforts to his government, and one interpretation even claimed that the precepts of provincial democracy were merely being extended to the state and national level. City problems multiplied, but no breaking point had been reached. In the bright new mill towns and factory villages and the booming new cities of the Midwest the opportunity for effective government seemed real. By and large, local communities showed signs of accommodation to demands for more responsibility and more democracy appropriate to the age. If the miniature republic was not working well, it was still working.

The Miniature Cracks

The gamble that the old ideal could be accommodated to the new conditions did not pay off. At least in its political aspects, the nation grew too rapidly to let the transition from Jeffersonian to Jacksonian precepts be completed. It was tripped up everywhere in the American government in the aftermath of the Civil War, of course, but nowhere was the deterioration of government and politics so painfully obvious as on the local level. From 1870 to 1900 inefficiency, scandal, and corruption characterized the larger cities in America, and suspicion mounted that even in the towns and villages all was not well. The Jacksonians had been wrong in supposing that universal suffrage and a long ballot were the logical extensions of the town meeting, and now the actual operations of local government exposed the error of their way.

The first crushing blow that preceded defeat was the overwhelming, apparently never ceasing tide of foreign immigration, and the second was the vast migration within the country itself. By the hundreds of thousands each year people from abroad and from the farms swept into the American cities. In the ten short years between 1880 and 1890, in the North Atlantic States three and a half million people moved into urban places. The population of New York City increased by 50 per cent; Philadelphia crossed the one million mark; Boston, Baltimore, Washington each had over a half million inhabitants. By the end of the decade, three fifths of the region's people lived in towns numbering 4000 or more residents. In the Middle West, four out of every five persons had been farmers in 1880, but only two out of three stayed on the land in 1890. Chicago, Minneapolis, St. Paul, Detroit, Milwaukee, Columbus, and Cleveland doubled or trebled their population. While the South and far West remained generally rural in nature, agrarian life in other parts of the nation showed signs of collapse. Farm population in New England, the Middle Atlantic States, and the Middle West fell off sharply, "civilization retreating before the advancing wilderness, farms, homes forsaken, villages abandoned, and deserted." The rural exodus and the foreign immigration combined to flood the cities and towns, so that by 1890, throughout the United States every third American was an urban dweller and thirty-nine of the 272 cities had populations exceeding 75,000.

The signs were unmistakable and the meaning clear: cities were no longer occasional aberrations set in a cluster of comfortable commercial centers and flourishing farm communities — they had become typical, a chosen way of life. Jefferson's "sores to the support of pure government" were cancerous now, spreading everywhere in the body politic. The majority of Americans had left the pleasant country seats, with their shaded streets, neat houses, and orderly central squares, for the sprawling, bustling city with its conglomeration of races living in uneasy associations, with "the same shops grouped in much the same way, the same middle class folk hurrying about their business, the same succession of unsightly telegraph poles, the same hotels with seedy men lounging in the dreary lobbies." Beneath the drab impression of uniformity, contrast and contradiction made the city more difficult to understand and to manage. Imposing six-story financial houses, churches, mansions, fine shops, blended quickly into row on row of monotonous common residences, shanty towns, stockyards, and warehouses. It was this congested disharmony of inhabitants, land uses, industries and commercial enterprises, always growing and always changing, over which local government was asked to preside, to offer communal services effectively in a democratic structure designed for an age long past.

One of the most fully documented chapters in municipal history records the failure of the old ideology to meet these new demands. The divergence of principle and practice became so complete as to make mockery of the historic rationale. There were accomplishments of an engineering and construction sort, certainly. City streets in the United States became the best paved in the world; the new Brooklyn bridge was the marvel of the age; transit cars, central power plants, telephone and telegraph systems, arc lamps for outdoor lighting, made mass living possible. Inventions kept pace with social needs, and there was cosmopolitan grandeur, wealth, spectacle, culture, intellectualism, variety to draw the hayseed from farm drudgery and to offer opportunity for the penniless immigrant. But whenever the city attempted to deal with the nontechnological problems of human relations and politics, the results were catastrophic.

Democracy, the keystone of the grassroots theory, suffered the most outrageously. "Government by common men" became common and coarse indeed. The public ethic disappeared and the private ideal of financial gain engulfed politics. This was the heyday of the boss, of personalized government, of sustained, systematic collaboration between the political and business leaders for municipal plunder, the era when election frauds and financial sleight-of-hand became professional in execution. In Jacksonian years, the early city politician could wear the mantle of "defender of the poor" with some grace. Now the bread and circus state arrived, and whatever humane impulses toward the immigrant the party organization once had were lost in an overriding and insatiable greed.

The connection between the boss, the contractor and the utility executive became direct and obvious. "We have undertaken to write something about the government of the City of New York," a writer in the *North American Review* reflected mournfully, "and yet we have fallen into a discourse on stealing." "If my worst enemy was given the job of writin' my epitaph," announced George Washington Plunkitt, Tammany district leader, as he concluded his famous disquisition on honest graft, "he couldn't do more than write: 'George W. Plunkitt. He Seen His Opportunities and He Took 'Em.'" City government to Lincoln Steffens was "the government of the people, by the rascals, for the rich."

More than rascality was involved, however; a systematic prostitution of the democratic process was taking place, so obvious and so universal that after visiting Chicago political saloons, H. G. Wells could write, "It struck me that I would as soon go to live in a pen in a stockyard as into American politics." The city machine was built on control and manipulation of the vote, on the one hand, and on granting business privilege on the other. Originally, control depended quite literally on the care and feeding of the newcomer, fresh off the boat, an assistance which resulted, quite naturally, in reciprocal political loyalty. This vote potential was organized, by district, ward, and precinct. It was supplemented by patronage, and by election manipulation — the graveyard vote, the repeater, the citizen imported from the neighboring city, the open ballot, the phony count.

But the immigrant was never the dynasty's sole or even major support. "The cities have no doubt suffered from the immigrant vote," observed Lord Bryce, "but New York was not an Eden before the Irish came; and would not become an Eden were they all to move on to San Francisco." Class tension, occasioned by raw industrial growth, heightened the persistent conflict between the propertied and the nonpropertied and created genuine issues on which the organization could take its stand. The great depression of 1873 and the severe if not as disastrous downswings in the next twenty years brought out in bold relief the inadequacy of welfare institutions, of outdoor and indoor relief. Politics, not government, could alone provide succor and hope, and on the broad base of simple poverty and human misery the machine set its foundations. "I think," said Martin Lomasney in Boston, "that there's got to be in every ward somebody that any bloke can come to — no matter what he's done — and get help. Help, you understand, none of your law and justice, but help." There was always, down to the First World War, a ring of truth in that sentiment.

No boss worth his salt was ready to wait for the spontaneous outburst of grievances, however, nor inclined to respond with the sincerity of Jacksonian city leaders. The second characteristic of the machine was its alliance with that part of the business community whose products and services the city used or could control. The overwhelming majorities turned out by the bosses were joined with the influence and finances of the business interests. Simple pilfering became sophisticated; the "fix" with organized crime, the party tax on job holders, the bribe, the kickback from city contractors were standard techniques. Utility franchises were for sale; so were nominations for office, architectural awards, land sites, bond issues, all activities of local government.

In this way the engineering and construction marvels of American cities were easily explained. Of course municipal governments believed in progress; their leaders lived off it. The roaring expansion of the country supported this corruption on an imperialistic scale. "New York is too rich to be brought into insolvency. Great cities, when badly administered, cannot be sold or abolished; they simply become dirty, unhealthy, unsafe, disgraceful and expensive." Across the nation the pattern was the same. New York had perhaps the most steady line of succession: Wood, Tweed, Kelly, and Croker. But there was the Philadelphia Gas Ring, Lomasney of Boston, Cox of Cincinnati, Ruef and Buckley of San Francisco, "Doc" Ames in Minneapolis and a reasonable approximation of boss rule in every city.

Nor was it simply in the cities that the political process was debased. The deterioration of the rural community, the constant drawing off of its youth, its decay and poverty, sapped rural government of its democratic pretensions. Pioneer spirit dwindled, and as the homesteader in the West settled in and the rural village of the East degenerated, the pitiful elite of the courthouse gang took hold. Here corruption was small-scale, concerned essentially with the acquisition of property and the dispensation of privileges and favors. The disposition of tax-delinquent land, the custody of public funds, the award of probate work, printing contracts, and county road maintenance, even the income from jury work, these were the prizes sought. The lawyer, the banker, the county clerk, the sheriff were the key figures, and the same characteristics of influence, power, discipline, and favoritism which marked the city machine appeared with the county ring. Money and votes everywhere converged to turn the miniature republics into small dictatorships, as hardbitten, ruthless, and cynical as the Old World had ever known.

There was one difference in the New World, however, which was vital. The local community was politically independent in theory to the point where its rights found sanction in some courts, but it was not sovereign in the legal sense, ultimately, and it was not sovereign in political fact. The degradation of democracy affronted the righteous, the rural and the conservative, and in their protest, they struck down the second historic principle, local autonomy. The states had retained the prerogatives of the colonial governors to grant city charters and regulate municipal affairs, although in their Revolutionary constitutions they had vested this power in the legislatures. They early set tax indebtedness limits within the charters they granted, and administered all but the lowest courts of justice directly. The right always existed, therefore, for the legislatures to dominate local government, and now this right was exercised to the point of virtual extinction of local home rule.

State after state reserved to itself the power to grant public utility franchises, chartered cities by special act, shaping each to the individual characteristics of the municipality involved, established special commissions to take control over municipal functions, and even abolished city governments outright. "Ripper Legislation" removed the police departments of Boston, New York, Chicago, and St. Louis from local control in this period. Special State Districts assumed water, park, and sewerage functions. The Alabama legislature abolished Mobile outright, and Tennessee revoked the charter of Memphis. Across the United States, hundreds of local laws went on state statute books, regulating the smallest detail of local government, setting salaries, creating new offices, organizing and reorganizing municipal departments, inquiring into every detail of local administration. Judge Cooley could assert that local self-government was "an absolute right" but neither legislatures nor the higher courts finally supported his dictum.

The destruction of local autonomy was not simply a result of city versus state antagonism or rural virtue pitted against urban cunning. Still less was the intervention of the state explained by efforts of reformers and "better elements" to throw the rascals out, although there was some impetus from this direction. Party politics played its part, for cities by now were staunchly Democratic, the split between "urban" and "upstate" was well established, and practical considerations of party control figured prominently.

But what moved the legislatures went even beyond party interests. The complicity of "big business and bad politics" extended to the states, and bosses, as politically secure in the state capitals as at home, often encouraged intervention to provide new opportunities for spending and new offices for patronage. Sheriffs, county clerks, boards of supervisors lobbied for the liberalization of the fee systems, contrived new ways for access to public funds. City, county, state, all were in the web of nineteenth century laissez-faire politics, and the assertion of state prerogative rarely meant the purification of local government.

So pervasive was the influence of business, so ingrained the notion of inviolate economic principles in the last half of the nineteenth century, that Lincoln Steffens was doubtless justified in distinguishing between the "machine" and the "system." Personal dishonesty and avarice were inadequate explanations of the debacle in local government, and the temper and the ethic of the time lent validity to Steffens' conviction that society in general was "a dictatorship"; "an organization of the privileged for the control of privileges, of the sources of privilege, and of the thoughts and acts of the unprivileged." The years from 1870 to 1900 saw the forces of reform at work in agrarian and labor protest, and in leaders with strong social conscience, and subsequent history was to make clear the limits of Steffens' analysis. But the muckraker philosophy, sympathetically and broadly interpreted, showed that the grassroots theory both as social and political fact was in shambles.

Technology and the urban culture it spawned had made the dominant form of social organization large, not small. The Victorian city was no longer isolated from its neighbors; the telegraph, the railroad, the telephone provided continuous contact with the outside world. It was no longer economically independent, for each city had become a specialist, exporting the materials it could produce most effectively from its own resources and importing the goods not natural to its environment. Within the city, the old conditions of equality had disappeared; classes, groups, and here and there lonely Horatio Algers sealed themselves off from alien elements. Wide social intercourse, neighborliness, familiarity diminished; ghettos were established for the rich and poor alike. Common standards, common values, and ultimately communion disappeared. In their place congestion, poverty, heterogeneity, crime, cold-bloodedness took over and made the urban world almost unmanageable. The basic prerequisites for the old forms of community life were gone.

Similarly, in politics, local autonomy had been overrun by the states, and local democracy had become a shibboleth that could not bear inspection. The people and the environment of the great city seemed to many observers contaminated almost beyond salvation. City size precluded the discussion, conference and consensus that was the essential of the old democracy. The variety of races, classes, and interests presented "baffling disharmonies," and the best that could be expected of city government was "bureaucracy tempered by occasional revolts of special interest." There was no direct or easy channel through which public opinion could effectively hold officials accountable or keep any check on administration. Factions had multiplied, minorities become insistent, and only the ward leader and the boss existed as conduits for transmitting the views of the humble. Lord Bryce and John Dewey both arrived at the conclusion that no city could function democratically or responsibly once its population exceeded 100,000. It was not that there was a lag in the accommodation of governmental structures to the industrial society; accommodation was impossible.

What is startling is not the reality of the American city or the breakdown of its government circa 1900. The facts of its social and political organization were well known then as they are well known now. Rather, what is startling is the imperviousness of the grassroots ideology to those facts. Common sense called for a reinterpretation of our democratic image either to accommodate the *realpolitik* of the times or to consider the new paths our great cities should follow. Extraordinarily enough, in the social and political philosophy which followed, neither course was taken. Men might be appalled at the actual conditions of their cities and the circumstances of urban life, but they never supposed that a new system might be in order, that something other than renewed doses of autonomy and democracy might be prescribed. The grassroots idealists tackled the twentieth century as if they had lost a battle, but not the war itself.

The Rejection of Reality

It is true that one camp of philosophers moved out of the fray entirely. The most renowned of all urban observers, Lincoln Steffens, discerned a sick society wherever he looked, in city, state, and nation, in Europe as well as America. He searched for but never found a break in the circle of corruption, and finally gave up in despair. It was not just the miniature republic he abandoned, but society as it was organized. Though he recognized the possibility of evolution and saw the United States experimentally moving in "his" direction, Russia remained for him "the land of conscious willful hope." In the end, he preferred revolution, and he was speaking generally when, in Los Angeles, he absolved Adam, Eve, and the serpent and fixed the blame squarely on the apple.

Most of those who retreated idealistically from the urban life of the post–Civil War period were more limited in their withdrawal. They were troubled by Steffens' indictment, but, for the nation as a whole, they kept perspective. They agreed with Henry Adams that "no period so thoroughly ordinary had been known in American politics since Christopher Columbus first disturbed the balance of American society," but they emphasized the relativity implicit in the remark and looked forward to better times.

What disturbed these observers was the economic and social existence of the city as such. In the most evangelical way they faced reality: they raised again the Jeffersonian standard. The theory of democratic, local self-government was valid enough, but its proper exercise was for Lilliput, not Brobdingnag. They could find no substitute for the "vitality and depth of close and direct intercourse and attachment," for the personal ties that characterized the first communities. They continued to insist that men always need to live close to one another, to know each other's private affairs with "devastating intimacy" if good government is to be achieved. To them liberty depended upon the discrete units of family and neighborhood, on the proliferation of hundreds of self-conscious governments across the nation, each closely connected by economic and occupational ties, each operating under conditions that favored intimate human cooperation and ultimate union.

If the facts were unpalatable to the theory, then, the neo-Jeffersonians would change the facts. Rejecting the classic vision of the city as "the fireplace of civilization whence light and heat radiated out into the dark, cold world," denying that "he who makes the city makes the world," they set about, politically or economically, to reshape the urban world.

A few recognized the necessity of modernity, the fact of industrialization, the established nature of urban life, even while they did not value these developments. They could not contrive a government for them, for chaos by definition could not be institutionalized, and the blatant forces of materialism, the pattern of urban economy, seemed too strong to be resisted at the local level. Their proposal was to reshape the pattern of representation in state and national government so that the rural communities could continue to carry the standard of democracy. Their platform was one of constitutional reform in which one yeoman was equal to a dozen mechanics, to maintain a balance of power and provide a counterweight to urban politics.

But there were bolder spirits, in new disciplines, who scorned political subterfuge and would remake the city itself. With tough-minded insistence, Patrick Geddes argued that the cities of his day were transitory, and that forces were at work within the economy that themselves would transform the world he saw. He classified his time as the last stage of the "Paleotechnic" Age, when the unfettered exploitation of land and resources was coming to a close, and Dickens' "Coketown" was no longer inevitable. New sciences and new knowledge had exposed the wastefulness and inefficiency of nineteenth century industrialism, and for Geddes the neotechnic age was dawning. We could rebuild our cities in the process of this evolution, design them and deliberately re-create the neighborhood, the small town within the larger framework. "The great city," he insisted, "is not that which shows the palace of government as the origin and climax of every radiating avenue; the true city is that of a burgher people, governing themselves from their own town hall and yet expressing also the spiritual ideal which governs them."

Ebenezer Howard provided in 1898 the specific model of reconstruction. In his *Tomorrow: A Peaceful Path to Real Reform*, he proposed to recast the urban environment in the form of garden cities. Resolutely, he put the past behind him, for "these crowded cities have done their work; they were the best which a society largely based on selfishness and rapacity could construct." The simple issue to be faced, he believed, was whether "better results can be obtained by starting on a bold plan on comparatively virgin soil than by attempting to adapt our old cities to our newer and higher need."

Thus the garden city was conceived, an ideal to be worked and planned for in the century ahead, a Newtopia as an alternative to Megalopolis. It was not to be just a further extension of the urban sprawl. In the biotechnic economy that Geddes had seen emerging, city and country would be reconciled, not by chance, but by plan. Land would be held by common authority, population growth controlled, a functional balance among home, industry, and market established, amid a balanced environment combining the urban and rural possibilities of modern life. "Life" values would supersede monetary values, for "town and country must be married, and out of this union will spring a new hope, a new life, a new civilization." In such a reconstruction of the physical city, the traditional theory of self-government could work again. Men interested in garden and home, living in communities planned as social units, could re-create the robust political life of the town meeting, see each other face to face, find the chance for political expression other than in the polling booth, renew their sense of public responsibility, and again exercise their rights with dignity and intelligence.

This vision, set forth cogently, appealing to all who worked with form and shape, allied both to art and science, made unnecessary any revaluation of the image. Men had only to wait a while, to correct the grievous error of the nation's adolescence, and shortly there would be new communities willing and ready to practice politics as it ought to be. The golden past was not gone but merely suspended, and if men kept faith intellectually with Jefferson's principles, localities worthy of their autonomy would be on hand again.

The Mechanization of Reform

While Geddes, Howard, and their disciples sounded the call to physical and social reconstruction, there were those who were unwilling to wait. More pragmatic, more optimistic, impatient with visions, these reformers persistently argued that the city in its present form could be redeemed and that local democracy and local self-government could flourish regardless of the size and scale of the community involved. Democratic government worked best, of course, in the smaller area; honesty and social tolerance came naturally there. But it could be made to work in the largest municipality, without recourse to the radical changes and controls demanded by the Newtopians.

The practical municipal reformers at the turn of the century saw nothing especially evil in materialism, and they wanted no reconstruction of American life in general. To them, it was unnecessary to approximate Jefferson's society in order to apply his principles. Indeed, it was foolish to reject the substantial accomplishments of the last fifty years. The commonsense thing to do was to invent new techniques and institutions so that the urban center had a consciousness of its own and means for self-government akin to the small town.

To these men, it was obvious that plain corruption was the source of most of the city's troubles and simple honesty could be a powerful corrective. Another step seemed to be to reconstruct the mechanics of the political process — voting, campaigning, party organization — so that it resembled more closely traditional grassroots politics. A third was to utilize the methods and techniques of the large society to maintain the essentials of small town life, however artificially. By a special blending of old and new, reformers undertook to preserve their heritage by applying skills of their own age of enterprise. Thus integrity, a rehabilitation of the rational, conscientious citizen, a special type of public organization, were the objectives of municipal reform, although the complete program did not emerge until after the First World War. Far more respected and acceptable than the dreams of Geddes and Howard, they constituted the mainstream of local politics after 1910.

So far as integrity was concerned, sporadic uprisings in its name took place from 1870 on in almost all large American cities. An awakening civic conscience achieved a new charter for New York as early as 1873; Pittsburgh, Chicago, and St. Louis underwent superficial face-lifting; civil service reform became widespread, and the secret ballot was almost universally adopted. Generally, however, civic renaissance based solely on indignation was short-lived. Tweed might be overthrown, but "Honest John" Kelly followed. The Reverend Parkhurst could triumph with moral fervor, but Tammany reappeared. Reform interludes were frequent, but they left few enduring results.

Gradually, it became apparent that "good men" in office unsupported by form and procedure were insufficient. If an adequate political facsimile was to be established, new political techniques to let urban democracy and autonomy function institutionally were needed. As the "permanent" reform associations appeared, the City Club in New York, the Municipal League in Philadelphia, and civic federations in almost every fair-sized city, they focused first on the management of the political process. By 1899, the newly formed National Municipal League crystallized these doctrines of municipal reform in its first Municipal Program.

Essentially the Program was a reassertion of the traditional theory of the republic in miniature with its social underpinnings shorn away. The League believed that the Jacksonian innovations in local government constituted an unfortunate departure from the original design. It took its stand for a government unfettered by artificial checks and balances, with a strong mayor, a rehabilitated council, and a municipal corporation possessing freedom and power unrestricted by state intervention.

The return to historic principles was accompanied by new devices to make them applicable to the times. Representative democracy was obviously a necessity, but the League sought to reconstruct as far as possible the image of the rational, informed, good citizen. To that end, the short ballot, the initiative, referendum and recall, nonpartisanship, proportional representation became cardinal tenets of reform. These techniques would refurbish direct democracy, while professional administration by experts would justify the return of power and prerogative to the city.

Richard S. Childs, a moving spirit of the League from its inception, proclaimed the new study of "democratics," and insisted that "we shall undertake to identify systems which will almost inevitably be democratic." Although necessarily the new local government had to be run by elected officers, this form of government could be as responsible to the people as a Town Meeting, given the proper mechanisms. Democracy could be made to work, and in the right sort of municipal government, "the will of the people where deliberately expressed will control, and the people cannot escape expressing their wills."

Childs saw three basic rules that governed the work of municipal reform: elective offices had to be visible, constituencies manageable in size, and governments well integrated. Long ballots, large electorates, the "scatteration" of powers were the deficiencies in urban local governments, but fortunately these were mechanistic — not moral — faults and hence "responsive to mechanistic corrections." Given a short ballot and proportional representation in nonpartisan elections to loosen the "old Kingopoly" of the two-party system, the way was cleared for a reconstruction of the public which could thwart minority rule and once again exercise the general will effectively.

Yet even with virtue re-established and the political process once again made visible and manageable, this streamlined reproduction still had to be made to function as effectively as it had a hundred years before. Now that the typical American city was large, not small, its populace divided among competing factions and classes, and a sense of communion hard to come by, some way of instilling cohesiveness and common purpose was necessary. The large municipality needed to look and act as if it were integrated, single-minded in its public objectives, even if it consisted, in fact, of the opposite characteristics.

It was at this juncture that the skills of the business world were called into play. Policy-making and bureaucratic institutions were invented to provide at least the illusion of simplicity and efficiency in the management of public affairs. In the revised editions of the League's model charter, the form of the city council was drastically altered. Ideally, it was to be a single body, a small number of members, all elected at large. These were to mirror the desires of the public much as a corporation board of directors represented the stockholders. Under the council, a professional expert, the City Manager, took charge, to bring together the growing array of municipal functions. Every department head was accountable to the Manager, and once the council set the course, he sailed the ship.

Happily presiding as "the minister who performed the marriage ceremony between the city manager plan as first thought of in Staunton and the Commission plan in Des Moines," Childs regarded this innovation as the capstone of reform. It provided public solidarity, a close-knit institution that compromised efficient and economic dispatch of the public business without the intrusion of political wrangling. By grafting the business corporation onto the Town Meeting, by reuniting popular government and private enterprise, the responsible members of society could once again become town fathers. The model could be universal throughout local government, in city, town, village, and county, a structural guarantee that even the biggest city would behave as if it were a small town once again.

The reconciliation which the mechanists effected with al-

most Newtonian simplicity between the age of materialism
and Jefferson's agrarian self-governing ward was no mean
feat. The logic of the comparability of private and public corporations might seem questionable, and men could
wonder if the unruly elements were really subdued. Still,
this optimistic, commonsense approach was a refreshing contrast to the radicalism of the neo-Jeffersonians, for to bring
the common aspirations of capitalism and democracy into
such tangible accord took Yankee ingenuity, at least.

With all the new ingeniously contrived structures and procedures, however, the greatest accomplishment of twentieth
century reform remained the resurrection of historic principles. The flood of political inventions, gadgets, and gimmicks
on the local scene never challenged the American heritage.
Nonpartisanship and proportional representation might seem
newfangled, but their assumptions about human nature were
in the Town Meeting tradition. Men living together in the
same area had, by and large, common goals for their community. Ideological issues in municipal elections were contrived and artificial, for "good city government is good house-
keeping and that is the sum of the matter." The only division
of interest was between "good and bad," and the majority
of citizens wanted the same results — adequate services
honestly provided.

If a constituency became too large, then proportional representation could serve the purpose of allowing individuals
to form nongeographical associations, based on race, occupation, or economic status. But at the same time, these associations would not be divisive, since no single minority could
exercise disproportionate power; ultimately they all had to
pull together. "Proportional representation," Childs proclaimed, "takes the chess play out of politics for the solidarity
and purposeful discipline of a group do not give it any added

power in such elections against an opposing group that is less united." The "mild and rational tolerance of Americans" would prevail, and freed from the delusion that voting Democratic or Republican had relevance in local elections, the people collectively — and not in factions — would rule.

Restored to its natural state of democracy, local government could then demand autonomy once more and become genuinely self-governing. Decentralization was established procedure for large business organizations, and, with a professional city manager, the expert on tap but not on top, the most effective administration of local affairs was by local officials. A scientifically designed civil service, a rational local tax system, model financial laws, uniform accounting and statistics systems, budgets, centralized purchasing carefully developed and installed — all these insured higher administrative standards. There was no need for strict state supervision and harsh intervention: "home rule" was as appropriate now as in colonial days.

The appeal of the package of modern reform was substantial. To be sure, educators held out stubbornly for separate school systems, breaking the golden rule of integration, and proportional representation, while its virtues were "mathematically provable," was too unfamiliar either for widespread adoption or for long continuation in cities where it was tried. The largest cities resisted the lure of the city manager and there were those who complained that municipal reform neglected the most obvious municipal problems: the tenements, care of the poor, education of the alien, working conditions in urban factories, health and sanitation for the populace at large.

These were exceptions, however: the emphasis on mechanistic reorganization predominated. The unicameral council with members elected at large became common; twenty-

three million citizens in 658 cities and towns adopted the
city-manager form of government; the short-ballot movement
was almost universally acclaimed; and civil-service and administrative reforms were everywhere installed. No one was
hurt but the politician, claimed the reformers, and scholar,
journalist, and layman applauded.

Revised and refreshed, the grassroots doctrine rid itself of
the shame of the cities, reasserted its validity and appropriateness to industrial society. Although much work remained
to be done, and the machine, the boss, and the inefficient had
not vanished completely, there were enough civic victories to
make the ideal seem possible of achievement. Generally
speaking, there had been, in William B. Munro's eyes, "an
almost unbelievable improvement all along the line." City
government, to William Anderson, was "much more honest,
efficient and democratic than it was a generation ago." The
reform movement had achieved a consensus as to what local
government should be and the consensus was a reaffirmation
of pre-Revolutionary beliefs. With only a scattering of articulated dissent, and with growing popular support, the republic in miniature continued as a legacy to the newest
American community, the suburb. Ultimately, it was to
prove almost the only justification for suburban existence.

CHAPTER 3

The Rise of Metropolis

Technology Redeems Itself

We will probably never know whether the political gadgetry of municipal reform could provide a reasonable facsimile of parochial life under urban conditions. Most of the largest cities never took part in the experiment; they refused to graft a streamlined superstructure of the town meeting onto their gargantuan communities. Usually they clung to party politics, rejected the city manager and continued to place their faith in a single elected executive dependent on a fickle and sometimes narrow majority rather than a council purporting to mirror perfectly the composition of the entire electorate. While they revamped their bureaucracies along modern organization lines, they refused to tamper with the urban political system based on classes, factions, and conflicting interests.

More important, however, the reformers never had the opportunity to test their propositions in any city, large, medium or small. They had scarcely buckled down to the task of reconstructing the municipality in the image of the town when the city, as they conceived it, disappeared. While they struggled to provide institutions to justify the continuation of local self-government on a grand scale, to repair the damage technology had wrought, technology redeemed it-self. It made possible the re-creation of the small town once again; it provided an alternative to urban reform. By turn-ing the city into a metropolis, by ringing the metropolis with suburbs, it offered what appeared to be at least a passable substitute for the small community of old.

Inventions had made the nineteenth century city possible; the steam power plant, the elevator, the water main, the elec-tric lamp. In the first half of the twentieth century, other in-ventions presaged its disintegration. The streetcar, the auto-mobile, and less romantically, the septic tank and cesspool, brought profound changes to the urban scene. The conges-tion of the city had since Jackson's time been notorious but inescapable. The daily demands for food, apparel, furniture, supplies, and workers had early created tangled traffic jams of horses, men, and carts which rivaled the best that Main Street can offer today. "Streams of walkers, two, three, and four miles long" converged on the central district in the morning and retreated each evening in the days in which Whitman wrote. Now there was an alternative to the cramped use of limited space; there were practical ways to be a part of the city but to live apart from it. Now there was the suburb.

Of course, the suburb was not unknown on the American scene; for over a century New York, Philadelphia, and Boston had been developing metropolitan characteristics. Popula-tion overflowed the boundaries of each city long before the Civil War, and first coach and ferry lines, later railroad and bridge facilities, had been established to handle the daily movement of commuters. Brooklyn was New York's "bed-room" as early as 1845, and civic leaders were even then com-plaining of the lethargy of citizens who considered themselves "lodgers" only. By 1850, the "true limits" of Boston were "those marked out by the business men for their stores, piers, shops, and dwellings" and not by her city fathers, and Philadelphia embraced "within her charted limits less than half her inhabitants." But historical precedent was no guide or true measure for the exodus of the twentieth century, and the quantitative difference had qualitative repercussions.

At first the exodus was limited by the pattern of transportation lines. Except for the very rich, who had used suburbia as a temporary means of escape — a summerhouse or an occasional retreat — the crowds followed the spokes of the iron rails diverging from the center of the city in all directions. The first new settlements for the middle class necessarily had to be within walking distance of the trolley line or the railroad station. By 1900, this pattern was distinct enough to be significant. "Each city," wrote Frederick Lewis Allen, beginning his account of *The Big Change,* "had its outlying residential areas; long blocks of single-family or two-family houses, rising bleakly among the vacant lots and fields; comfortable lawn-surrounded houses for the more prosperous. And there were many who made a cindery railroad journey to work from the suburban towns . . ." While initially the suburbs were small, distinct settlements, backed by open land, as the radiating fingers thrust out, the countryside "thickened up," jurisdictions multiplied. The Main Line in Philadelphia became a row of discrete entities, and so did the towns beyond Dorchester in Boston and those in Westchester County, New York. Two population movements were now going on concurrently, the influx of the farmer and the immigrant into the central city and the settlement of former city residents around the outskirts, and gradually the second trend became predominant.

The coming of the automobile intensified the migration, for now the open spaces between the spokes could be filled in.

Henry Ford, stubbornly pushing the logic of production to its ultimate conclusions, offered the Model T as a car both cheap and reliable, and other manufacturers followed suit. The public response was miraculous in the exact sense of the word; in 1900 there had been fewer than 14,000 automobiles in the United States, in 1915 only 2½ million, but by 1920 there were 9 million and by 1930, over 26½ million. No longer dependent on the streetcar or train, or at least having new access to them, families could settle where they chose. Given a breadwinner sufficiently healthy and complacent to endure the commuter schedule, access to work was assured. Highways began to ring the city and pierce it directly and buses and trackless trolleys went wherever the population grew. The metropolitan area was in being, and as land values soared within the city and along its farthest perimeter, the intermediate land filled up.

Physically speaking, the city absorbed outlying village and hamlet, abandoned the sharp boundary between town and country, sprawling aimlessly as it grew. The "motorized suburb became a reality, filling in the vacant tracts with stucco villas, Cape Cods and English cottages" where "the children would have the benefit of light and air and play space and their parents the benefit of constant battles over the policies of the local school boards, where the wife would gulp down her coffee at 7:52 to drive her husband to the 8:03 train before driving the children to school and doing the family errands." Except for terrain limitations on individual sites, a citizen could live anywhere within twenty miles of downtown and be a part of the urban economy — given the money to support his choice of residence.

In the 1920's, for many Americans the money was forthcoming. The notion of purchasing power and its potential function in the new economy, however incompletely articulated or realized, infiltrated business doctrine. Ford had startled the industrial world with a $5 daily wage, and, applauding, skeptical, or grumbling, other industrial leaders fell in line. Average hourly earnings doubled, from 32¢ in 1915 to 70¢ in 1925. Total private production income was 25 billion dollars in 1910; by 1920 it was almost 61 billion dollars. The gross national product averaged 88 billion dollars annually in the decade between 1919–1928, almost twice that of the turn of the century. Total national wealth — real property, improvements, equipment, utilities, inventories, and personal property — doubled between 1912 and 1922, reaching 320 billion dollars. The value of residential land and improvements kept pace, totaling 37 billion dollars at the end of the decade.

It is true that the new wealth was not widely distributed. Ten per cent of the nation received 35 per cent of its income; only 8 per cent of American families had incomes over $5000 and some 60 per cent less than $2000. But in the booming optimism of the twenties, more and more professional, small business, and upper white collar people felt their personal prosperity to be assured. If there was no money immediately available, they could acquire or at least anticipate it. The middle-income class which comprised the bulk of the migration usually owned homes in the city at the outset. The increasing value of urban land allowed many to sell their city homes and with the proceeds to buy new ones farther out, in the belief that land values would be constantly rising. For those seeking their first home, whose personal resources were insufficient, access to credit was never easier.

While the typical American waited for his fortune, innovations in home financing and home building added the multiplier of speculation to available wealth. Not all the savings held by the upper-income groups went into the stock market, or even into the Florida land boom. The fever of real estate speculation rose through every American city, and the sale and resale of suburban property became a national pastime. Title searches and the recording of deeds were perfunctory formalities; a binder of 10 per cent would close the deal. Margin was not for the market alone, and the confidence of Coolidge prosperity could persuade "the four-thousand-a-year salesman that in some magical way he too might tomorrow be able to buy a fine house and all the good things of the earth." There was money to be made in real estate — and in the twenties, capital was forthcoming. Expenditures for new non-farm residential construction amounted to 950 million dollars in 1915; by 1925 they had passed the $4\frac{1}{2}$ billion dollar mark. In 1915, 414,000 urban dwelling units were started; in 1925, 752,000. Outstanding mortgage loans from 1926 to 1929 annually exceeded 5 billion dollars — a volume they would not reach again until after World War II.

A natural appetite for space, a desire for home ownership, and an American penchant for basing present expenditures on future expectations were now expertly abetted by the subdivision developer. He had been a familiar figure on the American scene since at least the 1880's but his operations in the twenties displayed refined techniques and assumed mass-production proportions. The "polite and insidious drummers" multiplied, and so did the newspaper advertisements, excursion trains, free lunches, and band concerts. No longer was an estate graded and leveled and a few houses built by a single resident contractor who chose his neighbors carefully and made sure vacant lots protected his own home. Now, thousands and thousands of acres were staked out, divided into lots, intersected by streets thinly laid with half-inch blacktop, and decorated with half-acre lagoons and pools. Real estate syndicates joined hands with transit companies, borrowed money on investment certificates, and subdivided enough land in Long Island to house the entire metropolitan population of New York, as many acres in Chicago as the future growth of the city would require for twenty years, sufficient parcels around Buffalo to absorb half a million new residents.

With increasing facilities for commuting, with growing and available wealth, and with a confidence in the immediate future, Americans listened to the developer, and chose to spend their incomes, realized or anticipated, for space to escape the city's increasing congestion. Between 1910 and 1920, in the urban territory adjacent to America's sixty-two largest cities, population rose 33 per cent, for the first time exceeding the growth of the cities themselves, and reached ten million by the end of the decade. Two years after the First World War the total suburban population surrounding cities of 50,000 or more topped fifteen million, so that over 15 per cent of the total national population — and nearly one quarter of all urban dwellers — had become suburbanites.

In the decade which followed, the suburban population grew at the rate of almost 40 per cent around the seventeen largest cities, while the rate of growth in the central cities steadily declined. Four cities with over 100,000 residents actually lost population, while the suburbs burst at the seams. Los Angeles provided the extreme example, when suburban Beverly Hills registered a gain of 2486 per cent, but Shaker Heights near Cleveland increased 1600 per cent, Grosse Pointe Park outside Detroit 725 per cent, and everywhere gains of 200 to 300 per cent were common.

This was migration in the short-haul style which made previous suburban trends dwindle into insignificance. In comparison with the tentative thrusts of seventy years earlier, the suburbs of the twenties were national phenomena, no longer restricted to the eastern seaboard. The peripheral communities they established were not counted in tens and twenties but in thousands. The social characteristics they represented were not atypical but typical, and verging toward the universal, and the problems they raised for government were no longer vexing difficulties, they were close to unmanageable.

The decades that followed 1930 witnessed variations in the rate of suburban growth but no change in the fundamental direction of the trend. The Venetias, Biltmore Shores, Royal Gardens, and Colonial Heights of the twenties never flourished to replenish the fortunes of the speculators who built them. Grass grew in their lonely streets before the Great Depression had even fairly begun, and for years fireplugs, the central gates at the subdivision entrances, and storm sewers were the only visible signs that the land was ready for residents. Between 1930 and 1940, many metropolitan areas lost population, and only Washington and Los Angeles grew substantially. Even parts of the suburban ring declined around most large cities.

Though the volume of growth slowed during the Depression, the rate did not. The relatively small number of people who moved still moved outward, and by 1940 every central city in every major metropolitan area was losing population. It would take time to inhabit the lots staked out in the frenzy of the Coolidge era, but the promise was finally to be realized.

Real estate speculation vanished with the downward spiral of the stock market, but the New Deal provided compensation by institutionalizing the opportunity for home ownership. Against the wave of foreclosures that deluged the early thirties, the Roosevelt administration, in one experimental program after another, moved to prop up the small homeowner. From a welter of boards, commissions, and agencies the Federal Housing Administration emerged in 1934 to insure over 35 million mortgages and housing loans in the next twenty years, covering 30 per cent of all the dwelling units started since then, and to make possible 17 million property improvement loans as well. It was joined after World War II by the home guarantee programs of the Veterans' Administration, which independently underwrote 4 million loans on 13 billion dollars' worth of property. The self-liquidating mortgage replaced the limited-term obligation in private banking procedure, and the way was cleared for Americans to hang on to their residences or to start new ones with low down payments and with amortization rates realistically adjusted to middle class incomes.

As the nation moved slowly toward recovery, the major impact of growth continued to fall on the outlying areas. Between 1940 and 1950, with the impetus of war moving Americans everywhere, the defense program created boom towns of its own. In the postwar prosperity that confounded economists raised in the New Deal tradition, interregional and local migration went on, with the suburban trend in the forefront. The acute housing shortage, resulting from the low levels of construction during the Depression and the phenomenal increase in marriages and births during the war, intensified the search for space. In these years, nearly half of the entire population increase of the nation took place in the suburbs of the 168 standard metropolitan areas. Only in the South did the growth rate of the central cities exceed that of the outlying areas.

By 1950, less than half the population of forty metropolitan areas lived downtown, and in over three fifths of metropolitan United States the growing suburbs showed a greater numerical increase as well as a higher percentage growth than the central city. By 1955, it was estimated that five million of New York's thirteen million residents were in the suburbs and two million of Chicago's total of six million. In Los Angeles, suburbanites outnumbered central city residents three to two; in Boston the ratio was two to one; in Pittsburgh almost three to one; and elsewhere the gap was closing. One out of every four Americans was a suburbanite.

Not only people left the central city in this exodus. More slowly, and with significant differences in the pattern of deployment, commerce and industry shifted locations as well. By the 1950's the shopping center and the one-story factory had become as much a part of suburbia as the rows of ranch houses, split-levels, and Cape Cods. By 1948, the suburban share of total metropolitan retail trade was 31 per cent, up 4 per cent from 1939 and growing at an increasing rate. By 1955, 1800 shopping centers had been built in outlying business districts of metropolitan areas, and almost as many were on the drawing board. Freed from dependence on the steam engine as a central power plant, industries also began locating in the mid-zone of the metropolitan area, adjusting to shifting transportation, land use, market and labor patterns. Though the adjustment was complicated by conflicting trends in regional decentralization, by the business cycle, and by variations in site requirements among different types of industries, the industrial peripheries of metropolitan areas grew steadily, if slowly, throughout the years 1899 to 1947.

Industrial diffusion did not approach residential migration; during World War II it seems to have stopped entirely. The postwar trend to 1950 was only incipient, though suburban industrial activity expanded more rapidly thereafter. The significance of this diffusion, however, was less its size than its irregular deployment; business was selective in the suburbs it chose, and suburbs were often wary of the industries which clamored for admission. Thus, although the suburban share of the total metropolitan value added by manufacturing was about 40 per cent in 1948, most of this activity was concentrated in only a few of the outlying jurisdictions. Of the 29 million inhabitants in our seven largest metropolitan areas, fewer than 500,000 lived in jurisdictions where postwar manufacturing employment had grown faster than the population. Industry and people had moved out but they had not moved out together — and the result was that all kinds of communities appeared to ring the city. The suburbs extracted one by one economic and social functions which had previously existed side by side. Each tended to emphasize a particular aspect of society — residential living, industry, recreation, gambling, retail trade. Even slums developed.

Thus suburbia, residential, commercial, and industrial, became a permanent characteristic of urban life in the United States, and urban life itself was transformed from compact, congested cities into "metropolitan areas." By 1957, 174 of these metropolitan complexes contained 108 million people and 15,658 separate governments. Over 47 million of those people lived outside the central city, producing 36 per cent of the national value added by manufacturing and accounting for over 20 per cent of national retail sales.

The metropolis, so formed, was a concomitance of many forces. Some of these made suburban living possible: the innovations in transportation and communication, the changes in housing construction and residential finance, mutations in the pattern of industrial development. Others encouraged people to become suburbanites: the shortage of housing in large cities, aspirations for space and separate family accommodations and for home ownership, a drive for higher social status, the rising birth rate, the tradition of restlessness nourished and intensified by the Depression and the war prosperity, and the family ethic.

But not the least of the forces at work was the persistent ideal: the image of small town life that every migrant held in his mind and that every real estate speculator raised as a conscious symbol. In some ways the ideal comprehended the forces which were at work: the desire for space, family life, and the homestead were part and parcel of the image itself. In other ways, the ideology determined the uses to which modern technology would be put. It diverted the urban population and their governments from efforts to rebuild their central cities on a substantial scale or to devise new residential accommodations there to house the growing number of children. Instead, it fostered investment in transportation facilities rather than urban renewal, in automobiles in place of more extensive development of urban land.

The net result of all these separate and individual motivations, old and new, was to provide an alternative to the urban world. No longer did Americans have to tolerate the crowded neighborhoods of the city, its impersonality, anonymity, rootlessness, nor endure the suspicion and misunderstanding which class conflicts provoked. No longer were they forced either to accept the corruption and arrogance of machine politicians or to join reformers to wage an uphill battle for the redemption of the city. Technology had made it possible for anyone who escaped the center of the metropolis to live in a city less than one hundred thousand in population. In this modern migration of the twentieth century, people were not just moving out in a physical sense; they were moving into new communities in the political and social sense.

And here political boundary lines indeed played a crucial role, for the structure and spirit of the new region was created by the separate political jurisdictions it encompassed. The quiet half-deserted villages and townships on the fringes of the cities, by-passed for fifty years, had clung to their corporate identity and independence to good purpose. Caught up in the exodus, repopulated and reinvigorated, they were ready again to demonstrate the blessings of small town life and politics in the midst of urban culture.

Crisis in Autonomy

The nostalgic image found a new frame then, in suburbia, and its popularity justified suburban independence. Faith in the ideology discouraged the creation of new political institutions to serve the entire metropolitan area and provided an appealing rationale for the preservation of local town halls and county court houses. It served to crystallize the new region into hundreds of small communities, each more or less conscious of its own identity.

But was suburbia a legitimate recipient of the legacy? Did it offer a genuine renaissance or only a pale counterfeit of the real article? The suburb, after all, was not an early New England town, a southern market center, or a western trading village. The United States was no longer rural, but urban and industrial, and destined to become more so. The pattern of large-scale organization, the values of togetherness, the political philosophy of positive government, all penetrated suburbia, made it something more and less than a replica of earlier times. There was an economic interdependence of the region as a whole, a new pattern of social intercourse throughout the area, and these developments had both direct and subtle influences on the reinvigorated jurisdictions. In the short run at least, the immediate answer to the question as to whether or not the suburb was the carrier of the grassroots faith depended upon the success of the local govern-

ments in maintaining their autonomy. If they went under
and were absorbed by the metropolis, then no amount of
imagery could re-establish the small community in its essential form.

In the beginning, this issue of genuineness and the critical
role of suburban independence was scarcely recognized. The
new environment was overlooked, and men took at face value
the revival of the small-scale jurisdictions surrounding the
large cities and the apparent renaissance of independent,
healthy community life after one hundred years of somnolence. The issue in municipal reform throughout the last
half of the nineteenth century had been so much the question of size — how to reduce urban congestion or manage it
in accordance with historic values — and the solutions had
been so tentative that its seemingly automatic resolution was
accepted with delight, and with little critical examination.

For those who had emphasized the necessity of breaking up
the mammoth city to guarantee a satisfactory local government, the suburb was an intimation of dreams about to come
true. More pleasing still, their aspirations were turning into
reality quite naturally, without the tremendous political
and educational efforts that Geddes and Howard thought
necessary. Writing at the turn of the century, Adna Weber
could view the development of suburban towns even then as
"the most encouraging feature of the whole situation." "The
rise of the suburbs," he wrote, "is what furnishes the solid
basis of a hope that the evils of city life, so far as they result
from overcrowding, may be in large part removed . . . It
will realize the wish and prediction of Kingsley, 'a complete
interpenetration of city and country, a complete fusion of
their different modes of life and a combination of the advantages of both, such as no country in the world has ever
seen.' " And twenty-five years later, Harlan Douglass could

speak of the suburban evangel, and after a biting indictment of the city, look to a new motivation for life in the satellite town of open land and cottage home. He could confidently predict, "A crowded world must be either suburban or savage." For the first planners, the trend was nothing awesome, but a movement devoutly prayed for and constantly encouraged.

Even the more pragmatic municipal reformers, those who believed they had solved the problem of size by political and administrative adjustments, never claimed that their program of reform was superior to the genuine article. Proportional representation, nonpartisanship, the short ballot, the small council had been offered as substitutes in a large city for the direct self-government possible in smaller places. Certainly these experts felt that the suburbs could profit by employing a city manager and business methods of organization and administration, but they did not believe that the suburban trend was contradicting their own efforts. Instead it appeared to reduce the size of their job, for now they could concentrate on the central cities of the metropolitan areas, secure in the knowledge that the surrounding towns could take care of themselves.

Of course, a nagging doubt as to what was happening to the metropolitan region as a whole tugged at the National Municipal League's conscience, and metropolitan problems were discussed spasmodically at annual meetings from 1917 to 1925. But the League did not publish its first report on the government of metropolitan areas until 1930, and although the study was hailed as "the first comprehensive survey of its kind," it arrived at no specific recommendations. Indeed, its conclusions were regarded as "so general in their scope that it is virtually impossible to disagree with them — a sure sign that they have little value." The perfection of the structural and procedural mechanisms of reform continued to hold the center of the stage, and though there were hints that suburbia might cause trouble, they received low priority on the agenda.

So the trend intensified, and far from vanishing, the number of governmental units within each metropolitan area multiplied at an astonishing rate. In 1900, the New York region had 127 minor civil divisions, by 1920, 204; in Cook County (Chicago) there were 55 in 1890 and 109 in 1920; around Pittsburgh, 107 units existed in 1920 where thirty years earlier only 91 were formally incorporated. For the seventeen largest cities, incorporations of new governments around the fringe of the city went on and on — most rapidly at the turn of the century, but steadily for the next fifty years. Between 1952 and 1957 alone, 170 new municipalities came into being in metropolitan areas and 519 new special districts were created. By 1957, there were over 3000 governments that could be said to possess more or less general municipal powers, and there was, of course, that awesome figure of 15,658 legally distinguishable local units. Village, hamlet, school district, city, county, town, they were each one equipped with the legal prerogatives of government, each claiming to speak for a separate constituency. They jostled one another in the crowded confines of the metropolitan backyard, jealous of their authority and suspicious of their neighbors.

These units were democratic, at least in the sense that their citizens popularly determined the course of their own affairs, and certainly they were independent. They squabbled incessantly over jurisdictional problems: the intersection of streets at town boundaries, the acquisition of water supply, the disposal of sewage, the health nuisances which one government visited upon another. They maintained their own schools, their own police forces, their own fire departments. They had the capacity to govern and legal and political weapons to preserve themselves. They were autonomous, then, in the sense of independence, but as the governments multiplied, observers took a second reading on the word "autonomous." Were suburban governments presiding over distinct and meaningful small communities, or had the foundations on which their political autonomy depended been swept away by the onrush of the growing metropolis?

The issue first came into the open by the drab route of public finance. Here, the intrusion of metropolitan life took concrete and specific form, for as municipal budgets and tax rates climbed and climbed, the suspicion grew that the new-found suburban grassroots splendor might be only Indian summer. Previously men had always assumed that the economic, social and political conditions of small town life went hand in hand; that legal and financial self-sufficiency existed naturally together. Yet in suburbia and the metropolitan region at large, established governing bodies, faithful to the requirements for independence and democracy, suddenly lacked the resources to govern. The communities flourished, their inhabitants were employed, and there was a rising standard of living, but there were not sufficient public revenues for communal purposes. Even the cities of the 1880's with their bosses, their treasuries pilfered by dishonest contractors, their incredible extravagances, had not known bankruptcy. Taxable wealth was always available to provide a surplus, whether to be squandered or preserved. But now the neat fit between supply and demand disappeared. The property tax, divided among so many jurisdictions, did not suffice; the sum of the parts did not equal the whole. The multiplication of jurisdictions brought to the entire region, in good times as well as bad, municipal poverty, and the principle of genuine autonomy for local governments, in the sense of the financial as well as legal capacity to manage their own affairs, went by the boards.

What had occurred, of course, as the suburban trend developed, was an uneven distribution of tax resources and service needs throughout the new metropolitan areas. The divergent pattern of residential and industrial dispersion, unnoticed in the first blush of enthusiasm, played havoc with the development of financially secure governments. These were not the balanced communities that Howard had envisioned; they were only slices of the metropolitan complex. Surrounded by political boundaries, some communities residential, some industrial, some mixed in the pattern of their land uses, suburbs and central cities alike faced unequal demands and commanded widely disparate resources.

The central cities felt the pinch first. With the middle class steadily abandoning their downtown residences, commercial districts, industrial sections, governmental centers, and slums became the major land uses of the metropolitan core. A two-way squeeze took place: in the daytime commuters poured into the city, shooting the working population up 30 to 50 per cent above its permanent number, requiring services in transport, streets, water, police and fire protection on a level artificially pegged for the crowds between nine and five. But taxable resources steadily declined, and as residential areas deteriorated, the slums took up 20 per cent of the nonbusiness area, siphoning off 45 per cent of total municipal expenditures but contributing only 6 per cent of the revenue. As a further complication, as the city became more and more the educational or civic center of the region, the amount of tax-exempt property increased steadily. With service demands at least as high as when most of the urban population lived within its limits, and with the tax base declining relatively or absolutely, most large American cities ran out of money. By 1930, tax rates were rising everywhere, and municipal borrowing was moving ever closer to established debt limits.

Boston provided the extreme example. In 1930 its assessed valuation of taxable property was $1,972,000,000; in 1939, $1,524,000,000; in 1947, $1,558,000,000; in 1951, $1,570,-000,000 — four hundred million less than the value twenty years earlier. Faulty assessment practices and other deficiencies of the property tax as such accounted for some of the difficulty. But during that same period, the value of tax-exempt real estate increased by 216 million dollars, an increase from 19 to 40 per cent of total real property value. Despite a policy of postponing capital improvements until schools, parks, hospitals and equipment were at the point of abandonment, expenditures rose from 80 million in 1937 to 95 million in 1947 to 132 million in 1951. As a consequence, Boston's assessment on commercial and industrial property rose to the unheard-of rates of 100 per cent of true value and the tax rate reached $86 per $1000, a point at which the business community could complain with some justice that an increase much "beyond the present level could well spell disaster."

But the runaway tax rates of the central city — Boston, New York, or Chicago — were not the only sign of incipient urban bankruptcy. Some suburbs were in trouble too. There were windfalls for a few but scarcity for many others. While exclusive towns could finance twice-a-week garbage collections, skating rinks, recreational centers, and miles of parkway, others scraped the bottom of the municipal treasury to keep the schools open and the streets repaired.

By 1930, tax rates among metropolitan suburbs in New York varied from $2.21 to $4.73; in Detroit from $1.89 to

$2.54; in Cleveland from $.93 to $2.19; and in Boston from $1.92 to $4.88. The inherent inadequacies of the property tax as an adequate source of revenue were compounded as rich suburbs sealed themselves off from the central city and their neighbors and industrial and low-income cities struggled to provide the bare necessities. With staggering new demands for urban services, approaching the 21 billion mark by 1953, the disparity between needs and resources seemed to reach the breaking point. If autonomy depended on financial independence, most of the local governments in the United States, in the opinion of many observers, were going under.

Nor was financial adversity the only difficulty which the American miniature found in its new environment. As suburbs ringed the central city, obvious conditions of interdependence appeared. When sixteen thousand separate jurisdictions carried out local functions in a land area comprising less than 7 per cent of the country, the determination of local governments to maintain separate services was not just expensive, it was frequently absurd. Separate water systems, separate sewer lines, separate street and highway programs, individual police and fire departments — these affronted common sense and, more significantly, the scientific principles of administrative management. How could efficiency and economy be assured when no central authority planned for the provision of transit facilities and utilities? Who would provide an "articulated highway system adequate for metropolitan transit?" What was to be done with the obviously common problems of harbor and stream pollution, of storage and distribution of water, of control of contagious diseases, integration of police work, and coordination of fire fighting systems? The maze of local governments, each presenting a full array of public services, confounded logic. In this new governmental congestion, autonomy obviously did not guarantee efficiency although, surely, efficiency was supposed to be a major justification of autonomy.

From the organizational as well as the financial point of view then, the failure of the city to expand concurrently with the growing urban area seemed disastrous. The "crazy quilt hodge podge of local governmental agencies" could appear to H. G. Wells as far back as 1910, "like fifteenth century houses which have been continuously occupied by a succession of enterprising but short-sighted and close-fisted owners, and which have now been, with the very slightest use of lath and plaster partitions and geyser hot-water apparatus, converted into modern residential flats." To Victor Jones, thirty years later, the problem of metropolitan government remained much the same: "The need for servicing a large population scattered under the jurisdiction of many units of local government, most of which are crippled by limited powers over a restricted area, by inadequate tax resources and by such consequences of premature subdivision as heavy indebtedness and extensive tax areas." And Betty Tableman, writing in 1951, insisted indignantly that "no governmental unit is an island. Sins of omission and commission of any one municipality affect not only its own citizens but all persons living in the metropolitan area." Criminals were escaping because no police jurisdiction had effective control; fires raged while unused equipment lay idle across artificial boundaries; sewage dumped in a river by one government contaminated the neighboring jurisdiction's lake; master highway plans could not be completed on an area-wide basis. The urban center was no longer, in Luther Gulick's words, "floating around in a great and green rural hinterland." Rather, "it is now elbow to elbow with other paved urban centers."

Suburbia was not, then, to slip smoothly into the modern world, as its first supporters had fondly imagined. It was causing trouble, real trouble, for the metropolis of which it was a part. The first tenet of its political ideology — independence for each locality — no longer had an economic or social base, and the justification for autonomy apparently collapsed. A collection of small governments, without financial self-sufficiency and some spatial isolation from each other, made for ineffective political structures, and the principle of autonomy no longer went hand in hand with its companion doctrine — democracy — to justify these small-scale reconstructions of an earlier culture. The two doctrines were turned against each other, and the close democracy a suburb promised almost guaranteed ineffective government for the region as a whole. The threat to American localism was not from Washington or the state capitals; the creed was doing itself in and its greatest virtue had been subverted into its greatest vice.

Suburbia Besieged

The realization that suburbs could not, realistically, be independent entities set loose again the theory of cultural lag. The conviction grew that suburban political institutions were, after all, only relics, "holdouts" against the rush of metropolitan culture, soon to disappear. From 1930 to the present day most experts in metropolitan reform have agreed that something has to give, and gradually they have crystallized their doctrine to the point of proposing the abolition or drastic curtailment of the last artifact of the ideology, suburban political independence.

At first, metropolitan reformers offered no quarter; they mounted a frontal assault on suburbia. Looking at the financial and service plight of the metropolitan area, they were appalled at the callousness with which the suburbanite viewed his neighbors in the city, the indifference he showed to the problems of the region as a whole, and the waste and confusion he tolerated in public affairs. If it were a question of faithfully preserving the legacy or meeting the demands of urbanity, the early metropolitan reformer sided with his own generation. Financial self-sufficiency for the region as a whole, orderly, responsible consideration of regional priorities, autonomy in the true sense of the word, was of first importance. If the social and political worlds on which the miniature republic rested had split apart, then the suburban renaissance must be illusory. There was no alternative but a return to the program of mechanistic reform, to force the American people to face the fact that the small community could not be re-created in an industrial society. Approximate grassroots political philosophy as closely as possible, these reformers reasoned, but give primary emphasis to attaining regional self-sufficiency.

The attack came in two waves: a blunt denial that the suburbs were in fact true representatives of the republic in miniature, and a subsequent drive to merge the outlying municipalities with the central city, abolishing their independent governments outright. H. G. Wells announced the broad strategy that later arguments were to utilize. He flatly rejected the suburb's claim to small town status in the Anglo-Saxon tradition. "These local government areas of today represent for the most part what were once distinctly organized and individualized communities, complete minor economic systems, and they preserve a tradition of what was once administrative convenience and economy. Today, I submit, they do not represent communities at all, and they become more wasteful and more inconvenient with every change in economic necessity . . . Probably you find the thinnest sham of a community . . . where a clerk or a working man will shift his sticks from one borough to another and move on to a third without ever discovering what he has done." Lewis Mumford scorned, as pitiful mockeries of what they might have been, the phony communities with "neither the intellectual penetration to analyze their condition nor the courage and imagination to transform it. The suburb was a pharisaic way of passing by on the other side; leaving the civic organism itself in the gutter."

These men recognized only the metropolitan community as genuine, and turned their efforts toward removing the suburban roadblocks that cluttered the road to progress. Disposing of suburbia as illusion, the metropolitan pioneers proposed that the central city annex all the territory that surrounded it. The simplest solution was the best: let Elmwood extend its boundaries until it was Greater Elmwood; and for a time it seemed that this formula might work.

Until 1918, America's largest cities managed to annex sizable territory without substantial difficulty. The ten largest at least doubled their area and some increased from three- to tenfold. In 1891, New York completed the greatest single extension of territory, adding over 250 square miles to the city; Boston doubled its size in 1914; Baltimore added 60 square miles in 1918; and St. Louis gained 43 square miles in 1876. For cities of more than 100,000 residents, 605 square miles were annexed between 1890 and 1900, 413 in 1900–1910, and 628 and 521 square miles respectively in the next two decades. In Virginia and Texas, "automatic" annexation procedures were established by the legislature, and in every urban state special legal provisions were made for the extension of municipal boundaries.

But annexation did not keep pace with metropolitan growth, and just at the time when the metropolitan problem became critical, annexation petered out. Despite a few sizable territorial additions to Detroit and Los Angeles, and a spurt of small acquisitions after the Second World War, political opposition to the absorption of outlying towns increased. Completely surrounded by the territory of the central city, enclaves in Los Angeles, Boston, Cincinnati, Cleveland, Detroit, and Pittsburgh clung to their separate governmental identities and they were joined by towns and villages on the fringe. By 1933 R. D. McKenzie could write that "annexation is no longer practicable as a means of coordinating with the central city the vast areas into which the automobile and the paved highways have poured urban population." Ten years later Victor Jones could echo, "Annexations in the past half-century have contributed little toward a solution of the problem of metropolitan government . . . The large American cities have never been able to keep pace, by means of annexation or consolidation, with the accumulation of population on the margin of the city." Cool expert logic was no match for emotional loyalties to the old image, and the frontal attack collapsed, even in the rapidly growing new cities of the West.

But scarcely had the suburbs silenced the cries for "one community — one government" and frustrated the building of Greater Elmwood when a more stealthy invasion was upon them. The second wave of metropolitan reformers were less openly hostile; they did not propose to abolish the suburbs, but only to compromise them. The new experts were quite willing to permit suburbia to continue its independent existence; they would settle for something less than maximum efficiency and financial stability. All the suburbs had to do was to relinquish those functions and programs which were most obviously metropolitan in character to a regional government in which they would have representation. The new breed of reformer did not ask the suburb to pass from the scene, but only to face the reality of modern life.

Partly, the change in plans was dictated by tactical considerations, since annexation was obviously not working. But in good measure, the members of this movement were — and are — sincere. They had genuine doubts about the kind of political process that would result in a single metropolitan government many times larger than any municipality that had ever existed before. Some of them suspected the earlier reform principles of "automatic" democracy, and almost all of them were afraid of the vastness of the enterprise which annexation would involve. Moreover, they were not ready to dismiss suburbia outright; they detected at least vestiges of small town life in the new communities. They valued these remnants, for the new reformers were members of the faith themselves. They believed in the ancient image.

So, in the 1940's and 1950's, a whole series of proposals blossomed forth, designed not to abolish suburbia but to tame it. The modified objective was to preserve legal autonomy wherever possible, to make only grudging concessions to urban growth. From scholars' studies and administrators' desks came an increasing flow of recommendations, analyses, and evaluations. In place of annexation, why not isolate only a few of the most critical metropolitan functions and vest them in, say, the county, that established agent of the state? Or if the county was too small to encompass the new urban complex, why not a multi-purpose special district, which operated not just bridges, tunnels, and airports, but every program that was truly metropolitan in nature? Or if this plan found popular disfavor, then what about consolidating functions one by one? Establish a single parkway authority, or water commission, or sanitary district, or transit agency, under the state or by agreement with the municipalities. Sooner or later, they would likely as not come together, and a genuine metropolitan government might be on its way. At least, create a regional planning commission to plot a sensible and systematic land-use map as a guide for zoning development among all the cities and towns, or pool tax resources to make sure that the basic metropolitan needs of water and sewerage are provided for. The proposals began as early as the limitations of annexation became obvious, and painstakingly, in each metropolitan region, research studies were authorized, experts hired and set to work, bills drafted to be presented to state legislatures.

Finding "solutions" to the metropolitan problem took on the aspects of an academic crusade. Survey tumbled after survey, following the injunction of the National Municipal League that "there can be no single answer to the problem of metropolitan organization, applicable to all conditions and times." In thirty years, in twenty-six states, 88 separate projects, studies, commission reports, surveys and programs came forth, all designed to bring order out of chaos, restore efficiency, rationalize the "ineffective arrangement of multiple jurisdictions" while preserving suburbia itself. Schemes for intermunicipal cooperation, for exchanges of services, consolidation of city and county, separation of city and county, special authorities, federations, mergers, solutions with "no structural changes," solutions with "structural changes," from Birmingham to Boston and New York to Los Angeles, all came off the drawing board, all seeking to make the suburbs reasonable, to find a new type of local government.

Far and away the most popular plan recommended was a federal structure for the metropolitan area. By 1950, half a dozen schemes for federation in different metropolitan areas had been put forward, and in 1952, Toronto broke the log jam and established a "genuine" federated government. The theory of these federal plans was simple: the twin principles of autonomy and democracy could be reconciled by a new method of representation. Keep the suburbs, but create a new limited government with the authority to carry out obvious metropolitan programs in planning, land-use control, water use, sewerage, and transportation. Give the suburbs membership in the governing body of the metropolitan organization. Establish two tiers of local government, divide up functions or aspects of functions, allocate them variously to the two levels, and thereby secure regional cooperation while preserving suburban democracy. Surely this was a workable compromise, and citizens in Boston, Miami, Atlanta, St. Louis, and Cleveland pricked up their ears.

But as a rule, the suburbs were unimpressed, and even though signs of limited breakthroughs were apparent after the Toronto story became widespread, suburbia hesitated. The federated scheme seemed a vast improvement over previous programs, but two implications became steadily more apparent. The first concerned the allocation of authority: how does one decide what is a metropolitan problem and what is a suburban problem? Theoretically, there were more or less objective administrative standards that could be applied, but the closer the suburb looked at the model of federalism, the more it became apparent that as one gave up functions, the significance of legal autonomy diminished rapidly. Just as suburban legal authority interfered with metropolitan self-sufficiency, so even limited metropolitan authority decreased genuine suburban autonomy. What meaning did independence have, if all the suburban citizen could decide was where to place traffic lights and street signs and how much to spend for the library? If highways, planning, police, water, and recreational services were removed from his control, what value did local government possess? And how were the boundary lines between local and metropolitan affairs to be maintained? Every previous federal model envisioned a judicial body to arbitrate the inevitable disputes between the levels of government. Where was the supreme court of the metropolis, except at the state level, to resolve the issue of authority with all the subtle niceties by which the legal profession justifies its existence?

A second difficulty seemed even more serious. What happened to grassroots democracy itself when the regional functions moved upstairs? By definition, the process of local representation in the "Greater Government" was an indirect one, with town officials representing their constituencies in the larger councils. But the justification for suburbia was based precisely on the fact that its political process was the closest approximation of direct popular participation. Abandon control over the important functions of local government and the direct method of accountability that kept the bureaucracy in check and what was left of the Town Meeting?

Instinctively, rather than by rational rebuttal, most suburbanites interpreted the plans for federation for what they were: not compromise but seduction. Even if they could not explain the inconsistencies in the scholar's logic, they recognized the end product: a reduction in the real significance of their legal autonomy, and a belittling of the political process they possessed. Metropolitan reform was depriving the suburbs of their options in deciding public policy and, although the region and perhaps some suburbs themselves experienced financial adversity and administrative chaos, the ancient legacy was what counted. Sadly viewing the metropolitan scene in 1950, Thomas Reed, consultant to civic groups and city fathers on the grand design of the metropolis for over a quarter of a century, concluded, "Many better and wiser city planners and political scientists than myself have poured out millions of words, by tongue, pen and typewriter, on the same theme, but frankness requires me to say that so far we have accomplished little more than the world's record for words used in proportion to cures effected."

Suburbia Triumphant

Annexation, consolidation, merger, country-city separation — suburbia considered all of them and concluded usually that it wanted none of them. It preferred legal autonomy and small town politics above all, and it continued to expand. The New York region by 1954 boasted 1071 separate jurisdictions; Chicago, 960; Philadelphia, 702; St. Louis, 420; until, all in all, 14 per cent of all local governments in the United States were in the metropolitan areas. Against all appeals that this multiplicity fostered political irresponsibility and defeated "both the theory of popular control and the government's ability to provide services," the suburbs were adamant. They knew that what reform actually entailed was a reunion, at least in part, with the central city and its corrupt politics, its slums, immigrants, criminals, and the vicious elements from which they had only recently escaped. The reformers had demonstrated the expense of maintaining this isolation, but to most suburbanites, the figures merely proved that the price of liberty was always high.

In only one way did the suburbs adjust to modernity. When obvious breakdowns appeared in basic public utilities, metropolitan-wide institutions were permitted, so long as they were not governments. Public corporations, authorities, special districts were popular with suburbanites; they were self-supporting and businesslike in form. They were allowed to assume the money-making activities of local government

— the building and operation of bridges, tunnels, terminals, and airports — and because they were run by state-appointed commissioners, aloof from the undignified ordeal of vote-getting, they were acceptable. By that curious *non sequitur* so appealing to Americans — that the authorities had "taken government out of politics" — the suburbs reasoned they had nothing to fear. These institutions could not be threats because they were not governments.

Thus the only way in which big organizations entered local government was by masquerade. The metropolitan agencies now at work are in the form of *ad hoc* special districts, in highways, sanitation, airports, mosquito control, water, garbage collection, hospitals, almost every conceivable local activity. The New York Port Authority, the Boston Metropolitan District Commission, the transit authorities, the Golden Gate Bridge and Highway District, these have been the novelties permitted. No period in American history saw more inventions in forms of pseudo government than the decades between 1920 and 1950, when the baffling array of "nonpolitical" boards, commissions, and agencies sprang up across the country.

They were, of course, pseudo governments. Victor Jones was quite right when he wrote that their lack of direct accountability and numerical addition to the local governments already in existence "confuses the citizens and voters and makes it difficult to secure responsible local government in large urban communities." But the suburbs were satisfied; if the small town could not carry out a local function, then it was better to remove the program from government entirely. Grassroots democracy or big business — no other vehicle is trustworthy in the United States.

There was stubborn resistance, however, to all proposals for genuine government. The answer could be found in the words of Arthur E. Morgan about Great Neck, Long Island, in the twenties: "All the people in that area moved in about the same time. They were young married couples with one or two children . . . the men have a volunteer fire department and have recently built a beautiful fire house which is equipped for recreational purposes as well . . . The women very often do the shopping cooperatively. If anyone is ill, everyone will do her bit to help . . . The church is a community church. The minister is young and has done much for all ages. A social is held once a month for the married couples. There are frequent dances for the young people. It seems that something is going on every week." Or it could come in the forthright declaration of the resident of Tarrytown that "I would feel that I had surrendered some of my manhood if I gave to the politicians in White Plains the legal right to control in the slightest degree the education of my children."

However presented, the suburban choice in the twentieth century had been to retain the form of government most closely resembling Jefferson's legacy — a choice, moreover, made in defiance of the compelling values of the modern world: large-scale organization, efficiency, economy and rationalization. Fortuitously supported by two decades of prosperity, the suburbanite has been able to brush aside the specter of municipal bankruptcy, ignore the obviously illusory nature of his legal autonomy, and retain his independent community. The nation's wealth for the moment supports his idol, and the Great Society, at least in the political sense, is excluded from his hearth and home.

This overwhelming victory implies, of course, some serious weaknesses in the doctrines of metropolitan reform. One tactical error seems clear immediately: for all their energy and ingenuity, for all their battle cries of annexation, merger and federation, the reformers have mounted only a limited offensive. They have challenged the feasibility of small government and small communities in the twentieth century, but they have never seriously questioned the desirability of small government whenever it can possibly be sustained. In the end, the reformers have offered only an alternative program for better metropolitan financial and administrative management; they have never promised a better brand of politics.

This reluctance to launch a full-scale attack on the ideology as well as the practicality of small government diminishes the prospects for reform's success. It allows the suburb the heroic role of defender of democracy, even though it remains the villain in the melodrama of metropolitan development. Thus the suburb possesses an almost impenetrable line of defense, for what citizen, faced with a choice of an ineffective government democratically controlled or an effective government less democratically controlled, will not wrap himself in high moral principle and choose the first?

By refusing to challenge the grassroots faith itself, reformers are forced back to a single argument: that the suburban claim to the status of a small community is necessarily counterfeit. Yet, even here, taking their stand as hard-bitten realists, they are on weak ground. They assume that the loss of financial self-sufficiency among surburban governments and the end of social isolation means inevitably the collapse of small town life and consciousness. On this assumption reformers conclude that the suburban commitment to the colonial legacy must be, of necessity, illusionary. And, on this assumption, they have constructed the best alternative structure they can devise in the belief that some day suburbanites will realize that their allegiance is nostalgia, a commitment to a shadow world which existed only in the past.

But it is a serious mistake to believe that an ideology simply reflects the social and political organization in a particular period of history, lingering for a while, but ultimately giving way to an expression of a new reality. When they are powerful enough, ideologies may shape — as well as mirror — the world about them. This fact metropolitan reformers are discovering today, for it is not the simple memory of the heritage which thwarts their efforts. It is the power of that heritage as a very real expression of the aspirations and values of the present generation which blocks the progress of reform.

In the final analysis, Wells and Mumford, as the early discoverers of the organization man, never challenged the suburban evangel to any real effect for a good reason: the more closely suburbs are studied, the more genuine their claim to provinciality appears. In many essential qualities many suburbs seem like the American small towns of the past, much more impervious to modern life than is commonly supposed.

PART II

CHAPTER 4

The Nature of Suburbia

The Case of the Disappearing Community

To interpret the suburb as defender of long-established and basic American ideals solves a good number of the puzzles on the urban scene. Obviously it explains the plight of the metropolitan reformer, for it exposes him as having mistaken an apparently flourishing example of small democracy at work for a relic of the past. It restores confidence in the behavior of the suburbanite himself, for he appears not as a helpless captive of the gargantuan society of the modern world, but as the representative of our best traditions. It interprets the suburban migration as the result of rational decisions by rational people, who, despite their special motivations, have collectively used the material resources of an industrial society to recapture elemental human values. In short, it appears to make the suburb a desirable development on the contemporary scene.

At the same time, an argument that suburbia represents a return to normalcy, in the best sense of the word, seems to fly in the face of what we have discovered about urban life. Certainly it seems difficult to believe that a social basis for small town culture is compatible with the rise of great cities, and certainly for over fifty years almost every study of the American scene seems to indicate the overpowering advance of mass society. In the light of the information available at the time, Bryce, Wells, Geddes, and Howard based their doctrines of reform on apparently irrefutable facts which indicated the disappearance of the small community. And today, modern reformers and planners can present impressive evidence and reasoned arguments to show that the modern suburb possesses none of the vital prerequisites for community life as it is commonly understood. On first inspection, the fringe satellites around the American city seem to lack the ingredients of intimate social intercourse, human interdependence, similarity of outlook and interests, and widespread participation in civic affairs which are essential to the ideology.

The case for believing that suburbs bear at best only the faintest resemblance to the genuine article begins with a rigorous definition of the word *community*. Those who see modern metropolitan life as a process of progressively weakening man's ties with his neighbors are using the "primary" community as a reference point, the "preliterate society, feudal holding or peasant village." In this social unit, almost every aspect of an individual's activity was bound up with the collective experience of his fellows. Each of the unit's members worked within a closed economic system, producing for his immediate neighbors and consuming from his neighbors' production. The place of work and the place of residence were one and the same, and travel was almost unknown. Political power was typically vested in a single authority and, in peaceful times, exercised without interference from the outside. Social intercourse was confined to a limited group of neighborhoods, and the common values, opinions, and tastes developed within this small area. Sufficiency, isolation, sustained and constant relationships among all members were the hallmarks of this basic model.

If these standards are accepted, then it makes a good deal of sense to relegate the genuine small town to the realm of nostalgia. The suburb today has, as countless writers point out, no truly independent economic status. It is only a part of the metropolitan economy, and this economy, in modern terms, is the smallest system which can lay claim to self-sufficiency. Within the metropolitan system, the satellite towns comprise only hinterlands of "the nuclear centers of dominance." They contain only fractions of the labor force, facilities, equipment, and capital which provide the variety of skills and resources necessary to create a valid economy. Taken individually, the suburb as a production unit is nothing, and the separation of residence and place of employment, the complicated transportation network, the commuter's schedule attest the breakdown of the conditions of economic autarchy on which primary communities were built.

Since suburbs have no economic independence compared to the reformers' prototype, it would seem to follow that social isolation has also disappeared. Thus, many authorities believe that the central city's dominance extends to other aspects of group life, and suburbia is increasingly absorbed into the larger urban culture. They point out that friendships have become scattered randomly throughout the entire metropolitan area; associations made in the course of work are now different from those developed in residential neighborhoods. They emphasize that the metropolis provides easy access to a variety of spectacles, and suburbanites become increasingly exposed to the temptations which the rich cultural and educational resources of an urban civilization offer. A wide array of economic alternatives encourages people to change from one job to another, to move their residence at a moment's notice, and to hold themselves aloof from any particular involvement in any particular circle of association. A restless, shifting pattern of flux and change characterizes metropolitan life, and barriers, physical and social, disappear as each individual knows more people and travels longer distances in his daily work.

Given the disappearance of economic interdependence and self-sufficiency, the passing of conditions of social isolation, these proponents of the disappearing community argue that the "density of intercourse" which promotes common values and provides a conscious feeling of communtiy tends to vanish too. Standard textbooks of urban sociology point out that as the suburb becomes enfolded in the metropolitan complex, neighborhood groups and institutions — local luncheon clubs, youth organizations, churches, fraternal societies — lose their community importance. While some suburbs still remain cultural islands, the majority seem to be coalescing with the central city, their populations almost completely indistinguishable from that of the metropolis at large. Although suburbs may still have more local symbols, more associations among neighbors, more local-oriented participation than the city, they seem to be growing less and less conscious of their own communal identity. The powerful compulsions for social groupings which a separate economic system and isolation begat are removed and suburban consciousness apparently rests on the weak and flimsy foundations of historic memories.

It is on the basis of this sort of analysis, of the findings of Park, Wirth, McKenzie, Queen, and Carpenter, that the interpretation of the suburbanite as a representative of a new mass culture is built. And it is from these conclusions that Riesman, Whyte, and other observers of the contem-

porary scene have developed the theses of the other-directed character and the organization man. For if the suburb
has lost the qualities of its ancient predecessor, it follows
that its inhabitants must find it difficult to distinguish themselves from other Americans. In these circumstances variations in provincial character and eccentricities tend to be
replaced by a single national character and only the ties of
kinship, work, and the stultifying communications of mass
media remain to bind men together.

Thus, while recognizing some remnants of the past, these
observers believe that the individual is left to commune
only with himself or his family, alone in the metropolis as
one by one the defenses of small town life crumble. In place
of a clear sense of local identity they find a vague ethos of
metropolitan culture, defined and directed by mass media,
the mass market, and the cult of the organization man to be
the closest approximation we now have to a sense of common
values. In place of a distinct civic consciousness and a feeling of belonging they believe that the individual usually has
a sense of unrelatedness to his surroundings. At best, the
urban man can retain only a weak notion of patriotism for
the metropolis, a New Yorker's superficial pride in being
part of the Big Show. Against the vision of suburbia as the
carrier for the grassroots faith, the tough-minded observer
sees only a continuing spread of the influence of the central
city, and the net of the metropolis is cast in larger and larger
circles, promising ultimately to engulf us all.

Second Thoughts on the Vanishing Act

Harsh and bleak as this judgment of the modern suburb
may seem, it is compelling only if one takes the primary
community — and the forces which created and sustained it
— as a departure point. But is that community the appro-

priate model to choose, and are economic self-sufficiency, physical isolation, and enforced neighborliness the only catalysts which create a sense of common consciousness?

To begin with, the abstract notion of "community" is extraordinarily difficult to define. Obviously, a community is something more than a collection of people in a given area, but how much more is difficult to say. Clearly the ingredients of time, space, economic activities, social structures, personal and group values go into the building of a community. But these factors touch on almost every aspect of group life and we speak simultaneously of the "community of nations," the "community of interests," the "American community," conjuring up a myriad of separate images as we do. Even the scholar finds it difficult to give the word a single meaning. Sociologists speak, for example, of communities as "spatial social systems" and "interaction space," or identify them as "sub-classes of collectivity" and "ego-oriented relationships on a territorial basis." But they do not pretend to have discovered all the qualities which give identity to certain people in a certain area, and they do not have a single theory of community. The "pure" model — against which all conceivable types of communities could be compared — is a proverbial will-o'-the-wisp.

Under these circumstances it is unwise to lean too heavily on any particular prototype. A concept that emphasizes a particular factor, such as economic self-sufficiency or interdependence, oversimplifies the problem. To attempt a single definition, to ignore the analytical quicksands on which the notion rests, is to run the risk of ignoring the variety both of communities and of the ways they may be studied. So most sociologists tend to speak in relative terms, to identify types of communities and degrees of "communization," to select "problems" and "aspects" of community, and to proceed cautiously from one specific historical checkpoint to another.

Yet even if the primary unit is used in a restricted and historical sense, to indicate only how far the suburb has departed from the community of old, a second difficulty appears. The best examples of the primary community — the medieval manor, the savage village, and behind them the more primitive patterns of group existence — never produced the conditions of small town life and government which modern political and social philosophy applauds. Their social systems were based on rigid gradations in rank and privilege, and when they produced political systems at all, they provided institutions totally incompatible with the American heritage of equality and democracy: chieftains, kings, dictators and feudal lords. The isolated village of ten centuries ago, the social organization of a South Sea island, might yield the highest degree of "communization" but it is unlikely that it offered the kind of social structure and politics the western tradition upholds. Suburbia cannot be judged by the degree to which it possesses the qualities of a historical primitive any more than it can be judged by its emulation of a theoretical abstract. The comparison to make is with the social organization and governments which began the American tradition.

In the historical context the model for the suburb is obviously the New England town of colonial times, the settlement of the Old Northwest in the early part of the nineteenth century, or possibly the Southern county of the same era — social organizations quite different from the "primary community" and indeed from each other. And here the differences between old small towns and new are substantially reduced. The New England town, for example, had a stronger measure of self-sufficiency so far as daily necessities of life are concerned than does the modern suburb, and, as we have seen, a stronger sense of physical isolation. But it was also far removed from the primitive world.

Neither the town nor the other acceptable early American models ever stood apart from the trade and commerce of the larger society. The focus of their economic activity and social interest turned outward, and it is not at all certain that isolation was the key variable in creating our legacy, however much it may seem so today. Thus, as Scott Greer has pointed out, Western society was already large in scale when America was colonized, and the fact that America was a colony insured its dependence upon imperial and international markets. Plymouth and Jamestown relied on England for their very existence; trade made the New England sea captains rich; exports and imports ordered the economic life of the early colonies and guaranteed their well-being and survival. There were never primitive communities economically unaware and economically independent of the outside world in the United States, just as there have been no primitive communities in this sense wherever governments legitimate in Western eyes have been established.

Neither were these grassroots prototypes somnolent, stable, and self-contained. The small community in the Western tradition never committed its members to a lifetime of isolation. Its inhabitants did not move as daily commuters do today, but almost all of them moved at one time or another and many moved constantly. The westward migration, by groups and by individuals, early established the tradition of a "commitment of limited liability" to the home town so emphasized in suburbia today, and mobility and restlessness is nothing new in the American character. We do not think, even in New England, of men irrevocably putting down roots in one location: not when communities splintered continually, sending portions of their congregations out into the wilderness. Most of all, we do not think of the colonists or the pioneers as people unconscious of their origins in other lands and ignorant of the conditions beyond their own fields and forests.

When one attempts to describe the archetype of the grass-roots community, then, the primitive ideal is left far behind. The economy is more complicated, the isolation less complete, the "density of interaction" among neighbors reduced. Americans may still, as Elkins and McKitrick point out, make the primitive, agrarian level "the one from which we have drawn democracy's folklore," and in their words, "it has been chronically difficult for our serious thoughts to go very far beyond it." Yet, the old "real grassroots" communities often had few "herbivorous overtones" at all; they were towns with relatively sophisticated forms of meeting economic and political problems, in which the enterprise of the speculator and the developer were true forerunners of urban capitalism, and the drafting of the Mayflower Compact and the exuberance of frontier political participation intimated governmental developments to come.

Tocqueville captured the essential difference between the typical American settlement and the primary community when he wrote, "The Americans never use the word 'peasant' because they have no idea of the peculiar class which that term denotes; the ignorance of more remote ages, the simplicity of rural life, and the rusticity of the villager have not been preserved amongst them; and they are alike unacquainted with the virtues, the vices, the coarse habits, and the simple graces of an early stage of civilization . . . The pioneer wears the dress, and he speaks the language of cities; he is acquainted with the past, curious of the future, and ready for argument upon the present; he is, in short, a highly civilized being, who consents, for a time, to inhabit the back-woods, and who penetrates into the wilds of the New World with the Bible, an axe, and a file of newspapers."

It is not even easy to select from the various prototypes the special characteristics of community which they had in common. As Conrad Arensberg has pointed out, the early New England town was famous for its compact ordering of space, its heavy emphasis on egalitarianism, its sense of con-gregation. It signified a special use of time and space, the development of particular social and economic structures, centering on the parish house and town meeting, and an agreement on the particular values of thrift, discipline, and civility. But the town of the Old Northwest is equally con-sidered a model, and here in the early 1830's localism was "open-country culture," a main street, then straggling lanes, dotted here and there with houses and disappearing into farm lands. A disordered land-use pattern, a flamboyant fever of speculation, a quite different feeling for neighbor-hood and community affairs, indistinct geographical bound-aries, an array of political jurisdictions not too different from the present metropolitan jumble, produced in the Midwest a political pattern acceptable to the grassroots tradition. Even the Southern county, for all its aspects of "palacio," its wide dispersion of residents and economic activity over many square miles, was deemed a passable basis for the develop-ment of local communities. The political intercourse of the courthouse sufficed to offer a regularized structure for com-munity life, despite the shadows of class stratification which the figures of the Virginia gentry cast.

If the various forms of community life Americans idealize were quite different from the primary unit, it is also possible that the forces which created their self-conscious identity were not the same. While relative isolation and relative economic self-sufficiency undoubtedly played their parts, they may not have been the only factors involved — and they may not have been the critical ones. Many factors besides economic self-sufficiency and physical isolation have been singled out and emphasized as critical, and while comparisons are necessary, as Albert Reiss has suggested, rarely are they conclusive.

Elkins and McKitrick, for example, explain the development of the American sense of community by a process which relegates economic and spatial isolation to a secondary position. They see the important factor as the flood of public problems which arise during the early stages of establishing a settlement. To them, "political democracy evolves most quickly — while the process of organization and the solving of basic problems are still critical." If the community involved is homogeneous in make-up and does not possess "a structure of natural leadership" — if it lacks deep cleavages in class and faith and an established order — "democracy presents itself much less as a bright possibility than a brutal necessity."

By this kind of definition, of course, many suburbs qualify as communities. Indeed, Elkins and McKitrick discover remarkable similarities among the activities and communal life of a modern housing development and of Hamilton County, Ohio, about 1802, and Deerfield, Massachusetts, during King Philip's War in 1675. The common fact is the establishment of a new social complex in a given territory; a "time of troubles." The variables are "a period of problem solving and a homogeneous population whose key factor is the lack of a structure of leadership." Suburbs, on the fringe of the new urban frontier, possess the essentials of this American spirit of localism even though they lack the isolation, the autarchy, the union of home and work which the earlier community reportedly presented. Their exploding populations, their inadequate facilities, their creaking political processes guarantee a period of problem solving, while they have inherited a tradition of unstructured leadership — in Louis Hartz's term, while "they have been born free."

The more the underlying assumptions of the thesis of metropolitan dominance are examined, then, the less satisfactory the thesis becomes as an interpretation of suburban community behavior. While the characteristics of American small town life can be fairly easily described, the catalysts which promote these qualities are much harder to identify. The conditions of primitive society, economic self-sufficiency, physical isolation, close and frequent contact among neighbors, are clearly not the only means by which a group of people in a geographical area develop consciousness, institutions, symbolism and values of their own. At any rate, no theoretical model can be built on these factors alone and the American tradition of localism never relied on them exclusively. As the provocative hypothesis of "settlements a-building" suggests, there are many ways to secure the limited size, the similarity in occupations and opinions, and the sense of common purposes, which are the hallmarks of the small town. Modern life may change the methods by which these characteristics are developed, but it may not change the final results. Far from vanishing, the cult of localism may be rising in suburbia again in a form which, while not the same as a hundred years ago, provides the propinquity, homogeneity, social intercourse, and leisure on which, in every age, it ultimately depends.

The Case for the Reappearing Community

Historically, a hypothesis which opposes the theory of metropolitan dominance and the breakdown of the small community takes as its point of departure the Victorian city of sixty and seventy years ago. This was the urban settlement most removed from the American prototype and most advanced in the process of communal disintegration. Far more than the city of today, the Victorian city presented a layered, visible "class stratification" and an "open-class pecuniary" society, acquisitive and impersonal. It was in New York, Boston, and Philadelphia in the 1880's and 1890's that social and political communication and consciousness broke down most completely, and that power, economic and political, flowed into the hands of the few. These were the dark decades of humanitarianism and local government, when escape from the city was impossible and civic authority to deal with problems of social welfare reached its lowest ebb. If the comparison is to the New England town, then, the bleak era for community life was a half-century ago, when the individual was most completely alone, swallowed up in the city or left behind in deserted rural hamlets. The very success of the boss in creating political organization by providing a calculated facsimile of community life in the political ward testifies to the degree to which the old town spirit had disappeared.

If we take the Victorians as a checkpoint, the subsequent development of the metropolis may be interpreted as a process of community creation as easily as it can be seen as a continuation of metropolitan dominance. While, economically, a single regional system of self-sufficiency is appearing, social and political fragmentation of the metropolitan giant is taking place as well. The dispersion of social groups and economic activities vies with concentration as a predominant trend; decentralization opposes centralization, and the forces of segregation in neighborhood residences stand against the forces for absorption. Compared with the American urban community of fifty years ago, the new metropolitan area may well contain many genuine aspects of small town life and small town culture.

From this perspective, a general theory of the reappearing

community can be built. Its basic premise is that urban
Americans use political boundaries in place of economic interdependence as the catalyst to create some of the most important social and symbolic conditions of grassroots life. The
suburb is not the African village, nor a perfect representation
of the early American town, but as the urban exodus goes
on, new communities appear, using the legal powers of local
self-government and the variety of classes and vocations
which industrialization has spawned to fashion islands of
small town life. Not every quality of Mark Twain's Missis-
sippi River towns reappears, and not every aspect of the idealized life of what sociologists call "a distinct social system" or
a "collectivity" is evident. But the essential qualities for
the grassroots faith — propinquity, homogeneity, a special
kind of interdependence, a disposition to democratic participation in the Western tradition — show signs of flowering
again.

In broad strokes, the thesis of the reappearing community
holds that the institutions and political processes of county
and municipality long established but rusty in disuse become
the basis for creating new and special kinds of small communities. Political authority aims to replace relative economic
isolation to engender the critical sense of separate identity
and to give the lonely metropolitan man a home again. In a
sense, the process of community building is reversed: old
and outworn governmental structures now become the
foundations for new social and economic groupings. As land
is changed from farm to suburban, as constituencies are repopulated, as suburban political institutions face problems
of community life, suburbanites are caught up in a tempo
as speculative and promotional as ever existed in the Old
Northwest, and relive the time of development which produced local government in the grassroots tradition.

The challenge the suburban community confronts is the immense scale of industrialization and urbanization of modern life. The response is a sorting out of the disparate, disruptive factors which modern specialization has produced and a reassembling of them in manageable clusters. Out of the great urban mass of occupations, classes, technical skills, income levels, races and creeds, particular variants seem to be coalescing into smaller units with definite conscious identity. This isolation, in the suburbs, of certain types of metropolitan people into groups is creating a new kind of homogeneity, participation, and equality. Instead of the economic autarchy that held a community together earlier, now similarity of occupation or of race, or some special bond unique in the area serves to set down the roots of a modern small town culture.

In this task of making new communities out of the Great Society of the metropolis, the pioneers may even be abetted by their lack of economic self-sufficiency and of physical isolation. The variety and prosperity of the urban age offers them a range of choices in setting the tone of their communities that earlier American towns never had. In terms of social structure and occupations, settlements in New England or in the West rarely differed one from another except in the bounty nature had supplied and the broad patterns of specialization regional differences decreed. In the modern metropolis, the technological revolutions in transportation, industry, construction, and home finance frees the inhabitants of a small community from the necessity of providing all the resources for livelihood within the borders of their home town. Modern innovations allow a specialization in community living that is realistically adjusted to the modern world.

At the same time, years of prosperity have allowed these

suburban settlers to escape the conditions of scarcity and marginal survival suffered by their predecessors. Civic frills can be provided to enhance a feeling of group unity: generous support of churches and museums, special recreational facilities, celebrations, and schools rich in community activities. This variety of possible resources and the wealth to get them offer lavish raw materials for the construction of an idealized small town, especially since that town has the opportunity and the means of keeping itself homogeneous in exactly the way it wants.

For if the powers of local government are used strategically, the original settlers of a suburban town can refuse to be overwhelmed by the onrush of population from the city. They can, by zoning, residential covenants, selective industrial development, taxation and informal patterns of segregation, literally choose their own fellow citizens. Because they do not have to reproduce all the parts of a self-contained economic system and admit clerks, craftsmen, and laborers within their boundaries, a degree of homogeneity can be achieved that was not possible before. The central city becomes a receptacle for all the functions the suburb dweller does not care to support. He can thus indulge his atavistic inclination, within his own circle escaping the greater community and making the best of both urban and suburban worlds. In this sense the suburbs may come to be not merely reproductions of the original small towns but, in many ways, improvements on them.

Of course the process of distillation necessary to produce the "pure" small town has a high price, for not all the unwanted elements in the metropolitan region can settle in the central city. For each suburban community which achieves a homogeneity and consciousness in keeping with American tradition, there may be another devoted to a less compatible function. Some suburbs take on a ghetto character, housing

residents who live within their boundaries because they are
not permitted to live elsewhere. Some receive the overflow
of industrial activity which makes them company towns or
pushes out all but slum residences. Still others perform services which are at least extra-legal and amoral according to a
strict interpretation of laws in other localities. These variations of the general picture of suburbia as the domicile of
the middle class means that a sizable number of suburbanites do not escape the modern world, and many more settle
for something less than an adequate reconstruction of earlier
communal conditions.

Nonetheless, enough suburbs seem to have succeeded in
the process to suggest that the differences in neighborliness
and civic participation between the central city and suburbia
in general are not just the lingering vestiges of old communities about to go under. Instead they are manifestations of
an incipient trend that will grow stronger, feeding on the
metropolitan economy. On balance, what is most significant
is not the influence of modern culture, but the general
suburban resistance to it. What is striking in the lives of most
suburbanites is the frequency with which they choose *not* to
avail themselves of the variety of experiences the metropolis
affords, the way they decline contacts with the larger society,
and the manner in which they voluntarily restrict their interests and associations to the immediate vicinity.

As transportation becomes more difficult and tiresome, a
journey to the city for any purpose other than work becomes
an increasingly rare occasion, indulged in by a restricted
number of suburbanites. The suburban newspaper becomes
as important as the great metropolitan daily; the do-it-yourself cult operates in the age of specialization, and although
the old-style Sears Roebuck catalogue may disappear, more
modern mail-order brochures styled to suburban tastes take
its place. On the fringes of the metropolitan area, in poorer

suburbs, conditions approaching the old frontier reappear in a more obvious way. Here, residents often build their own homes with their own tools, rejecting the expert as they painfully learn again the skills of the pioneer jack-of-all-trades.

Even theology has recognized the suburban effort to reclaim village life. The Reverend Truman B. Douglass explains the success of American Protestantism in suburbia, and its failure in the central city, not in terms of a modern suburban character which typifies the metropolitan man. Instead he sees it as a coincidence of outlook between the American Protestant churches and their suburban congregations. There is, to Douglass, a common hostility to the cities' "vast agglomeration of human beings, its monstrous vitality, its myriad future"; and there is a common acceptance of the "ethic of rural and small town traditions." Protestant sects find a warm welcome in the middle class suburb because of "the huge prejudice of Protestant leadership in favor of nonurban culture as being more favorable than city life to the growth of religion and of human good and therefore as being in some sense more pleasing to God."

If these indications are reliable, in church, recreation, shopping, and civic interests — in every activity except for work — the life of the suburbanite begins and ends within the political jurisdiction he calls home. The center of suburban attention turns increasingly inward, and daily contacts become more and more provincial. Change is going on in the metropolitan area, but it is not primarily a process of absorption. Instead, under the alternative hypothesis, it is an intimation of new communities in the making.

Proper People in Proper Places
The existence of two theories about suburban commu-

nity development complicates tremendously a judgment of the nature of suburbia today. The problem of arriving at an understanding of the suburb is not a matter of choosing one thesis to the exclusion of another, for countervailing forces are at work. It is more one of estimating the prevalent trend, in terms of the historical prerequisites for small governments.

Obviously, the American suburb is not a medieval village, but the American grassroots belief would not tolerate that kind of small community if it appeared. Obviously, it is not the garden city of the planners, a neoclassic expression of hierarchy and organic balance, but that is not a part of our classless faith either. The critical question is the evaluation of contradictory trends and forces: the impact of metropolitan influences of mass culture against the suburban effort to find a substitute for economic and physical isolation. Is the metropolitan dominance continuing to spread across the hinterlands, enfolding all the territory within the region in a shapeless, gigantic social system to portend a metropolitan elite superimposed over a lonely crowd? Or does a scatteration of society accompany the scatteration of government to promote a "huge mosaic of massed segregation of size, class, and ethnic groups," a "crazy-quilt of discontinuities," in short, a bundle of small communities?

There is as yet no conclusive evidence to document the superiority of one of these trends over the other. Our tools for isolating and measuring the forces and direction of metropolitan change are as crude and imperfect as our attempts to define the notion of community. Yet we know that, whatever the sources, there are certain necessary conditions for small town life — limited size, a population more or less reasonable in behavior and possessing a sense of civic obligation, a strong agreement about social and political values, and relative equality in prestige among the inhabitants. For the American model the check list is more specific: the size of the acceptable town has certainly not exceeded Lord Bryce's limit of 100,000; its people, in the tradition of the yeoman and the rustic, have generally been pictured as from Anglo-Saxon stock, sober and industrious as befits our rural folklore. Their life has traditionally centered on the family, and they have been believed to be God-fearing, law-abiding, respectful of learning, and ambitious to increase their possessions and advance their standing. The standards are inexact and unscientific, to be sure, but when available data are assembled, some inferences are possible about the way the battle is going.

On the matter of size the evidence is clearest — the suburban assault on the metropolitan area has already achieved considerable success. The 1950 Census shows that 1316 incorporated places with populations of 2500 or more, containing 70 per cent of the suburban population, surrounded the central cities in the urban areas then identified. Only one of these places had a population exceeding 250,000 and only 48 exceeded 100,000. There were 71 suburbs with between 25,000 and 50,000 residents, and 231 between 10,000 and 25,000. But there were 268 in the 5000 to 10,000 range; 241 between 2500 and 5000, and 457 under 2500. Even more important than the fact that places under 5000 population accounted for over 50 per cent of the total number of suburbs is the distribution of the total suburban population among the various political jurisdictions. One third of all suburbanites lived in places of less than 25,000 population, and more suburbanites lived in towns between 10,000 and 25,000 than anywhere else.

Suburbs possess small enough constituencies, then, provided their residents retain the flair for politics, the capacity to manage public affairs with common sense, the sturdy devotion to family and property which is supposedly our national heritage. On this second point — the similarity between suburbanites and their forefathers as they are idealistically remembered — there is also reason to believe that the suburbs measure up. Statistical series are on hand which, although they lead to no startling new conclusions, support the suburbanite — not the reformer — in his instinctive feeling of civic superiority over other Americans.

The first series is based on Census data as presented by Otis D. Duncan and Albert V. Reiss, Jr., in the Census Monograph, *Social Characteristics of Urban and Rural Communities, 1950.* It speaks to the success of the suburban population in differentiating itself in certain ways from the mother-city in its own metropolitan area and the nonmetropolitan city of comparable size. These figures (compared and analyzed more extensively in the notes for this chapter) show what has already been generally accepted on partial evidence — that the suburbs are well on the way toward capturing the major share of the social and occupational classes which have always seemed best suited to the Anglo-Saxon political tradition. When the suburban population in the United States is compared with that of the central city, the former is revealed as younger, more equally divided between men and women, and with a larger proportion of native white inhabitants. It contains a higher percentage of children, more married persons and many more family units. Its men are more regularly employed in more managerial and skilled occupations, average suburban income is considerably higher, and the majority of both men and women are better educated. If youth, a commitment to family life, relative economic well-being and education are helpful in organizing a community, and producing a feeling of "moral integration," then the suburb dwellers are clearly better off than their big city neighbors.

Suburbia not only has advantages over the central city in the metropolitan region, however, but over independent cities of comparable size located away from the metropolitan areas. When suburbs with population ranges between 10,000 and 25,000 and between 25,000 and 50,000 are compared to independent cities of the same size, there is little difference in the balance between men and women, and not much in age distribution. But, so far as ethnic composition is concerned, the non-white proportion of the independent cities is twice as great, and so far as family orientation is concerned, the suburbs have a substantially higher number of married persons and larger households. The suburb leads again in the number of working men, and in the concentration of employment in upper white collar jobs. More of its women are housewives. Suburban education is higher and suburban income is much higher. So is the number of home-owners and, contrary to popular belief, suburbanites move less often. Isolation from the great urban centers by physical distance, then, no longer assures the possession of the characteristics that provide citizens in the small town sense. The suburb has apparently succeeded to some degree in triumphing over its location and drawing together better population resources despite the fact that it is not a separate entity.

A third set of data documents further the thesis that the suburbs possess a population aggregate well equipped to support community consciousness. When suburban characteristics are compared with those of the urban fringe — that part of urbanized areas, largely unincorporated, which lies outside of places of 2500 or more residents — a different set of suburban advantages can be imputed. There is no national statistical series available for use here, but in its place is an

intensive investigation of the fringe of Chicago, undertaken
by Duncan and Reiss. This can be taken as at least a provocative sample, and the results show two separate trends
occurring in the hinterland. On the one hand, the fringe has
a closer balance between men and women, larger families,
more married people, and fewer transients than the suburbs.
The fringe population is younger, has a higher birthrate and
more children, and in all these characteristics may seem
more like the town of old. On the other hand, the average
fringe resident has less education, a lower income, and is
far more likely to be employed in blue collar trades than
white collar professions. If Chicago's experience is typical,
then, fringe people appear to be moving away from that combination of qualities which suburbia had to order its communal affairs.

One final comparison, more speculative and heroic in its
basic assumptions, may be in order as we test suburbia's
claim to defend the grassroots faith. This series of data,
again developed from the Census Monograph, concerns the
degree to which the characteristics of the suburbs correspond to those of the farm villages of between 1000 and 2500
population in the United States. Though we are an urban
nation, these villages still account for about one twentieth
of our total population, and their residents number over
six and one half million people. If we assume that they
may be taken as vestiges of the "natural" communities in
the American rural tradition, then perhaps a semi-histori-
cal checkpoint exists to compare with suburbia.

When the characteristics we have been using are arranged
in this series some interesting comparisons develop. In terms
of education, occupation, and income the rural villages are
substantially different. Their work is farm-oriented and
their income and educational level correspondingly lower

than the suburbs. But in terms of homogeneity of occupation, family orientation, and population balance, the similarity between suburb and village is striking. Extraordinarily close values obtain in median age, the balance between men and women, fertility ratios, proportion of native white inhabitants, family units, and mobility. Suburbia, in terms of these qualities, is closer to the small farm towns than it is to any other organized community.

It would be a mistake to read too much into these figures. The relative importance of the factors that go into creating a community pattern remain obscure. But the similarity is at least striking enough to lead Duncan and Reiss, in their study of urban and rural communities, to conclude that the village groups tend to "belong with the group of small urban places" — with the smaller suburbs or the urban portion of the fringe. The rural man and the suburban man are certainly quite different creatures, but their motivations and the way they go about ordering their social life seem to have more in common than we generally suspect.

Suburbs and Suburbs

So far we have dealt with national comparisons of the characteristics of the suburban population within the framework of the individual qualities which suburbanites bring to their home communities. The assumption has been that literacy, common ethnic and occupational backgrounds, family orientation, and home ownership enhance the possibilities for a conscious small town life and political system which the American heritage defends. The inference is that despite their position as satellites in the metropolitan economic orbit, the suburbs taken as a class have placed people with social and political competence in jurisdictions of small size. They have situated the majority of the educated white, professional family population of the United States in circumstances where they can participate in public affairs. Certainly, if any contemporary Americans retain a sense of civic obligation, a belief in the efficacy of direct participation, and a capacity to produce leaders in the tradition of localism they come from this group. The raw materials for good citizenship and good government are at hand.

The fact that these materials are at hand does not necessarily mean that they are employed to build communities, however. Averages are misleading, and it is possible that the way the population is distributed throughout the suburban ring works against the development of separate civic consciousness. If the figures for the indexes we have been quoting here are spread randomly throughout suburbia, then each suburb would tend to look like its neighbor and each would still contain a diverse mixture of races, occupations, degrees of education and family size comparable to the characteristics of the mammoth city population. Under these circumstances, the small town qualities would be so widely scattered that the existence of separate political boundaries would have no significance at all. Instead of hundreds of small communities working to restore conditions of communal life, only small reproductions of modern city society, with all its disharmonies and conflicts, would exist.

To make any reasonable deductions about the social and economic characteristics of suburbia, then, two additional kinds of data are needed: evidence that the suburbs are not alike and evidence that there is a pattern in how they differ. The by-products of the suburban "distillation" process have already been impressionistically described. In every metropolitan area, "exclusive suburbs," "workingman's suburbs," "sweet little communities" and waste lands of subdivisions and mass developments are recognized. Textbooks formalize these impressions when they classify suburbs as dormitory, industrial, service, recreational, and educational, with various subcategories under each. Investigations in the pattern of land use show major differences, even among suburbs serving the same economic functional purpose, in the ways they employ space. There are even indexes of the differences in moral qualities among cities and suburbs according to the degree of "goodness" they exhibit.

More systematic investigations confirm this general evidence that the average suburban characteristics just described are in fact a composite of a wide range of different types of people and attitudes. An analysis of characteristics reported for 394 suburbs in the 1956 *Municipal Yearbook* shows that 180 were predominantly residential, 121 essentially centers of employment, and 93 "balanced" between residences and commercial or industrial activity. By one measure of rapidity of growth these suburbs in 1950 were almost evenly divided: 90 per cent of the dwelling units in 126 of the suburbs had been built before World War II; at least 75 per cent of the homes were prewar in another 128; and less than 25 per cent of the existing residences were constructed before 1940 in 140. In the same report, there were eleven different classifications of the basic economic activities of the suburbs studied, from heavy manufacturing to amusement and education, with the ratio of employment to residents ranging from well over 100 per cent to less than 4 per cent. Though the dormitory nonmanufacturing suburb appears most frequently, as a class suburbs cover the spectrum so far as their basic economic functions are concerned.

Sociological studies report the same abundance of variety with respect to social and ethnic groupings. A comprehensive study of the St. Louis metropolitan area, emphasizing differences according to indexes of status (occupation-education) and ethnic composition (proportion Negro and non-white) reports ranges in the suburbs as broad as in the central city, both in terms of census tracts and suburban municipalities. By standards of social characteristics, as well as economic activity, then, the term suburbia covers a multitude of community experiences.

When the most rapidly growing suburbs are studied, the existence of variety is further confirmed. In six major American metropolitan areas 106 suburban municipalities, each less than 50,000 in population and each growing faster than the national suburban average, were selected, representing about one fourth of all the suburbs in these regions. Four characteristics of all 106 were first grouped in five intervals which correspond to the national distributions for all American communities. While the largest number, of course, clustered around the national average, suburbs were represented in every category, as indicated in Table I on the next page.

Each metropolitan area was then studied separately, and the sample suburbs were grouped in intervals which represented the distribution of all municipalities within that particular area. Table II shows both the ranges of experience of suburbs in the different areas and their distribution for three characteristics reported in all six areas. Table III gives the distribution for three additional characteristics for four of the metropolitan areas. Again, the wide disparity is evident, most particularly with respect to income, occupation, and the balance between men and women.

These limited excursions into quantitative comparisons make it clear that the overall suburban disposition to gather together a disproportionate share of middle class, better-educated Americans is, within itself, fragmented and divided. The broad tendencies toward homogeneity in occupation,

Table I

DISTRIBUTION OF 106 SELECTED SUBURBS BY SOCIAL AND ECONOMIC CHARACTERISTICS, 1950

	Very High	High	Medium	Low	Very Low
Median Income	(over $5500) 7	($4500-$5500) 11	($3500-$4500) 58	($2500-$3500) 26	(below $2500) 4
Per cent white collar of total employment	(over 80%) 2	(60%-80%) 24	(40%-60%) 47	(20%-40%) 32	(under 20%) 1
Per cent population over 21	(over 70%) 17	(65%-70%) 43	(60%-65%) 31	(55%-60%) 14	(less than 55%) 1
Sex ratio	(over 105%) 8	(100%-105%) 23	(95%-100%) 46	(90%-95%) 18	(under 90%) 11

Source: *1950 Census of Population*, Vol. II, *Characteristics of the Population*. Quintiles for each characteristic represent national distribution. Sex ratio refers to the number of males per 100 females.

Table II. DISTRIBUTION BY METROPOLITAN AREA—106 SUBURBS

Characteristics	Area	Highest	Median	Lowest	Very High	High	Medium	Low	Very Low
Median Income	St. Louis	$6000	$2966	$2488	5	4	1	1	0
	San Francisco	$4420	$3250	$3013	3	3	3	1	0
	Los Angeles	$4134	$3101	$2448	2	4	4	3	0
	Philadelphia	$4581	$3030	$3122	15	4	2	0	0
	Pittsburgh	$4906	$3060	$2841	9	11	5	0	0
	Chicago	$6155	$3497	$2095	18	7	0	0	1
Sex ratio	St. Louis	105.8	96.1	91.7	3	2	3	2	1
	San Francisco	137.8	94.4	91.5	4	3	2	1	0
	Los Angeles	101.2	92.4	73.5	2	6	3	1	1
	Philadelphia	104.1	93.7	85.8	2	7	6	2	4
	Pittsburgh	106.0	93.3	85.1	7	9	5	2	2
	Chicago	105.8	96.1	89.3	9	10	6	0	1
Median age	St. Louis	n.a.	33.0	n.a.	0	0	5	6	0
	San Francisco		32.9		0	1	2	7	0
	Los Angeles		33.7		1	3	4	5	0
	Philadelphia		32.6		0	6	13	2	0
	Pittsburgh		31.2		0	4	16	5	0
	Chicago		33.1		0	1	9	15	1

Source: *1950 Census of Population,* Vol. II, *Characteristics of the Population.* Quintiles for each characteristic represent distribution of all municipalities in each metropolitan area. Sex ratio refers to the number of males per 100 females.

Table III

DISTRIBUTION BY METROPOLITAN AREA—55 SUBURBS

Characteristics	Area	Highest	Median	Lowest	Very High	High	Medium	Low	Very Low
Per cent white collar	St. Louis	82.5	56.1	23.2	1	3	1	2	4
	San Francisco	62.1	51.1	25.5	0	4	2	2	2
	Los Angeles	64.8	47.4	28.3	5	0	2	2	4
	Philadelphia	41.1	54.2	28.3	2	5	4	5	5
Per cent native born white	St. Louis	97.3	94.2	89.0	0	0	8	1	2
	San Francisco	94.3	88.9	82.7	1	1	5	2	1
	Los Angeles	94.7	92.9	88.1	0	2	6	5	0
	Philadelphia	95.4	93.7	79.3	0	3	13	1	4
Per cent foreign born	St. Louis	2.8	12.3	1.1	2	1	2	2	4
	San Francisco	11.4	9.5	4.4	0	3	4	1	2
	Los Angeles	10.9	6.4	4.2	0	3	8	2	0
	Philadelphia	9.7	5.4	3.6	1	3	9	8	0

Source: *1950 Census of Population*, Vol. II, *Characteristics of the Population*. Quintiles for characteristics represent distribution of all municipalities in each metropolitan area.

education, orientation to family life, and age are intensified
in particular suburbs, and their differences from other American communities are even further exaggerated. This spectacle of suburban variety confirms and magnifies the reappearance of small localities capable of distinguishing themselves from their neighbors.

Suburbs Coalescing

But is there rhyme or reason to the welter of places and
people suburbia has come to encompass, a discernible pattern that can serve as a straw in the cross winds of metropolitan dominance and small town revival?

The traditional theories about spatial organization in metropolitan areas group people and economic activities in terms
of four major patterns, in addition to geography: by con-
centric zones, by sectors, by "multiple nuclei," and by cultural
components which interlace simple economic land uses with
intangible considerations important to the specific community. The concentric-zone theory envisions the metropolitan
region as a series of rings, beginning in the center with the
business district and moving through successive rings of in-
termingled industrial and residential uses, residences of
gradually increasing cost, and special types of manufacturing,
until finally the open spaces are reached. The sector hypothesis divides the regions into sectors of different land uses, by
which rich residential areas and industrial concentrations
may exist side by side, expanding outward through the rings
in the same direction. The area becomes sliced like a pie, as
people and economic activity move out along transportation
lines, with the richest succeeding in getting the best access to
the central city. The "multiple nuclei" theory emphasizes
the tendency of financial, legal, and administrative functions
to cluster closely together in the center because of the con-

stant communication their businesses demand; industry following transportation routes; residential areas separating themselves according to their ability to pay and simple prejudice. Finally, the symbolic values which residents attach to particular historic landmarks or special neighborhoods may be critical factors in determining the use of space and the development of land, and may give a community a special flavor all its own.

All these land-use theories speak for certain types of homogeneity. They serve to soften the harsh picture of the metropolitan community as an aggregation of classes and activities scattered randomly throughout the region, and lonely individuals who associate impersonally with their neighbors only in contractual terms of getting and spending. All of them give clues to the ways in which the suburbs surrounding the central city may find different and distinct personalities. While none of them at the present stage of development is completely persuasive on empirical grounds, they sound the theme of suburban homogeneity and social intercourse.

The different ways in which space is used in a metropolitan area also suggest the development of different social systems as well. As the investigations of suburban variety indicated, suburbs tend to separate themselves along several lines — by social status, ethnic composition and family structure, for example. These patterns are fairly regular in nature and they are closely related to the land pattern of the region. They provide additional evidence that there is purpose and direction in the suburban migration.

One useful current interpretation about the way in which these physical and social arrangements are tied together emphasizes the relation of occupations to residential distribution. Studying the Chicago metropolitan area, Otis and Beverly Duncan ranked occupational groups according to social status and then investigated the way the groups located their homes. They found no random distribution of members of a given occupation throughout the area, but rather a tendency of people with occupations highly separated in social status to put physical distance between them as well. In terms of an index of residential segregation — the tendency of one occupational group to have a different pattern of distribution from all others in a given area — professional workers vied with laborers for the highest rank, and clerical workers and craftsmen showed the least tendency to congregate.

In terms of an index of dissimilarity, which measures the variation between the occupational distribution in an individual suburb and that for the metropolitan region as a whole, a similar pattern emerges. If a low percentage of laborers and a high percentage of professional workers in a given area implies that the two try to put space or other barriers between themselves within the region, then the Duncan study shows an almost perfect scale of preference for neighbors of the same or similar occupation and status. Managers locate next to the professional class, and sales workers next to managers, and clerical workers or skilled blue collar workers next to sales. Contrariwise, laborers and service workers live more frequently together in the same area, and service workers are closer to operatives. Each area tends to find its residents associated according to the social ranks the occupations hold.

Moreover, although the occupation of a metropolitan resident is a strong influence on his choice of a neighborhood, his father's occupation appears to be a stronger one. In the Chicago study, the greater the difference in the occupations of the parents, the more physical space separates the homes of the present generation. The pattern of dispersion and segregation which emerges from studying the parental background of the metropolitan residents is more consistent than the pattern which emerges from identifying their present job. In short, prestige values inculcated in childhood seem to carry over more strongly than occupational, income or educational characteristics acquired in adult life.

In the suburbs, as might be expected, occupations and family backgrounds of the residents are typically those of higher social rank. Professionals, executives, managers and salesmen, in descending order, live furthest from the central city. Industrial workers concentrate in their own suburbs, and clerical and department store workers undertake to join the more successful white collar associates whenever possible. All the white collar occupations show the greatest aversion to low-rent districts, and the central city is inhabited primarily by service workers and operatives.

Throughout the study, the Duncans found exceptions and variations to an exact correlation between occupations, social standing, and residential location. The relationships were obviously affected by factors such as proximity to the place of employment, ethnic prejudices, and to some extent, income. A desire to climb up the social ladder, especially on the part of sales workers, helped prevent a perfect fit between occupation and prestige, and residential restrictions against Negroes and other ethnic groups affected residential locations for some occupations. Yet the striking conclusion of the Chicago study was how closely both occupations and family backgrounds produced a clear rank-order of social prestige, and how closely connected social prestige is to residential location.

The consistency shown in the Duncan findings indicates that each suburb tends to have a special character and feeling. People holding similar jobs, of similar ethnic back-

grounds and like incomes, tend to congregate in a few jurisdictions. As proximity to a man's place of work becomes less
and less important in the location of his home, given his ability and willingness to commute to work, the character of his
neighbors and his neighborhood becomes more important.
The substitute for the economic interdependence and physical isolation that created old communities is a conscious
choice of a location in which values and customs are most
likely to be shared.

Many of these new neighborhoods possess the characteristics of the old small town in extreme degree; others represent
quite different types of economic activity and ethnic groupings and undoubtedly are far removed from the ideal. But
all have those basic ingredients which foster some type of
community consciousness, institutions, and identity. The
great difference between the old American small towns and
the new is not to be found in size, in the political capacities of
its inhabitants, or in their homogeneity. The difference lies
in human volition; the colonials lived in small towns because there was no alternative; the suburbanite re-creates
them because he wants to, and thinks that they are good.

Natural Neighborhoods Plus Politics

The tendency to find one's own — whether defined by
similarity in jobs, race, or education — is apparent, of course,
throughout the metropolitan area. It existed in the Victorian city, for the urban humanitarians at the turn of the century recognized this propensity and built their neighborhood
houses on the basis of these instinctive groupings. The settlement idea of Jane Addams and Robert Woods was predicated
on the knowledge that a church, a charity organization, a
boy's club, a recreational center, could serve within a small
area of the great city as an institutional focal point for re-

constructing some aspect of parish life. More spontaneously, the corner drugstore, the bowling alley, the political ward heeler's office, served the same function, though with less lofty aspirations. At least in the beginning, the political machines which suburbanites scorn today relied in great measure upon providing personal associations, opportunity for congregation, and the preservation of old cultures. Probably there have always been these persistent clusters formed to combat the impersonal dominance of the metropolis and to resurrect small town ways on urban sidewalks.

It is not surprising, then, that the political jurisdictions of suburbs often comprehend natural neighborhoods with a cluster of similarly inclined residents. Burgess, Hoyt, the Duncans, regularize our knowledge about these groupings, but their basic conclusions are not likely to be startling to either urbanites or suburbanites. It is natural to expect that local organizations — athletic leagues, college clubs, American Legion posts and auxiliaries, religious organizations — draw local people together. It is also natural that in one suburb or neighborhood the Veterans of Foreign Wars is an important organization, and in another, the American Legion; that the social life of one revolves around the Holy Name Society and the Knights of Columbus, while the activities of a nearby suburb center on the League of Women Voters, the Rotary, and the Wednesday Night Bridge Club. Neighborhood and suburb alike have social institutions and activities largely supported by local membership, enhancing local self-sufficiency, and different from the next geographical area. The pattern of differentiation and of the special social life that it engenders goes on regardless of jurisdictional lines.

What distinguishes suburb and neighborhood, however, are the additional dimensions of community which separate political boundary lines contribute. The status of government that a suburb bequeaths to its inhabitants — thereby making them citizens — creates at once another sense of community — a cultural *sui generis* brought forth by legal fact, which Firey discovered — and the means to enhance and perpetuate that particular sense of community by public policy. Superimposed on group values and land values and economic values is a cultural component provided by the simple fact that a political entity is in existence.

Because that entity exists, it differentiates the neighborhood consciousness of the suburb dwellers from that of the residents of a particular sector within the central city, or of the unincorporated fringe lying about the suburb. It provides ways and means by which a suburb can retain the uniqueness that the population grouping has brought to it. There can be differences in the quality and design of the houses that are built, differences determined not by a great municipality's master plan but by the neighborhood itself. There can be differences in the type and quality of public services provided, in the expenditures set aside for public schools, in the relative emphasis given to highways, welfare, recreation, within the limits of the local budget.

Above all, there are political institutions established and in being by legislative fiat, public officials to be chosen, and an electoral process to be gone through in every suburban town and belonging to that town alone. In short, the suburb has one vital advantage over any city neighborhood in its struggle to preserve itself against metropolitan dominance and to build a small community again. It has power to pit against power, and, in and of itself, that power strengthens the community.

Re-enter the Metropolis

There is a final defense, however, for those who support the thesis of metropolitan dominance. It is possible to admit the tendency of the metropolitan population to divide itself into clusters homogeneous in their skills and out-look which have achieved municipal status and erected social and political barriers against invasion, and still argue that these groupings make no real difference. Conceivably, the impact of mass media and the great organization, the influence of the national "peer group," has been so pervasive as to affect all occupations, all ethnic groups, all neighborhoods. The new American character may not be limited to the cocktail set of the exclusive residential suburb in Crestwood Heights or to the developments in Park Forest, Illinois. The other-directed man may be, as Riesman suggests, the metropolitan man wherever he is found within the area. Differences in outlook and value caused by differences in income, age, occupation, and race may pale into insignificance before the pressures for conformity and adjustment which play upon us all. Metropolitan dominance may be achieved not by absorbing every suburb into the city's sphere but by psychologically invading the mind of every metropolitan citizen and instilling the same urban habits and values one by one.

The response to this variation on the theme of the metropolitan dominance is to explore its historical benchmark in much the same way as we investigated the departure point of the disappearing community. Those who saw the suburban communion as an artifice reached past the relevant historical model into primitive society to build their case. Those who see a new metropolitan character never reach the appropriate model historically at all. They stop short to take a particular type of nineteenth century man as their "old American." He was the rugged, independent individualist, pioneer or capitalist, guided by moral principles inculcated by parent and teacher, insensitive to those around him, impatient of restraints, unhappy in crowds. He appeared as frontier man, incapable of conformity in a settled society,

searching always for elbow room, or he appeared as a robber
baron believing that rules and regulations, public or private,
were made to be broken. Gauged by this character type, the
modern American, urban or suburban, is new indeed.

But this "old American" never lived in a grassroots community, never participated in the small government we idealize today. His habitat was the physical wilderness at the
fringe of the frontier or the moral wilderness of the Victorian
city. The inhabitant of the early small town was a much
different sort of fellow. He was the American Tocqueville
described: friendly, gregarious, subservient to public opinion, uncertain of his values. Even earlier, he was a resident of
Hadley, Massachusetts; in 1659 he was Joseph Kellogg,
farmer and proprietor of a ferry, "most active in the public
affairs of his community." Kellogg was no lonely individualist, antagonistic to society, but "esteemed in the memory of
his fellow citizens" for his service on the school committee
and as selectman, and his military leadership in King Philip's
War.

Later on, this second type of "old American" appeared in
the Midwest, gravitating toward the town, "promoting" its
business and political future, throwing himself into a "mael-
strom of politics" and by "placation and cajolery" entering
the life of the community. So James Lathrop is described in
Stark County, Ohio, in 1816, ". . . a young Connecticut
Yankee, brimming with talent and ambition . . . plunged
instantly into public life . . . organizing Canton's first library, appointed Receiver for the Bank . . . elected county
auditor . . . serving in the legislature . . . and heading
the committee which wrote Ohio's first compulsory school
tax law."

This strain of socially oriented man is persistent in American history, living generations earlier than the "inner

directed" individual on whom we focus today, with strong traits of adjustment, conformity, and a proclivity for congregation. He also needs to be recognized as a representation of American character when we gauge the distinctiveness of our contemporary culture. When he is recognized, when the homesteader as well as the pioneer, the promoter together with the industrialist, is brought into view, the modern suburbanite does not seem so new and strange. The contrast with the past is not so sharp, because there was an earlier man, more tamed and more adjusted in our modern sense, who initiated the grassroots ideal at the time when Daniel Boone and Horatio Alger were bequeathing the separate legacy of individualism.

Certainly, the suburban man has new characteristics. As Riesman emphasizes, there may be an important distinction in the earlier American's orientation to work in comparison with standards in our present economy of abundance. But just as clearly, the suburban type has much in common with the resident of two hundred years ago as well. What we may be witnessing now is the small town character's re-emergence as a reaction against Victorian man in the same way that the suburb is a reaction against the city of fifty years ago.

At the very least, there are intriguing similarities between the suburban man so emphasized today and the small town man of old. Is propinquity, which Whyte believes so injurious to personal privacy, a result of the mass living arrangements in modern suburban developments, or is it the more timeless quality which Sumner saw whenever small communities arose — small town public opinion as "an impervious mistress . . . Mrs. Grundy held powerful sway and Gossip was her prime minister"? Whyte's same apartments, set in the center of the city where no expectation of small town life exists, almost guarantee privacy. There no one knows, or cares, about his next-door neighbors.

Other qualities now taken as typical of suburban behavior present the baffling problem as to where semantic differences leave off and substantive ones begin between the grassroots chroniclers and the investigators of modern life. Much is made of the decrees of the peer groups to which everyone must adjust — in schools, at home, or in the club. Are they so different from the dictates which church and town fathers early imposed along the Atlantic seaboard? Are the neighborhood parties to welcome new arrivals in Park Forest, the cooperative baby-sitting, the car pools, modern innovations in character or contemporary expressions of a tradition of cooperation? Is the community construction of a swimming pool so different from a barn-raising? Or is the exchange of lawnmowers instead of reapers an inappropriate comparison? Modern interdependence among neighbors is not expressed in fighting Indians or gathering crops, but in sharing children's clothes and alternating trips to the supermarket.

Cooperation in the New England town was encouraged by the scarcity of collective resources; it is engendered again in the suburbs today by economic pressure. When the suburbanite burdens himself with debt, courts financial disaster with each time payment he assumes, he edges closer to dependence on his neighbor in the communal affairs of life. Even the egalitarian instinct reappears: there is more than superficial correspondence between the old injunction that "you are as good as any man — better than none" and the modern conviction that one should "keep down with the Joneses" and make "inconspicuous consumption" the rule of the day.

So the checklist of old virtues contrasted to new foibles runs: town meeting versus civic association, PTA and the League of Women Voters; the town moderator, Scattergood Baines, cautious, familiar, without airs versus the fashion setter, " 'the wheel' . . . intelligent, affable, resourceful,

democratic, and approachable," who again is at the forefront
of the group but not beyond it. And as for time: are
our schedules cluttered today because of inexorable vocational demands or because of committee meetings voluntarily
instigated to improve our towns? Perhaps one result of the
thirty-five hour work week is that it provides again the leisure that small town residents found when crops were in, and
that they used for cracker-barrel politics — the optional
dabbling in community affairs which gave local democracy
its broad base of support. Whyte's description of the duality
in the modern suburbanite's character, the tensions between
individual and community, may be suspect when presented
only as a picture of modern culture. Perhaps it always
existed, in considerable degree, in small towns everywhere.

Small Communities en Masse

From this welter of the crosscurrents of change, inadequate and impressionistic as the evidence may be, one
major conclusion emerges. The proponents of the disappearing community and the new metropolitan man cannot have
it both ways. They cannot take individuals who rejected the
notion of a community almost entirely, place them in a savage
village where their individualism would not be tolerated for
a moment, and present this combination as the ideal community life by which to judge the suburb. If our ideal is the
republic in miniature, then the model was a less perfect community than the primary village and its typical inhabitant
a more tamed and outgoing person than the unbridled en-
trepreneur. The appropriate model becomes the American
small town, which never approached the isolation of its primitive predecessors, and the American householder, accustomed to the dictates of his neighbors.

Nor need we try to turn the modern suburb into the village

on the green or make the suburbanite and the Minuteman indistinguishable. We need not deny that day-to-day mobility, the new role of women, modern communications, and an economy of abundance have left their mark. Of course, the thesis of metropolitan dominance is not to be gainsaid in explaining aspects of modern man. For our purposes, the issue as to how the American character has changed is largely irrelevant. We seek only the appearance of qualities, values, and behavior patterns that support the concept of the small community.

In this more relative framework, the suburban town emerges equipped with a limited constituency, a homogeneity, a type of civic attitude and an amount of leisure which bid fair to put small town democracy into practice for more people and for more governments than has been possible for a hundred years. The overwhelming majority of suburbs are relatively small in size and their populations manageable in number. Suburbanites, by and large, tend to exhibit the qualities of enterprise, education, and responsibility which, variously mingled, have served as the stamp of competent citizenship in the American tradition. Even in the suburbs where those attributes seem absent there is a tendency for like to seek out like — quite clearly by the occupational test, and in all probability, by ethnic and religious standards as well. This process of coalescence and clustering takes the place of the economic independence and physical isolation which in earlier days served as the critical agent in building a community. It makes possible a plausible inference that each suburb has values and institutions all its own.

Most important of all, each suburb has public problems and political institutions to heighten the sense of community. Even the raw new suburb, hewed out of potato fields, composed of mass developments, encompassing a variety of backgrounds, and divided by antagonisms between races and religions profits by these political mechanisms. The law may be only paper, but by the law, campaign races must be run, public facilities provided, political battles fought and public decisions made. As the decisions are made, someone wins and someone loses, a group joins the majority or the minority and the direction for further suburban development is set.

In all these ways, limited essentials of the grassroots faith seem satisfied. At least a good number of suburbs make attainable again the ". . . opportunity for companionship and friendship, for easy access to local services, and for certain forms of security" which the city did not offer. They promise a new version of open-country culture to stand against the metropolis as the "focal point not only of our material activities but of much of our moral and intellectual life as well." Within the metropolitan region, the significance of the suburbs is their actual representation, in their spatial organization and the character of their residents, of the ideal which has governed local government in the United States. In the final analysis, the dictionary as usual is close to the truth: the suburbs are a commingling of rural and urban characteristics. As Americans flock to them they represent a reconstruction of the ideals and the conditions on which our tradition of localism depends.

CHAPTER 5

The Politics of Suburbia

The Theory of Conversion

According to the line of reasoning advanced so far, suburbia dissects the metropolitan giant into small pieces, capping each with legal authority and some degree of civic consciousness. Suburbanites, to be sure, use space differently from their ancestors in New England towns, southern counties, and western hamlets. The economic and social functions of the suburbs are not the same as those in earlier American communities. Yet by a particular process of adaptation, the homogeneity, propinquity, and interdependence of small town life reappear. In many suburbs, precisely because the variety of urban life is all around them, suburban consciousness is subtly heightened and the values of smallness are displayed conspicuously. Technology, material abundance, the large organization have their impact, but it is at least an open question whether or not the pressures of modern life have ridden down the old aspirations of Americans at the local level. In many ways, the spirit of the old settlements has its counterparts in the urban frontier of today.

There is a double level of reality involved here, however. One may admit the existence of the ancient ideology in the minds of suburbanites. One may demonstrate a statistical reshuffling of population that may seem to substantiate, at least logically, the impact of that ideology. Conceivably, a Gallup poll might ferret out these suburban convictions as the reason why each suburb goes its different way. But, on a second level, what difference does the existence of these beliefs really make? Do men live by them, use them as guides for social and political conduct? Or do they mouth their small town loyalties, store them in mental compartments to be unlocked on the Fourth of July and Town Meeting night, and then act in different and possibly opposite ways? The spectacle of men equipped abstractly and emotionally with one set of convictions and operating practically and instinctively to the contrary is notorious. As with any thesis concerning the influence of ideas, the definition of suburbia as renaissance faces ultimately the stubborn test: what evidence is there that ideology and practice coincide?

One group of investigators looks to election results for evidence. They reason, with V. O. Key, that "the strand of rural and small-town politics contributes a special color and tone to the American political system," and they go beyond Key to impute to suburbia the selfsame disposition. Philosophically, their assumption is that the Lockian values of property and equality are most easily united in the small community and their potential conflict obscured. Small property owners in homogeneous communities express traditionally an instinct for conservatism, a distrust of government, and a preference for preserving existing arrangements. Since small town citizens are, by and large, homeowners, with a stake in private property, they face none of the tortuous conflicts vis-à-vis the national scene that plague the urban resident and the liberal, as Louis Hartz defines him.

Consequently, except for sporadic and historically fruitless deviations, small towns typically join rural areas in a display of preponderantly conservative sentiment. They ally themselves, politically, with urban business in the Republican Party, or they produce, as in the South, a special temper and philosophy within Democratic ranks. In upstate New York, downstate Illinois, western Massachusetts, across the nation, the small town, rural counties deliver consistent majorities in support of the American right. Even the occasional defections to the party apparently left of center are explicable by special circumstances in which the small town voter sees his preference best defended by changing his allegiance.

Suburbanites, according to this analysis, escaping from big city politics, are ready converts to the small town set of political values. They may have precious little equity in their houses, but they think of themselves — and are thought of — as homeowners. They may fail to find the suburb where their own kind already lives, but wherever they locate, they seek eagerly to be accepted. The first property tax bills they receive reinforce the voters' recognition of their new status. The first local organizations to which they are admitted enhance their desire to belong to the community *in toto* and erase latent tendencies for deviation. Green grass, fresh air, and new social status, in Louis Harris' words, work their magic; class and ethnic appeals lose their potency. Differences in nationality, religion, and occupation become submerged by a predominant identification with locality. The ownership of land, the symbol of community, these provide the sources for suburban loyalty and interest. Suburbanites shed their big city ways and embrace small town qualities of mind and outlook as quickly as they accept the backyard barbecue and the commuting schedule.

The proof of this process of assimilation, according to its advocates, shows up in the ballots — in the overwhelming shift to Republicanism that has taken place in metropolitan areas since 1946. The Republican Party lays claim to the suburban vote, it is argued, because it better protects their new interests and status and because it is the political faith of the old-time residents whose friendship is cultivated by the newcomer. Why retain allegiance to the Democrats, with their big city machines, corruption, and handouts? Loyalty to the party of the city conjures up memories of personal problems of the city — "a thousand images of an indecent, uncivilized past, perhaps necessary for the poor and ignorant" but not for the suburbanite. As homeowner and taxpayer, he is the man "economically coming up." Why risk social ostracism when "everyone knows that the town had an eight-to-one Republican registration" and no one has heard of Democrats in the suburb?

Moreover, the Republicanism of Willkie, Dewey, and Eisenhower supposedly eases the intellectual and emotional pains of transition. There is room for new blood within the party, and the conservative shift is mitigated by accepting the best of the New Deal and the best of responsible internationalism. Thus Eugene Burdick creates his fictional Joe Wilson of Burlingame "who was once Jere Wilzweski of Pittsburgh," who moved occupationally from the blast furnace to a white collar job, and physically from downtown to the suburb. Changing their sedan for a station wagon, their funny papers for *Fortune,* the Wilzweskis changed their registration too. They "put a Dewey sticker on their car and eagerly said harsh things about Truman, and finally even began to reconstruct their memory of Roosevelt and remembered him as socialist, father of much-marrying children, fomenter of discontent, upsetter of the peace, and heard and believed that Eleanor had never loved him."

So the theory of conversion goes. The Wilzweskis are taken

as typical of the majority of suburbanites who "politically, during the war and before they left their city homes" were Democrats. Today the suburban majority is Republican, and that majority is so large as to require an entirely new interpretation of party politics in the United States. Just as class politics in the first half of the twentieth century replaced the sectional politics of the nineteenth, the suburban vote renders impossible those uneasy coalitions of ethnic groups and diverse classes that Roosevelt so skillfully assembled. Just as Democratic dominance of the big city overshadowed Republican strength in the hustings, Republican supremacy in the suburbs renders the urban working-class vote impotent. Hailing the new hope of Republicanism, Robert Taft could say with satisfaction in 1952, "The Democratic Party will never win another national election until it solves the problem of the suburbs." Reflecting the same conviction, from the opposite perspective, Jacob Arvey could comment dourly, "The suburbs beat us."

Voting returns seem to support the politicians' statements. In 1952, the suburban pluralities in six states for Eisenhower outweighed the Stevenson city pluralities by 243,000, enough to be decisive in the outcome for each state. In the same year, 17 of the 24 suburban Congressional Districts around the 20 largest metropolitan areas chose Republican representatives. Between 1948 and 1952, the suburbs in the fifteen largest metropolitan areas increased their Republican plurality from 773,000 to 1,688,000. By 1954, the Democratic vote in the New York City suburbs averaged only 35 per cent; the suburban Democratic vote around Chicago was barely 40 per cent. On the fringes of Philadelphia, St. Louis, San Francisco, Minneapolis, Buffalo, Milwaukee, and Cincinnati, Democrats never represented more than 47 per cent of the total suburban vote, and more frequently their proportion ranged between 35 and 40 per cent. Even around the Democratic strongholds of Detroit, Pittsburgh, and Cleveland, traditional Democratic majorities waned as the suburban exodus went on. A 7 per cent advantage was the highest suburban majority the Democrats could muster in any given metropolitan area in 1954, even though that was a non-Presidential election year.

As the flight from the central city continues, Edward C. Banfield, plotting the redistribution of population in metropolitan areas, can predict a dramatic shift from Democratic to Republican dominance for the entire metropolitan region. According to Banfield's population projection, and his assumption of a 60 per cent Democratic plurality in the core city and a 60 per cent Republican suburban plurality, the metropolitan-wide Democratic advantage disappeared shortly after 1956. By 1975, the imbalance between city and suburban population will be so great that the Republican metropolitan plurality can be expected to exceed two million.

By the conversion theory, as the suburbs continue to grow, the crisis of the Democratic Party deepens; the appeal of home ownership and the symbol of community overwhelm old loyalties. On-the-spot surveys confirm the statistical interpretations. In New York, the *Times* reports the settled convictions of suburban politicians that a change in allegiance has taken place: "A sense of property rights and a concern for tax rates comes with the key to a suburban home . . . a desire for social status and a feeling that it can be achieved by belonging to the 'right' social groups . . . a feeling that local conditions require a Republican enrollment if there is any hope of a consequent political career or political favors." In Chicago, the *Daily News* parrots the same rationale, and in a sample of 500 suburbanites finds that one in every ten has switched parties in a three-to-one ratio favoring the Republicans. Suburbs have, since the 1920's, always been Republican; in the 1950's, they continue to be so. If assimilation is going on in the way most generally believed and the suburbs are aping small towns everywhere, then the legacy has impact indeed. It is responsible for the success of the New Republicanism and its political role is more important than it has been for a hundred years.

The Theory of Transplantation

But do suburbanites change their votes *because* they live in suburbia? Perhaps the process of assimilation is the dominant force at work, or perhaps the newcomers seek out suburbia because other forces earlier changed their political outlook and disposition. Perhaps the Republican fortunes rest on ticket-switching in the suburbs, or perhaps the new loyalty to the Grand Old Party is engendered by the selfsame factors which encourage suburban migration. Suburbia and Republicanism may both be symptoms of other changes taking place in the American scene.

Election returns can be read in several ways, and prominent political analysts are as prone to emphasize changes in income and occupation and the dwindling significance of ethnic loyalties everywhere as they are to stress place of residence. References to the growing middle class and the new outlook of descendants of immigrants are inevitably intertwined with studies of the suburban vote. The cause-and-effect pattern involved is difficult to untangle, for after all Jere Wilzweski changed his name and his job before he moved to suburbia. Connections exist between locality and party affiliation, but they also exist — and probably even more closely — between party and social characteristics, religious affiliations, occupational status, and simple historical accident. Unraveling the relative importance of each of these factors in political behavior is a complicated job.

Thus, though Samuel Lubell readily conceded the importance of the suburban vote in a straight party analysis, he viewed it essentially as a projection of the growing middle class trend in America, an offshoot of a generalized search for acceptability. The second- and third-generation immigrants, to him, were consumed by a hunger for social standing and respectability. Living in the suburbs was one way to satisfy their drive, voting Republican was another, and frequently the two coincided. To Lubell, the factor of timing — the period when a family arrived at a "state of middle class blessedness" — was the critical explanation. Those climbing upward through the depression and the war could still look on the Democrats as the party of prosperity and reason: "I own a nice home, have a new car, and am much better off than my parents. I've been a Democrat all my life. Why should I change?" Those who arrived earlier with Coolidge or later with Eisenhower, when inflation was linked with a Democratic Administration, chose the Republicans.

In the same way Louis Harris makes the white collar symbol as important as the suburban one in tracing the rise of postwar Republicanism. The suburb happens to be a melting pot, to him, and happens to be the home of the new middle class. Influences at the office, and desire to escape from a foreign heritage, merge with the fact of home ownership and social standing in the new community. Essentially, Harris does not try to separate the factors as he characterizes the suburban vote. The suburbs produce Republican majorities; they are likely to continue to do so. In a very broad way these majorities result from the new white collar respectability, from prosperity, home ownership, subtle differences in outlook and residence; but, perhaps wisely, Harris does not try to gauge the relative importance of each factor.

From this perspective, a theory of transplantation is just as plausible as one of conversion. It is possible that as more

and more big city residents move outward, they simply carry
their convictions with them, and that changes in their political sentiments arise from their other affiliations. To the degree that suburbs become less the province of the middle class,
in the strict white collar sense of the word, and exhibit the
homogeneity within variety described in the last chapter,
each suburb may cater to quite different political outlooks.
These outlooks may be shaped by a number of influences,
and the suburbs could be merely the stage on which a vast
reshuffling of the metropolitan population is taking place.
Once living side by side, voting in wards and precincts, different city neighborhoods may resettle themselves in different suburbs retaining their own consciousness and political
disposition. Lubell recognizes this possibility, arising from a
more careful analysis of the characteristics of the suburban
population, when he speculates that "the suburban exodus
appears to have revived the old patterns of discrimination.
Around New York City there are suburban districts which
have become as heavily Jewish, or Italian or Irish in family
ancestry as were the ghettos of 'little Italies' or 'New Erins'
of the Lower East Side twenty-five years ago."

Facts as well as abstract logic support the transplantation
theory of the suburban vote. If the metropolitan ballots cast
since 1948 are examined more closely, the size of Republican
Presidential pluralities in these areas become the result of
Democratic defections in the city, not Republican gains in
the suburbs. Between the 1948 and 1952 elections, the central cities in the fifteen largest metropolitan areas shifted to
the Republicans, in the aggregate, to a greater degree than
did their suburbs. In the fourteen areas showing increasing
Republican strength in 1952, the gain in eight central cities
was greater than in their suburbs. If their ranks had held
firm in the five largest of the big cities, the Democrats would

have given Stevenson a majority in these metropolitan areas. The dwindling Democratic city vote, plus the growing absolute numbers of suburban voters, were the decisive factors in these elections.

In 1956, the crack-up of the Democratic urban strongholds was even more apparent. Republicans gained another 4 per cent in New York City over the 1952 returns; 6 per cent in Boston; 5 per cent in Chicago; 4 per cent in Milwaukee, and over 3 per cent in Pittsburgh. Only in San Francisco and Los Angeles did the Democrats manage a slight comeback. If the metropolitan areas as entities are going Republican, then something more than a simple move to the suburbs is involved.

Presidential returns, however, particularly in the last decade when personalities and issues have figured so prominently, are notoriously unreliable in indicating long-run party preferences. As with the conversion theory, there are case studies and spot surveys to give support to the theory of transplantation. Investigating voting behavior in suburban St. Louis County, Charles Edson discovered that in Congressional elections in this traditionally Republican county, Democratic strength rose sharply in all the townships between 1946 and 1954. The percentage increase in the total Democratic vote over the total Republican vote ranged from 308 per cent to 13 per cent, and those suburbs which were growing most rapidly in population were generally growing most rapidly in Democratic strength as well. Party preferences followed relative housing values and ethnic groupings more closely than they did jurisdictional boundaries. By the end of the period, in Congressional, state, and county elections, the Democrats were registering steady gains.

Edson pushed his analysis further by polling two subdivisions in suburban St. Louis, one Democratic and one Republican, which had similar income and ethnic characteristics. Questioning white, Christian residents whose income ranged between $4500 and $5000 a year, with an equal Catholic-Protestant ratio, he found no evidence of ticket-switching after residents moved to suburbia, no rush of independent voters to join the Grand Old Party, and no dissipation of Democratic loyalties among those who had been Democrats in the city. What Edson did discover was that party preference was most directly related to occupational status, combined with the influences of income and parental party loyalties. Particularly in the skilled labor bracket, a preponderant Democratic allegiance was observed regardless of the subdivision in which the worker lived. The greatest switching in party allegiance (defined as a change from the party of the voter's parents) took place among junior executives, moving up the ladder of social status.

A similar finding that a change in residence need not result in a change in party allegiance is reported by G. Edward Janosik in his analysis of Bucks County, Pennsylvania. When this suburban area experienced an influx of almost 17,000 people, stimulated by the location of a new steel plant and the establishment of a Levittown, the traditional Republican majority dwindled rapidly. The new residents were by no means all steelworkers — 28 per cent commuted to Philadelphia and another 22 per cent worked outside the county — but the net effect of their political participation was to increase the strength of the Democratic party fifteenfold in three years, while the absolute number of Republicans barely doubled. In the 1951 elections the Republicans polled 14,000 votes and the Democrats 2500. By 1954, in the gubernatorial election of that year, the Republican vote totaled 32,000 and the Democratic 31,000. Charges of corruption against the local Republican organization and personalities affected these elections in Janosik's opinion, but clearly the newcomers were not changing political labels to gain acceptance by their established neighbors.

The conversion versus transplantation problem can be approached from still another angle. Theoretically, at least, if suburban development represents primarily a redistribution of population within the metropolitan area, without significant party-switching, two checks seem possible. First, no overall change in the Democratic-Republican balance for the metropolitan region as a whole should take place, except that resulting from national trends which presumably reflect general pressures on party allegiances. Second, party loyalty can be matched, suburb by suburb, with the economic and social characteristics of the residents in each. To the degree that voting records correspond with differences in population characteristics, a presumption in favor of the predominance of occupation and income over residence as a determinant of voting behavior could be established.

An investigation of suburbs in the Boston metropolitan area lends some credence to this hypothesis. The voting records of the eighty-three cities and towns surrounding Boston were compared with the state two-party vote over a fourteen-year period from 1940 to 1954. For each town, in Presidential, gubernatorial, and state legislature elections, the difference between the percentage of Democratic votes in the suburb and in the state average was established. For the entire fourteen years, the change in these differences was calculated to give an indication whether the suburb was moving with, against, or faster than the state trend. On the assumption that the Boston metropolitan region as a whole experienced relatively little immigration of population from outside the region during the fourteen-year period, then its relatively constant Democratic percentage (a differential of 2.5

per cent from the state trend) should be composed of offsetting gains and losses among different types of suburbs. Further, the suburbs showing marked changes toward Republicanism and Democratism should be growing farther and farther apart in their population characteristics. If these tests held up, a fair inference that party loyalties were being transplanted, not converted, might be made.

The results of the investigation showed no substantial change in the Democratic vote for one half of the suburbs in any of the elections. The other localities divided into fifteen increasingly Republican towns, nine increasingly Democratic towns, and thirteen towns Republican in 1940 but Democratic in 1954. The towns showing increasing Republicanism were predominantly Republican to begin with, and the increasingly Democratic towns were also Democratic at the start. Significantly, perhaps, no Democratic suburb changed into a Republican one; rather the changes from one party to another were all in favor of the Democrats.

When the social and economic composition of the fastest-changing suburbs were compared, the expected differences showed up: the increasingly Republican suburbs have higher educational levels, higher incomes, higher rents, more home-owners, and better jobs. Basically, the pattern of political behavior followed the spatial organization of the metropolitan region. Suburbs closest to Boston, with either stable or declining populations, were most heavily Democratic. Suburbs with no change in political disposition or with an increasing Democratic vote occupied the second ring or extended along a transportation route in which housing and income patterns corresponded to those in the second ring. The Republican towns occupied the outer fringe of the metropolitan area; they displayed the highest income and professional characteristics and the fastest rate of growth. Their growth rates, however, were exaggerated because of their relatively small populations at the beginning. Thus, in absolute numbers, they did not represent the largest bulk of suburban migration, but probably only that portion made up of the relatively well-to-do.

With these figures in hand, one can speculate that population turnover — rather than assimilation — is the major source of the changing fortunes of the parties within the suburbs. Increasingly Democratic suburbs gain their new pluralities from direct Republican losses, occurring because the Republicans have simply moved out and their former residences have been occupied by Democrats from the central city or left vacant. In formerly Republican towns now tending to become Democratic, a steady population growth occurs, but the character of the population inclines downward in income and occupational terms. In the increasingly Republican suburbs, the rate of population growth is faster still, but occupational and income classifications are in the top white collar bracket. Since seven of these ten "most Republican" towns were already 65 per cent Republican in 1940, the likelihood is that Republicans leaving the Democratic suburbs move quite naturally into these areas, thereby swelling the already substantial Republican majority.

The transplantation thesis is thus consistent with the migration theory which Coleman Woodbury has described — that most suburbanites come from the central city by a series of hops. As their income and status rise and space requirements and social aspirations grow they change neighborhoods, and through a series of moves, they find the communities most harmonious to their new outlooks. Somewhere along the "old tenement trail," former political loyalties may break, and a shift to the Republican ranks may be made. Yet the critical reason for the switch is the individual family sta-

tus that has been achieved and, depending on the generation involved, the break may never come at all. Whatever the
political outcome, the change — or lack of change — is pre-
cipitated by reasons quite apart from residence. The suburbs
merely reflect a more pervasive transformation of American
society.

The Fruits of Electoral Analysis: "Not with a Bang . . ."

Despite the superficial rationality of both these theories
of conversion and of transplantation, it is most likely that
neither rests on firm foundations. The data by which they
must be tested are crude, for the election returns conceal a
myriad of motivations, and population figures, traced over
time, are subject to sizable errors. We have no adequate information concerning the former place of residence of newcomers to the suburbs, nor for that matter any method of
distinguishing between oldtimers and those who have just
arrived. Moreover, we cannot be sure whether the actual
Republican or Democratic votes cast represent persistent allegiance to parties. In fact, we can be quite sure that they do
not, for issues and personalities peculiar to each campaign
play an important part in the final decision of many voters.
Finally, we can be certain that Republicanism and Democratism have quite different connotations across the country.
Party labels by no means reflect accurately a voter's propensity toward conservatism or liberalism as implied by property
ownership or white collar status.

There are also logical snares and delusions in both theories. Even if the metropolitan vote is completely attuned to
national and state trends, and therefore relatively constant,
the theory of transplantation is not proved. True, it may be
more logical under these circumstances to think of the metropolitan population's redistributing itself by seeking out com-

munities that already express appropriate political and social attitudes. But it is at least possible to speculate that Democratic suburbs are assimilating Republicans and Republican suburbs are assimilating Democrats, and, in effect, a massive double ticket-switching process is underway.

There is also a danger in relying on national trends to set the standard of general changes in party sentiment, and then regarding metropolitan deviations from that trend as indicative of the suburban factor at work. Metropolitan regions now contain so large a part of the nation's population that their voting behavior is a decisive determinant of the national trend. To the extent that the metropolitan vote comprises the national average, we are using the same phenomenon to test itself.

Finally, there is the problem of deciding which type of election — Presidential, Congressional, gubernatorial, state legislative — most faithfully reflects party allegiance. The differences, at least in the Boston study, were substantial and at times contradictory. It was found, for example, that in towns "going" Democratic much faster gains were registered in state legislative races than in Presidential or gubernatorial ones. In towns increasingly Republican no such spread existed. One could reason, as Wallace Sayre has done, that some suburbanites have recognized a closer affinity to the big city and become Democrats in state matters while retaining a national Republican allegiance. Many suburban voters may have one attitude about international affairs and federal taxes and quite a different one on the grants-in-aid formulas for highways and education which the state establishes. The same suburb may elect the most regular of Republicans as Congressmen and yet support state legislators who regularly join city Democrats to do battle with upstate legislators over city aid, highway location, and school-building programs. This thesis of differential voting is, at best, highly tentative, for personality and issue factors obviously intrude, but its very possibility emphasizes the complications in interpreting suburban voting behavior solely through election returns.

These problems of data and logic imply that even the most detailed nationwide investigation is not likely to establish the origins of suburban voting behavior. Analysis of the facts at hand results in considerable skepticism about the theory of conversion as a generalized explanation, and establishes a presumption in favor of the transplantation hypothesis. But the evidence is not conclusive, and very likely both factors are at work. It is, for example, probably important whether the new suburbanites arrive individually or in groups, whether they settle in a development or more isolated individual homes, or whether they select an established neighborhood or enter a newly opened subdivision. Perhaps the most sensible conclusion is to accept both forces as being of some importance, with the magnitude of their respective impacts varying from one locale to another.

Yet whether more suburbanites switch votes than continue their old allegiances, one common inference seems possible on the basis of existing information: there is at work a political tendency toward homogeneity within each suburb comparable to the social and economic homogeneity traced in the last chapter. If assimilation is the major motivation on the part of the individual, the homogeneity comes about by conversion. If a desire to seek out one's own predominates, then the homogencity results from transplantation. In either event, the end product is the same: an increasing differentiation in political sentiment among suburbs, a correspondingly wider range of voting behavior for suburbia *in toto*, and a dwindling minority group in any given suburb.

Coincidental with a tendency toward one-party dominance in any given locality, or perhaps as a consequence of it, there seems to be a decline in the importance of partisan association as such. As Harris suggests, suburbanites, at least initially, have little time or motivation to busy themselves with political affairs. A striking feature of the St. Louis analysis is the high and apparently increasing proportion of voters who think of themselves as "independents." Even more provocative is the finding in the same survey that the partisan alertness of the citizens interviewed is at an extraordinarily low ebb. The majority of those polled did not know how their neighbors voted. Many did not know the majority party in the country at large and many of those who did express an opinion were factually wrong. Traditionally, few Americans wear their party allegiance on their sleeves, and it is not at all certain that party politics is a matter of great interest or great discussion in suburbia. Party assimilation may have little correspondence to social assimilation, and pressures for political conformity in the partisan sense simply may not exist.

In the end, a predominantly party-oriented analysis, focused on national and state elections, yields relatively few rewards. It seems clear that the existence of comfortable majorities in most suburbs and the growing tendency toward independent voting de-emphasizes politics and more especially dampens the flames of partisan politics. On state issues, suburban attitudes appear forged by a peculiar complex of contradictory forces: on the one hand, obvious coincidences of interest with the central city, and on the other, an emotion of anti-urbanism akin to the anti-metropolitanism that upstate areas so often exhibit. On national issues, the suburban factor becomes submerged amid a host of other influences and, in effect, is indeterminate. It may be that in particular areas and at particular times the place of residence is important in determining voting behavior, but the evidence at hand does not justify this presumption.

Politics at the Local Level: Symbols and Beliefs
    If no spectacular discoveries of suburban influence in state and national elections can be seen, the same does not hold true for local elections. Especially at the municipal level, suburban politics appear to differ, at least in degree, and probably in substance, from those of other American communities, both urban and rural. In the end, this difference has important implications for the state and national pattern.

One indication of this difference, which Harris has described, is the relative respectability and restraint of suburban politics at the local level — the yearning to shed the disreputable political habits of the big city. Another bit of evidence, which Whyte and Henderson have discovered on a sample basis, is the strong sense of community consciousness and civic responsibility that impels active participation in local affairs. Deeply concerned with the quality of schools, conscious of their new status, suburbanites are inclined to "care" about local affairs — zoning regulation, recreational plans, garbage collection, school curricula, street paving — in an especially intense way. As the logical converse of their apathy toward strong party affiliations, suburbanites approach the politics of the community on the basis of individual preferences; they are, more and more frequently, nonpartisan, sharply distinguishing their local public preferences from their views of national and state affairs.

Suburban nonpartisanship takes several forms. Sometimes, as in the Washington environs, it is simply a way of interjecting another party on the local scene, an organization closely identified in attitude and outlook with a national party but separately organized to overcome the minority status of its big brother in the area. In these cases nonpartisan groups parallel the earlier efforts of municipal reformers in the large cities to overthrow an established — and in their eyes — unpalatable party machine. Sometimes, as is customary in New York and Connecticut suburbs, nonpartisanship takes the form of the inclusion of members of the minority party in local councils in a ratio that preserves the majority party's control but that the minority could never achieve on its own. Finally, and apparently most frequently, local politics have no association, open or covert, with the established parties at all. Public affairs are the province of essentially political organizations — civic clubs, social leagues, or improvement organizations — whose members are loosely tied together and whose announced goals are "what is best for the community." There are exceptions amid the variety of suburbs, of course; some remain staunchly and overwhelmingly partisan in outlook. But the general trend is in the other direction — nonpartisanship is legally recognized in 61 per cent of the suburban governments reporting in the *Municipal Yearbook,* and for those under 10,000 population, the percentage is probably even higher.

This emphasis on nonpartisanship is, of course, a familiar element in the local politics of many communities which are not suburban. As the authors of the Federalist Papers early noted and as V. O. Key has more recently pointed out, nonpartisanship reflects a highly integrated community life with a powerful capacity to induce conformity. "Party, as such, often has no meaning except as a combination to fight the opposition. It is rather an expression continued from generation to generation of the consensus of a more or less individual community or at least of a majority in such overwhelming command that it is unaware of any challenge to its position. The politics of the locality is a politics of personality and of administration rather than a politics of issues." In this broad sense, suburban nonpartisanship does resemble the politics of all localities, stressing the candidate and not the platform, and exhibiting a high degree of disorganization.

Yet there is a significant distinction between the no-party pattern common to suburbia and the one-party localism that Key identifies, just as there is a distinction between the structured homogeneity of a relatively isolated town, with its banker, lawyer, merchant, farmer, clerk, and workingman, and the more unified composition of an individual suburb. In traditional one-party politics, intramural competition among factions, interest groups, and cliques within the same organization is accepted as normal at the local level, disruptive as it may sometimes be for party leadership. This kind of factionalism, prevalent in one-party states and large cities, is not antagonistic to the idea of partisanship as such and does not preclude organized group action at higher levels. On the contrary, party regularity beyond primary or convention fights is expected and encouraged; the existence of the party structure, tightly or loosely organized, is taken as natural, and the politically minded work within it.

The no-party politics of so many suburban governments, however, often exhibits quite different characteristics. There is, first of all, an outright reaction against partisan activity, a refusal to recognize that there may be persistent cleavages in the electorate, and an ethical disapproval of permanent group collaboration as an appropriate means for settling public disputes. "No-partyism" eats away at the idea of partisanship by outlawing party influence to "outside" elections and by discouraging outright displays of party allegiance in the community as indicative of bad taste. The political animal is tamed; as the suburbanite approaches the ballot box in local elections, he is expected to strive for a consensus with his friends and neighbors, to seek "the right solution" as distinct from favoring one or another faction of his party.

One explanation for this rise in the number of independents is that this view of citizenship spills over into national and state campaigns. The "local political man" dampens proclivities of the party political man, restrains his condemnation of the Man in the White House or his suspicion of big business or his conviction that labor racketeers spell the downfall of the nation. Instead, the nonpartisan is more likely to believe that the good citizen seeks the best man and the right answer in every campaign, so that the almost inarticulate loyalties common in one-party localities are consciously rejected.

Thus, Edward Janosik, after an investigation of politics in 57 suburban counties around the 20 largest metropolitan areas, concluded: "Many suburbanites in the United States seem to take pleasure in cultivating a politically independent state of mind. Some counties normally designated as suburban have population densities as high, if not higher, than sections of the core city. Even so, the pattern of political favors and resultant political obligations characteristic of older urban areas has never been strongly established in suburban communities."

A second feature of nonpartisanship is the suburbanite's acceptance of an obligation for extensive civic participation on the part of the lay constituency. So far as general political activity is concerned, this proclivity shows up in the large proportion of eligible voters who actually get to the polls in national elections. Janosik estimates that for these elections the chances are nine to one that the eligible suburban voter will cast his ballot. On the local level civic interest may express itself in the citizens' inclination to undertake the supervision of the local bureaucracy directly, or in his suspicion of the role of the professional political leader. Here the image of resurrected grassroots democracy commits the citizen, theoretically at least, to a do-it-yourself brand of politics, in which as many issues as possible, simple and complex, require his personal sanction, and the acceptable elected official is the part-time amateur, taking his term in office just as he once led the community chest drive.

Finally, and most fundamentally, no-party politics implies some positive assumptions about political behavior that go beyond simple antagonism to partisanship. Inescapably, there is a belief that the individual can and should arrive at his political convictions untutored and unled; an expectation that in the formal process of election and decision-making a consensus will emerge through the process of right reason and by the higher call to the common good. Gone is the notion of partisan groups, leaders and followers, and in its place is the conscious or unconscious assumption that the citizen, on his own, knows best.

This set of convictions, of course, marks the basic distinction between one-party and no-party politics, for it establishes a standard for acceptable political behavior that antedates the party system. As a theory, nonpartisanship harks back to the traditional concept of local government, to Jefferson's high expectations for the rational capacity of the yeoman, and to that strand in American political reasoning that relies on unfettered individualism, and that manifests itself in the agitation for primaries, referendums and recalls. It is in these assumptions that the suburbanite is linked most directly with his small town ancestors, and not in a coincidence in political attitude, which the theory of conversion tried to establish between the two.

This resurrection of conscious nonpartisanship so evident in the suburban brand of politics — as distinct from big city and rural patterns — has some quite specific consequences in the modern world. The antagonism toward party, the obligation for extensive citizen participation, and the expectation that there is likely to be a single right answer to a political problem results in an unwavering commitment to political forms in which direct democracy can be applied. This commitment, in turn, leads to an important redefinition of the relationship between the citizen and the bureaucrat, and an equally important de-emphasis on the role of the politician. Most important, under the cloak of local nonpartisanship, specific patterns of small, informally organized cliques develop which interact against the doctrine of nonpartisanship itself.

As we shall see, in the context of the modern service state, rather bizarre methods of conducting public business result. They are not evident in all suburbs at all times, and sometimes they are indistinguishable from practices in medium-sized independent cities and other localities that have adopted municipal reform's reinterpretation of the republic in miniature. But essentially they resemble more closely American political practice of two hundred years ago, as it grappled with contemporary public problems, than they do the more typical political process of twentieth century America.

Institutions for Nonpartisanship

The most obvious consequence of the suburbanite's insistence on the management of local affairs uncontaminated by partisan considerations is his preference for small governments which permit the greatest degree of individual participation. The most perfect institutional expression of this preference is found today, as it was found originally, in New England. Here, nonpartisanship relies on the same governmental structure which existed when the American theory of

localism began — the Town Meeting — and here the principle of the enlightened, unselfish citizen dedicated to the general advancement of his community can be applied in undiluted form.

In the environs of Boston, Portsmouth, and New Haven,
every citizen who wishes to crowd into the town hall, studies
with care the town warrant, judiciously considers the recommendations of the selectmen and the finance committee. He
deliberates the advisability of replacing the pump on fire
engine Number 52, and delivers, in consort with his neighbors, his decision. As the evening wears on, he listens to the
careful pros and cons of the School Committee as to the site
and construction of the new high school or the recommenda-
tion of the Planning Commission for a new building code.
He examines the details of gymnasium construction, the efficacy of outdoor exits for each classroom, and studies the implications of the load factor for four-inch joists. If he detects
a flaw in the expert's judgment or discovers a better method
for achieving the common objective, he rises to his feet, and
walks thirty yards to the nearest microphone. There, succinctly and with good-humored wit, he exposes the error or
suggests the improvement before five hundred of his neighbors. By such a process of debate, forethought on the part of
each citizen, and the leisurely development of a consensus —
not infrequently crystallizing at two o'clock in the morning
— the affairs of the town are popularly ordered.

Only the suburbs of New England are blessed today with
these institutional arrangements to ensure that the collective
knowledge of the town is brought to bear on all major problems and to guarantee the airing of grievances. In the other
sections of the country, the form of government is a municipality, a borough, a village, a township, or even a county. But
the principle of maximum participation remains the same
throughout the country. When suburbanites cannot congre-

gate physically they prefer to choose directly their mayor, their councilmen, aldermen, supervisors, board members, and to ensure that each citizen has free and easy access to his government. Elaborate appeal systems before the zoning board are established; open hearings on all important actions are required; the proposed budget is published in advance; volunteer advisory committees flourish at every turn.

Almost always, the governing body has several members, and rarely is the executive equipped with decisive powers. Every effort is made to "bring in" the minority in local decisions, by identifying their cooperative and responsible members and thereby ensuring that they have the chance to work as good citizens too. Should individual problems arise — a broken water pipe, a problem with the building inspector, an inconvenient new schedule for rubbish collection — the citizen goes straight to the top and expects to have his problem handled on a rational, objective basis. If direct participation by all members of the constituency is not possible, public affairs can still be carried on with the reassuring conviction that the government is readily accessible. The always difficult relationship of individual to state, so the theory runs, is eased by the sure conviction that there is no party hierarchy, no structure of leadership to stand between the man and his government.

To be sure, there is the additional problem of identifying which government is in fact appropriate for given problems. The metropolitan reformers were quite right in emphasizing the scatteration of governments, for the good citizen may have trouble knowing who is responsible for what in the provision of local services. Typically a separate school district or system exists with its own elected officials, to oversee public education quite independently of the municipality or town or borough. Quite frequently special water districts, fire districts, garbage districts, and highway districts, each independently organized and financed, appear on the scene. When a resident of Hempstead, Long Island, receives a tax bill composed of the levies of a half dozen separate taxing jurisdictions, conceivably he may have difficulty in determining the drift of local financial affairs. When he is called on to elect five or six different boards and commissions he may be excused for not being intimately familiar with the qualifications of all the candidates. Yet if these are unfortunate departures from the town-meeting model, they at least generally continue faithful to the principle of direct participation. The thousand-odd separate suburban jurisdictions around New York City may be difficult to fit together, and they erect additional obstacles to the exercise of prudent enlightened citizenship, but they are nonetheless of limited size and they offer an abundance of elected officials.

This insistence on easily accessible avenues into the decision-making arena, this passion for being able to participate without formal organization or selection, are the first fruits of suburban non-partisanship. Because local politics is viewed as a thing in itself more clearly than in one-party localities, it is no mere stepping stone to higher office. On this point suburbanites differ sharply from big city dwellers or rural folk; their political action expresses the conviction that a man *can* beat city hall, or that it is undemocratic to let the sheriff or the county judge "run things around here." So the suburbanite resists the lure of the larger, more efficient units, even as he becomes bewildered by the number of public decisions he is called upon to make, secure in the conviction that his preferences can make a difference in the way his government is run.

The Management of Issues

The second consequence of no-party suburban politics follows from the first; given a structure designed to encourage as much participation as possible, the citizen is expected to handle, on his own, the hot issues of the day. No barrier stands between him and his government; he takes pride in calling the police chief by his first name. As a consequence, the quality of the police force is the citizen's responsibility. Ideally, he is always in charge; and, ideally, he is committed to the tasks of constant surveillance of the public's business.

The reality of this energetic, civic-minded model citizen is frequently questioned by observers. As the activities of suburban government grow more complex, the town meeting or the public sessions of the borough council are sometimes described as "government by wisecrack" and written off as mechanisms too cumbersome to make real decisions. It is pointed out that even the most earnest voter is not able to give sensible decisions about water mains, fire engines, school curricula, and zoning patterns. It is suggested that while his present political institutions may serve a useful purpose in creating a sense of community, they rarely serve as effective instruments of popular government.

This less romantic interpretation of the actual results of nonpartisanship suggests that it is not the citizen but the local bureaucrat who is most influential. As the citizen finds the substance of public affairs growing increasingly intricate he finds ways to whittle down the size of his civic job. This feat is accomplished by a redefinition of what falls within the province of popular decision-making and what does not. Because nonpartisanship is built on the assumption of a like-minded constituency, contemplating no fundamental disagreements, it is a short, logical step to classify a whole range of public activities as entirely nonpolitical.

Thus, by making budget preparation the province of the professional finance director, zoning decisions the responsibility of the professional planning director, and supervision of the local bureaucracy the duty of the professional city manager, the burden on the citizen is mercifully lightened. Street repair and traffic control, it is argued, are no longer matters of each resident filling in the potholes in the public ways adjacent to his own property and warning the teamster that the bridge down the road will not bear his wagon's weight. They are properly the province of the highway department and the traffic engineer. Issues of public health can no longer be decided by public debate, or even by general practitioners in medicine; their resolution requires the scientific investigation of public health specialists. It is not enough to maintain a jail for the unruly. Criminology and penology are complex subjects, and sentences and prison routines need to be guided by the latest findings on juvenile delinquency. A modern welfare program is not a matter of Thanksgiving baskets for the poor, but a complicated process of interview, determination of need, case investigations and evaluations in which many specialists may take part.

So, function by function, more and more public activities in suburbia are called administrative and professional, removed from the list of subjects to be discussed and decided by public action, and routinized in budgets too large for scrutiny, let alone understanding. Since the average citizen cannot in fairness be asked to comment upon building codes, methods of water treatment and the relative merits of various types of police equipment, no citizen should have to comment at all. The exercise of popular control is restricted to only the most important of local issues, carefully culled to ensure that the citizen will have the time, energy and capacity to deal with them, and the arena of popular debate is kept small.

But exactly what are the issues that remain? With so many of the activities of local government the special province of the expert, acceptable matters for debate, so far as the general suburban government is concerned, are usually reduced to three: honesty, the tax bill, and land development. The question of outright corruption and wrongdoing on the part of public officials, by its nature, arises only sporadically, and, in a nonparty suburb, usually as a result of the suspicions and energy of the local press. It is likely never to be a major problem, if only because of the growing professionalization of the administrative side of local government. Even when skulduggery is detected, the average citizen can be expected to be indignant but not especially useful in either investigating or punishing it. Public action can express itself only by locking the barn door after the horse is stolen.

Nor does the issue of taxes offer the public much more opportunity to make rational policy. A higher tax rate can call forth cries of anguish and protest, but without familiarity with the budget and adequate information about the relative priorities among the locality's public needs, citizen action is not likely to be effective, and it can quite easily be harmful. Organized legislatures on the state and national level, equipped with committees and featuring an opposition party primed for attack, have difficulty enough in establishing a reasonable budget process. Town meetings, city councils, and commissions run into more trouble; and the voter's role, in a nonpartisan atmosphere, is usually reduced to accepting or rejecting bond issues at election time. Conflicts between the professional administrators and the elected officers quite frequently arise, but the lay citizen rarely finds an effective channel for participation.

Roughly the same situation exists so far as the control of land use and zoning is concerned. In suburbia, most residents reserve their strong opinions for the topic of the community's future development. Home ownership is, after all, a distinguishing characteristic of the residential suburb, and the instinct to protect property values is strong and widespread. Yet once again the effectiveness of citizen action is questionable. Planning has become the preserve of the specialists, and if the planner goes unheeded, a vast range of alternatives faces any locality. Shall developments be permitted or excluded? Shall the design of residences be regulated, to make sure that ultra-modern or ultra-conservative homes are kept out? Shall architects be permitted to experiment with newfangled construction materials and techniques? Is there to be a commercial sector or an industrial zone to relieve pressures on the tax rate, and if so, where and how big? What reservations are proper for recreational purposes? What attitude should be taken toward the location of the new express highway, other than the obvious position that it should not be allowed to come through the town?

Even assuming a collective, public, nonpartisan answer to these questions and a consensus about what the suburb wishes to become, stubborn technical problems of law and zoning remain. Private property rights still have sizable defenses, and the complicated procedures of zoning, regulations, appeals, and exceptions permit many modifications of any suburb's master plan. If the citizen were truly to fulfill his obligation with respect to land use, he would spend evening after evening listening to individual pleas for extending the building line in this instance or that, constructing a "nonconforming" garage, or putting a commercial building, by spot zoning, in an established residential area.

It is quite true that citizens of the metropolis as well as of more isolated cities face the same problem of understanding the technicalities of modern government and of controlling the burgeoning ranks of bureaucrats. Where nonpartisanship holds sway, all these municipalities may be in the same boat with the suburbs. Where party politics exist, however, even if predominantly one-party politics, there are professional politicians who make it their business to know developments and there are party organizations which, in the end, and, if the situation becomes too outrageous, may be held accountable.

Suburban municipalities, committed for the most part to part-time mayors and selectmen, resentful of open claims to political leadership, dependent upon the energy and zeal of the individual citizen, do not often possess this intervening layer of surveillance. Despite the classification of more and more problems as administrative, and the most energetic displays of public spirit, the average suburban citizen's capacity to deal effectively even with the issues which remain in his province grows more questionable. Nonpartisanship may faithfully preserve the image of Emerson's restless, prying conscious man, and the resort to professional expertness may limit the range of issues into which he is expected to inquire. More and more frequently, however, the reality of control seems to rest on the shoulders of relatively few, either elected officials or informal leaders, who stand between bureaucracy and the nonpartisan public.

The Suburban Boss

The conclusion that few citizens are capable of living up to their own ideology is not startling. The same sort of gap between the aspirations and practice of democracy exists almost everywhere in the United States. Yet the ineffectuality of citizen direction and control in many suburbs indicates a quite different pattern of decision-making and manipulation from that existing in other localities. In cities and rural areas the vacuum between constituency and government is usually filled by avowed political leaders; in suburbia, this alternative is typically not available. In a nonpartisan community the professional politician very seldom appears, and when he does, he operates under special circumstances.

It is true that some suburbs feature highly partisan and professionally organized elections; the Jersey City of the late Mayor Hague was, technically speaking, a suburb. Party competition can be strenuous in those outlying municipalities undergoing rapid changes in the character of their populations, as is the case in several suburbs around New York. Some suburbs attract the politically ambitious or idealistic, who chafe under the restraints of the city organization and hope for more successful or rewarding political careers outside the city limits. Occasionally, as Charles Adrian has made clear in his study of a Detroit suburb, a single political figure appears to dominate a municipality, especially when the suburb is industrial in character. Nonpartisanship is only a major and not a universal feature of suburban politics, and even its doctrines can be turned against themselves to produce a strong man.

Nonetheless, in most suburban municipalities, and especially in residential ones, the same conditions of suburban life that encourage nonpartisanship restrain the exercise of local political leadership as it is commonly understood. By his very migration, the suburbanite proclaims the fact that he does not need the help of the politician in managing his personal affairs. He is, as Louis Harris points out, no longer looking for handouts, jobs, or entry into the kingdom of American citizenship. He does not even require the intercession of a higher authority between the landlord and himself: his residential finance problems are with the institutionalized forces of the bank, the Federal Housing Authority, and the Veterans' Administration. Undoubtedly, personal adjustments and favoritism take place in the process of financing a new suburban home, but this complicated pattern of corruption involves collusion between sectors of private business and federal agencies more frequently than between local officials. A bank lawyer or vice-president, a federal employee, as Congressional investigations testify, are often more strategically located than a suburban political leader. Studying the results of his fifty-seven county investigations, Janosik concluded, "Traditional and flagrant types of political favoritism, such as interceding with law enforcement officers or conferring unofficial health and welfare benefits have never played an important role in suburban politics and do not today."

With the traditional function of the party leader as a dispenser of favors absent from the suburban environment, other community characteristics make the development of effective party control more difficult. In the residential suburbs it is harder to put together an effective ward organization, both because of the spatial dispersion of the community and the unpopularity of party associations as such. As far as votes are concerned, patronage no longer has substantial appeal, access to the welfare rolls is not a major aim of the middle class residents, and fewer suburbanites are likely to be engaged in illicit enterprises that require the connivance of the local police for their existence.

It is also more difficult, by reason of the limited size and scope of suburban government, to generate the pressures and inducements to finance a healthy machine. In the city, an alert boss can subject small or large business to pressures via the assessment, licensing, and regulatory routes; in the suburb, business is likely to reverse the process, for the wealth and income it offers to the community is likely to result in public concessions in the form of zoning, inspection and service adjustments rather than the payment of private tribute. Even in large industrial suburbs, the psychological influence of nonpartisanship, the generally higher income status of the population, and above all, the yearning for respectability, make the rule of the boss more difficult. The nonpartisan basis of local elections requires that the activities of a would-be boss be especially subtle, and the standard techniques for appealing to groups and classes and for manipulating voting procedures are not countenanced.

The same forces of respectability, prosperity, and the limited potential for outright corruption work against the appearance of the rural machine. The strength of the courthouse gang depends essentially on amateur administration and relative community poverty. As municipal professionalization increases, opportunity for juggling tax assessments, making special contractual arrangements, farming out legal business, and manipulating property records decreases. The fees which the clerk or sheriff once found a comfortable increment to his other occupations are abolished; once these officials are put on a regular salary, the temptation to contrive phony events to bring additional fees diminishes.

The necessity for "getting the county's business" also declines: the lawyer no longer finds that service to the local government is a major part of his income and competition for official favors diminishes. Both the rise of the professional administrator and the decline of the community as a place of business remove the local government from a favored position as the dispenser of munificence. Undoubtedly, special favors in real estate and legal businesses continue, and special exceptions in the use of the police power are made. But these gifts can rarely be translated into votes. The suburban man remains psychologically, economically, and institutionally oriented toward independence.

The suburban "boss," when he appears, then, bears little

resemblance to the traditional American image. This is not surprising, of course, for the political machine as typically understood has lost ground throughout the nation. Generally, however, the place of the boss has been taken by the party leader, a term denoting a man more interested in the fortunes of the organization than in personal prerogatives and power. It is in this respect that suburban politics begin to diverge from those of other localities.

A suburban party leader is needed in the general party framework. Someone is required to maintain contact with the state organization, to recruit candidates for the state legislature and for Congress, and to claim for his suburb the proper share of favors and appointments. Since the suburban government has extensive dealings with the state, in education, welfare, and most especially, highways, a man who knows his way around the capital is useful. Since both parties face today a growing problem of maintaining a semblance of grassroots organization, they have an interest in promoting devoted party work at the suburban level. In this sense, quite frequently a local party leader appears, usually at the county level, where the ties to the state government are most direct, and sometimes he receives, deservedly or not, the appellation of boss.

The circumstances surrounding suburban party leadership, however, place the leader in a position that is both more comfortable and more restrained than his urban or rural counterpart. His job is made easy in the sense that the vote that he is expected to deliver generally delivers itself. Situated as he is in a community preponderantly of one party whose members are indoctrinated with the responsibility of good citizenship, he faces neither the possibility of sporadic minority uprising nor the obstacles that physical distance and personal apathy impose on the rural organization.

He can generally count on a good turnout at the polls without much effort on his part; he does not need to stimulate interest by dispensing money or liquor, rounding up jobs in the county highway department, or providing transportation to the voting booth. Impersonal means of communication — flyers, mimeographed letters, and posters — suffice to inform his party members of the dangers that await them if the opposition triumphs in Washington or at the state and county levels.

To a considerable degree, then, the leader can talk issues rather than provide personal favors, however much he may distort and exaggerate their substance. Alternatively, he can devote himself to protecting the residents of his jurisdiction from invasion by what appears to be an undesirable wave of immigrants from the city or surrounding municipality. In either case, however, he is more likely to reflect adroitly his constituency's sentiments than to shape them. Demands for vigorous and disciplined action on the leader's part correspondingly diminish, for in a very real sense he has the best of two worlds: the small town homogeneity that creates a party consensus quite naturally, coupled with the sense of civic obligation which brings voters to the polls largely on their own initiative.

At the same time the suburban party leader is likely to work under restrictions which his urban and rural colleagues do not share. They live in an environment in which traditionally local offices are used as stepping stones for more responsible party posts. Party leaders are expected to indicate their preferences for local offices and an association between active party work and local office-holding is viewed as natural. In the New York political world of Carmine De Sapio, the Chicago of Mayor Daley or Senator Byrd's Virginia, municipal, county and state offices are tied together by the operation of the party, and politics at these levels blend. In this environment, the limitations of urban political activity are most usually determined by the growing professionalism of the city's bureaucracy.

In the suburbs, however, the party leader intervenes extensively in local nonpartisan affairs below the county level, somewhat at his peril. While a few are influential in local affairs in the same ways as their urban and rural counterparts, more typically the ethos of nonpartisanship makes their involvement more dangerous. The local candidate is considered suspect if he is too obviously an outpost of the party organization for state and county activities. It is frequently best for a local official to belong to the right party but not to be prominent in it. So Janosik reports that, particularly in the newer and less densely settled suburbs, "the independence of the voter is so fierce that the extent of political activity on election day is the distribution of small sample ballots at the polls and occasionally bringing an elderly lady to the polls . . . Political workers of both parties in these sections assert that the electorate resents the slightest attempt to encourage a citizen to avail himself of the right to vote, much less induce him to support a particular party. The voters' adherence to political independence compels party activity of an oblique nature, quite different from that associated with party organization."

Under these circumstances, a party leader is usually well advised to remain aloof from municipal, town, or village elections and to allow opposing candidates to fight it out for themselves, as long as they both come from the ranks of his own party. He comes to expect and even to encourage local government uninfluenced by partisan considerations. At the minimum, he undertakes to strike a pose of neutrality and to insist that nonpartisan efficiency is his ultimate local goal.

Although his philosophy of conscious self-restraint relieves the party leader of considerable headaches, it may occasionally pose some problems. Apart from the obvious fact that he is not in control over all aspects of political activity in the way other party leaders may be, the restrictions make it more difficult to grant rewards for party fidelity and to recruit new blood. The leader still has the obligation of caring for the struggling young lawyer who in ten years may make a good Congressman, and he still needs money for campaign coffers, especially when his suburb does not encompass the entire electoral district in question.

Generally, the leader finds the solution to the first difficulty in the appointive and usually uncontested offices which special districts provide. No one really cares who mounts the guard over Fire District 37 or who belongs to the commission that runs the garbage district. Only lawyers are aware of the counsel jobs authorized for the multitude of special jurisdictions and only lawyers are qualified to fill them. The very number of local units in the suburbs, abetted by the conviction that the public need not be concerned with technical services, gives the leader a certain leeway in patronage of a high type, which does not arouse nonpartisan indignation. Quite frequently this patronage is all he needs in the environment of middle class respectability.

So far as money is concerned, the state today operates the major highway programs and the award of really important construction contracts is often apart from local control. As long as the leader makes sure that his suburb is adequately provided for in state allocations and that local contractors receive their just due, he is likely to find campaign funds available. So long as he exercises the deciding vote in judicial appointments, he is satisfying the major aspirations of the suburban legal talent he needs in order to make his limited party organization work. All these matters are not the direct concern of local government, and his power here does not bring forth charges that grassroots democracy is being prostituted. To be sure, there are advantages if the local officials heed party requests, and certainly partisan considerations are at times bootlegged into local administration and policy, but the suburban "boss" does not absolutely require them to fulfill party obligations.

By and large, then, the party leader represents an additional dimension to suburban politics, standing beside but to quite a degree apart from local government. The two worlds are defined by the boundary line of nonpartisanship, and to the degree that the local government is not party-oriented, the partisan leader may actually be strengthened. The contrast with the old boss whose image lingers on in many voters' minds, is a point in his favor, and in the sphere where party activity is acceptable, the leader may find voluntary converts simply because he steers clear of local activities. Operating primarily within the party framework, supplying occasional assistance in local affairs but more generally oriented to the state level, he is able to receive credit both for the good government he does not control and for the big majorities he does not produce. In his own world of inter-governmental relations and a few ambitious personalities, an intimate knowledge of law and administrative procedure in state departments and an accurate feeling for the temper of his suburb are better sources of strength than popular and flamboyant action in behalf of the discontented.

In the final analysis, the specter of a dominant political personality is not a particularly realistic one in suburbia. Outlooks, institutions, and election habits work against this sort of development, with the party leader tolerated only within his own backyard, or if accepted, severely restrained in the demands he can impose upon the locality. But the absence of a single personality does not mean the absence of politics by personality. On the contrary, since the environment discourages formally organized political activity, politics by personality is about the only kind that exists.

In place of the outright politician, the professional who works full time at his job, residents look to "wheels" to spark civic affairs — men and women who engage in politics as their avocation, and occasionally as their recreation. Sometimes regarded as conscientious citizens, sometimes as simply incurable extroverts finding release for their energies, the amateur dabblers in public affairs shape local policy. The pattern of politics which emerges from their efforts often provokes intricate maneuverings among competing groups, lively conflict and sharp disagreements; and it is volatile and complex. But it is rarely partisan in the accepted sense of the word — and it is seldom managed by the professional politician which the city breeds.

Suburban Decision-Making

If the earnest citizen has surrendered control over many local issues, if few party leaders intervene, and if public affairs are the responsibility of the nonpartisan amateur, how are the politics of suburbia managed? A detailed answer is difficult to come by, but it is at least certain that in one form or another, alignments and associations exist to form some sort of power structure. As V. O. Key points out: "A consolidation of electoral strength must be accomplished to govern; that consolidation is accomplished through some combination of leadership elements capable of gaining majority electoral support ordinarily against the challenge of some other clique or cliques of persons with the ambition to govern . . . Party may be found, at least in rudimentary form, in any going democratic society, save perhaps the most tranquil or stagnant in which the governing processes are reduced almost solely to habit and tradition."

Suburbia is no exception to this rule. Yet even if it is reasonable to expect an assortment of special interests in that environment, it is exceedingly difficult to generalize about them. An investigation of the impact of the suburbs on party loyalty produced enough evidence for a tentative generalization that the relationship was overestimated. In gauging the influence of the nonpartisan ideal, with its consequent reduction of the numbers of public issues, the evidence was even more limited. Yet we know at least the extent to which nonpartisan elections prevail in the suburbs and the number of streamlined city-manager forms of government that have been established. In a negative sense, the characterization of the suburban boss makes it clear that the customary party pattern of formal majority responsibility and minority criticism does not usually apply to suburban officials. But when the nature of decision-making comes under inspection — the specific network of personal relationships and group interests that constitute a "power elite" — a systematic empirical basis for evaluation does not appear. Except for bits and pieces of information, the field is open for the exercise of logic and speculation.

Scattered studies do exist to demonstrate that in this particular suburb or that, on one special issue or another, a particular combination of forces comes into play. The "metropolitics" involved in the success or defeat of proposals for metropolitan-wide government has, for example, received considerable attention. Occasional research forays have been made into the influence of the party organizations that are organized primarily for state and national elections. The politics of city managers, in terms primarily of their success in retaining employment, have come in for investigation.

There are side observations on the political action of particular groups and classes of suburbanites as a by-product of general community social studies, and here and there a particular suburb is taken apart in exhaustive detail.

But by and large no muckrakers have appeared on the scene to describe in chapter and verse the inner workings of suburban politics in the way that big city bosses and urban political-business alliances were detailed fifty years ago. This is not surprising; the number and variety of possible suburban political patterns make the documentation needed for sound generalizations an exceedingly formidable job. It is little wonder that we know most about our national, less about state, and least about local politics. The task of research expands geometrically as we go down the scale.

If speculation from the fragments of evidence now available is an unhappy necessity, however, it can at least be done in an orderly manner. At one end of the spectrum of possible political patterns is the "vacuum" suburb in which no real pressures play overtly on local officials at all. Where the suburb approaches true homogeneity, where it is already settled and has become irrevocably one kind of town, where new population pressures do not rise to plague it, the management of affairs is likely to be a routine matter. Conflicts, demands for special decisions, issues of great local moment, simply do not arise, and the apathy that ensues results not from frustration but from contentment.

Even in rapidly growing, changing suburbs, the vacuum pattern may exist. When the commitment to nonpartisanship is strong, the tradition of professionalism well established, the income and social status of the residents high, local officials may be left alone to use their own best judgment in dealing with emerging problems. So strong is the belief in the individual political man that the mere fact of organizing an interest brings down the wrath of the majority, regardless of the purpose the group may seek. In these circumstances, the pressures on the legally constituted officers may be only in terms of personal associations derived from matters of personal importance, and may arise so naturally and informally as scarcely to be recognized.

It is doubtful, however, that the vacuum model applies to many suburbs. A consensus of political opinion may be a tendency and a goal, but it is rarely an accomplished suburban fact. Much more frequently, a pattern of conflict exists between old residents and new, frequently intensified by ethnic, religious, and occupational differences. This conflict arises both in the election of local officials and in the politics of individual decisions, and though it may be subdued by the common aspirations of the rising middle class and the desire "to belong," it is nonetheless quite real. Thus Charles Ball, writing of Winchester, Massachusetts, describes a continued struggle between old Yankees and new Italian and Irish residents, with the Yankees, having the prominence of social status on their side, usually winning. Ball traces an election contest for selectman in which the Italian candidate sought to go his Yankee opponent one better in the matter of respectability. He widely advertised his family coat-of-arms, first bestowed in Naples in 1337, thus topping the *Mayflower* passengers by three hundred years.

More generally, Ball documents the effective organization and participation of the established residents both in election campaigns and in town meeting. In Winchester, only one Yankee candidate files for a vacancy while regularly two Italians, two Irishmen, and one or two other relatively recent arrivals compete for the non-Yankee vote. At town meetings, Yankee precincts turn out over 70 per cent of their residents, while the precincts representative of mixed populations muster a little over 60 per cent and the solid non-Yankee areas scarcely 50 per cent. The power of length of residence and social status, intermixed with ethnic divisions, clearly operates here to place political predominance in the hands of the established people.

In the same way, Stanley Aronoff has described the unsuccessful efforts of "upstart" elements in Brookline, Massachusetts, to prevent the abolition of rent controls in the early 1950's. Temporarily victorious because they organized the newcomers as a body in a special town meeting, their power was gradually worn away through a series of special hearings, referrals, and postponement of action, until the older residents mobilized a majority and the organization of the newcomers was torn with dissension. Similarly, Frank Mann, in analyzing the politics of the suburban city of Newton, Massachusetts, discovered that for over twenty years an incumbent has always been in the race for City Council. Whenever a councilman decides not to stand for reelection, he considerately resigns prior to the expiration of his term, thus enabling his fellow council members to make the appointment to prevent an open race between two new aspirants.

Further south, in the Virginia counties adjacent to Washington, an open battle has been raging between old and new residents since 1940, when the growing number of federal employees spilled over into homes across the Potomac. In Arlington county, two nonpartisan organizations emerged, one representative of old Virginia, the other of new federal workers, and sharply competitive elections for county board, school board, and planning board have been the rule for over a decade. Complicated by the special strictures of the federal statutes which limit the political activities of civil servants, the interest and influence of the Byrd organization, and the occasional intervention of the state judiciary, the political attitudes in this county seem nonetheless essentially determined by a resident's time of arrival.

A second pattern of relationships and influences affecting political power exists, in some suburbs, between the commuters and the stay-at-homes. These groups may be indistinguishable as far as race and religion are concerned and they may all belong to the business community in the larger sense, but their place of work may have an important effect on their political influence. Generally, though by no means always, the commuter versus stay-at-home conflict centers around the residential-family character of the suburb. Since commuters have usually moved out of the city because of their children and their search for space, they are often antagonistic to commercial or industrial development. They are also likely to support public services more strenuously and to be more prepared to pay for them.

Yet commuters are unlikely to develop a political influence commensurate with their numbers. They tend, generally speaking, to be less directly affected by local decisions than are those who work as well as live in the suburb. Decisions on zoning and tax rates affect the latter intimately and, frequently, local businessmen have the opportunity to provide goods and services to the suburban government. Some businesses, notably real estate, depend in an ultimate sense on municipal decisions. And though the commuter pays his taxes and wishes to preserve his property values and the tone of his neighborhood, he is a good deal less involved than those whose livelihood rests in the town.

Also, in terms of time and breadth of association, the commuter is unlikely to have the opportunity to participate as completely and intensively as the stay-at-home. Keats' generalization that for practical purposes commuters de-

liver their franchise over to their wives and follow distaff
recommendations as far as local politics are concerned is undoubtedly too broad, but it also has considerable truth in it.
Since Brooklyn became a dormitory for Manhattan before
the Civil War, complaints about commuter apathy and lack
of interest in local affairs have matched the reformer's charge
of commuter neglect of central city civic conditions. Today
E. B. White discovers the commuter's natural habitat to be
his train "buried in the mud at the bottom of the East
River." Not only is he ignorant of the wonders of the city
except for the "time of arrival of trains and busses, and the
path to a quick lunch," his suburb is a "mere roost where he
comes at day's end to go to sleep."

It is unlikely that the commuter disengages himself as
completely from local affairs as Keats and White suggest, but
it is also clear that his time and energy have limits and that
his roots are more shallow than those whose entire day is
bound up within the suburban confines. His absence frequently results in the concentration of political power in a
relatively small group, and even when he participates, his
actions, consciously or unconsciously, are likely to be shaped
by the group. Ball, for example, in arguing his case that
the governments of metropolitan Boston were by and large
Yankee-controlled, suggests that the actual management of
suburban affairs rests in the hands of an even smaller minority of stay-at-homes. In particular, he believes three
groups hold the balance of power: retired people, local
businessmen, and middle-aged ladies. Their spokesmen are
"men of middle age who are Harvard or Dartmouth educated, and who have law offices or middle management positions in Boston or Cambridge," but the groups themselves are daytime dwellers. While some commuters are capable of being drawn into local affairs, they depend on the

stay-at-homes for intelligence, support, and, quite typically, the formulation of the objectives they seek.

The composition and attitudes of the stay-at-home electorate will vary, of course, according to the suburb. Almost always, women's organizations, whether self-consciously community-oriented, as the League of Women Voters, or serving ostensibly another function, as in the case of nursery schools, garden clubs, and church guilds, form one source of political gossip and action. Small business interests often make up a second, and real estate a third. If the suburb is big enough, these interest groups usually organize formally, in taxpayers' associations, business luncheon clubs, public expenditure councils, and the like, or contribute a special orientation to local clubs of national fraternal organizations — the Elks, Kiwanis, and Rotary.

Generally speaking, the women's groups fall into the categories of the "spenders" who are the most conscious of unfulfilled public needs, and the "aesthetic" who are out to preserve the charm or residential quality of the suburb. Business interests are more prone to emphasize the value of a low tax rate, or the advantages to be secured by commercial and industrial expansion, or perhaps the desirability of smaller-house developments in order to expand their local markets. In some suburbs, a single industry may be so large a factor in the tax base of the town that, although few of its workers or managerial staff reside in the locality, the business can exercise an influence in ways reminiscent of the company town of old.

Although we know that political lines between old residents and new, between commuters and stay-at-homes, and among the stay-at-homes themselves exist in particular localities, the universality of these patterns as well as their particular details remains largely a matter of conjecture.

There is a fourth political pattern, however, which is undoubtedly much more widespread. This is the influence and activity of bureaucracy itself, the stream-lined counterpart of the courthouse gangs in the small towns and rural areas. The rise of professionalization in suburban political administration, the intimacy of contact with the public, the supposedly close supervision over public programs that local electorates are able to exercise, does not diminish the influence of full-time municipal or town employees in suburbia. In many ways it extends their power in the realm of policy and decision making. The doctrine of nonpartisanship, the very informality of the political structure vis-à-vis the electorate at large, provides wide opportunities for those whose personal livelihood depends on the government.

In investigating Winchester, Ball found that sixty-nine public officials, divided equally between elected officers and town employees, held town meeting seats under Winchester's form of limited town meeting. Further, in terms of participation, these officials and employees accounted for over 36 per cent of the actual attendance in meetings, year in and year out, and other studies of Boston suburbs come up with much the same result. These officials participate actively and vigorously in deliberations. At a minimum it is customary, as the town warrant is presented, for the head of each department to make the defense of his budget, speaking both as an administrator and as a citizen.

In suburbs operating under the city-manager form, an even more effective channel of influence is opened up. Although the plan exists in theory only because policy-making and administration are capable of separation (the council deciding "what to do" and the manager determining "how to do it"), the dividing line is in many ways fictitious. Over the years since the plan first became popular, the original concept of the manager as technical administrator and expert has gradually been modified until now his role is frequently defined as "community leader." The original Code of Ethics of the International City Managers' Association, for example, contained in 1924 the flat injunction, "*NO City Manager Should Take an Active Part in Politics.*" The revised 1952 code provides more equivocally that the city manager "recognizes that the chief function of the local government at all times is to serve the best interests of all the people on a non-partisan basis."

In the same way the old code instructed the manager to leave "to the council the defense of policies which may be criticized," while the new code simply establishes that the manager "defends municipal policy publicly only after consideration and adoption of such policy by the council." For many managers the revisions mean that only partisan political activity is barred and that they now have "tacit or implied consent to enter other forms of political activity where municipal policy is the basic issue." One manager put the case more succinctly: "God bless all civic associations," he said. "They are the city manager's ward machines."

The impossibility of dividing the bundle of services into packages neatly labeled "policy" and "administration" literally forces the manager into a political role, for he is the figure on whom suburban attention focuses. Some managers openly enjoy this role and conveniently picture city councilors as ultra-conservative hacks, dependent on existing programs and patronage to garner the votes and campaign funds necessary for re-election. Others do not blame the elected officer, for "in order to be elected he needs votes," but they belittle, even in nonpartisan communities, the electoral process . . . to a city manager, votes are secured only by an exchange of favors.

Thus, whether the elected official is personally incompetent or only the unfortunate victim of the democratic system, the pressures to which he is subjected justify political activity on the part of the manager. As an appointed administrator, he is "above all concerned in the whole character and overall welfare of the total community, in financial programming, and in the improvement of governmental procedures." Quite naturally, he "tries to formulate policy, 'sells' it, and if necessary forces decisions distasteful to the city council through the indirect rallying of public opinion."

The "indirect rallying" does not follow the usages of bureaucracy perfected by the city machine; quite the reverse pertains. The bureaucrat's participation in suburban politics is not that of the political leader mobilizing support through patronage and payroll kickbacks. Rather, it is the activity of the pure-in-heart professional, defending the science of administration against the onslaughts of popular government. He has cleansed and fumigated bureaucracy and now he must carry the fight to the political process itself. So the prudent city manager early finds friends in suburbia; he speaks before the luncheon clubs and civic associations, he confers with the League of Women Voters; he discusses problems with the Taxpayers' Association. Piece by piece, he builds his own basis of support, though it is uncertain how great a price he pays to secure professional purity. Generally, the logic of his situation places him on the side of the business group and the forces in favor of low tax rates. But wherever he finds support, he is nonetheless a factor in suburban politics.

Of course, by changing titles and names, a similar picture could be constructed for many nonsuburban governments, especially those operating under the aegis of nonpartisanship. All that may set the suburbs apart as a class is the differences in degree of rate of growth, the rise of new problems, and a more passionate and widespread attachment to non-partyism. But if the pattern is not unique to suburbia — and even all suburbs may not fit it — it nonetheless stands as the most accurate description available evidence allows of suburban political behavior. And, to the degree that it is accurate, one predominant impression emerges: the conflicts and relationships among political groups are necessarily subterranean. Under the blanket of nonpartisanship, the suburbanite may neither give these associations formal recognition nor admit in public their appropriateness. He cannot acclaim leaders openly; he cannot join in local political organizations unless their aim is for good government in general. He can only wrap the cloak of nonpartisanship more tightly about him and go on behaving as if he had arrived at his preferences through the workings of his own mind.

The Special Issue of the Public Schools

A sketch of suburban politics as the power relations of a relatively large number of personalities and of relatively few and generally harmonious interest groups operating under the cover of nonpartisanship needs to be qualified in at least one important respect. The program and expenditures of suburban schools are quite likely to engender a brand of active, if not frenzied, political behavior that stands in stark contrast to the more controlled decision-making in other parts of suburban government. Part of the pattern of school politics is explicable in universal terms and is likely to be found in all types and sizes of American communities; part seems to be peculiar to the suburbs. Regardless of its source and motivations, however, the operation of the public schools results in more extensive public participation in political affairs, more heat, and not infrequently less light than any other function.

The quantitative magnitude of the school problem is one aspect of school politics. Since the suburbs represent the growing edge of the American population, the provision of school facilities is their major public problem. The central cities wrestle with deteriorating land values, slums, and blight, and concentrate on renewal and redevelopment programs to restore physical and fiscal soundness. Rural areas find highways perhaps the most persistent and politically sensitive public function. But the suburbs grapple with the growing tide of children who invade their borders. Following the Pied Piper lure of better schools, family after family lists consideration of their young as a primary cause for the suburban trek, and they tumble over one another to find governments with "good school systems."

In this context, the relative youth of the suburban population, the social acceptability of large families in the growing middle class, the almost universal practice of the present generation to complete at least a high school education, all combine to raise enormous quantitative demands on public education. In all local American governments, educational expenditures account for almost one half of the total budget; for suburban governments it is frequently a good deal more. Metropolitan school systems spend considerably more per pupil, adopt advanced techniques in instruction more quickly, and expand curricula more readily. Because the schools have the largest bureaucracy, take the greatest part of the tax dollar, and represent the most rapidly growing public demand, they are the most important function suburban governments perform.

Viewed in these terms simply of quantitative pressures, the school problem exaggerates whatever conflicts and disagreements already exist. Cleavages between established residents and new, commuters and stay-at-homes, young residents and old, industrial and residential taxpayers, are naturally intensified. And new dimensions in the power pattern are likely to come to the fore, expressed by the sharply different attitudes of Catholics, Protestants, and Jews toward the proper role of public education. The conflicting pressures of population and finance are likely, in and of themselves, to ignite public debate.

Yet quantitative pressures alone do not generate the suburban school battles which are so evident at the present time. Americans, and particularly suburbanites, care deeply about the qualitative aspects of public education — how "good" the additional teachers and the expanded curricula are. In part, this strong popular interest results from the suburban preoccupation with family and children. In part, it arises from the demands for literary and technical skills in our highly developed economy. In part, too, it stems from the social responsibility education now provides.

But the qualitative aspect of school politics stretches back beyond the values of our contemporary culture. A full explanation of school politics, its emotionalism and agitation, lies buried in the American political tradition as it is interpreted in educational philosophy. The national commitment to education began with the eighteenth century belief in man's reason as a prerequisite for popular government. Given that conviction, it follows that the development of the power to reason deserves the most careful attention any democracy can manage. If man is perfectible, in the sense of becoming progressively more reasonable, then the schools are the critical force in guiding and shaping his advance.

The twentieth century emphasis on irrational and emotional factors in human nature — the discounting of pure reason as a major determinant in human affairs — does not diminish the importance of the school. On the contrary, as the educator interprets the new philosophies, they extend its responsibilities. No longer does the cultivation of rationally acquired skills suffice; the proper qualities of attitude and outlook, psychological balance and social poise, need also to be instilled. To reading, writing, arithmetic, and vocational training, modern educational doctrine adds instruction in social skills and group behavior, to ensure the development of the well-rounded personality. The "whole" child has to be considered, and his orderly adjustment to the world around him becomes a major function of the school. Even the techniques of teaching traditional subjects must be altered to ensure proper motivation and incentive for the student. In a curiously distorted way, the liberalism of Dewey has fused with the liberalism of Locke and the function of public education becomes no longer "schooling" in the restricted sense of imparting definite skills and knowledge. Now its responsibility is even greater: it is nothing less than the successful ordering of man's relationship to man, the happy adjustment of the individual to society.

Take the outright quantitative pressures on schools, add the requirements of modern culture, and mix philosophical assertions that raise fundamental issues about human nature, and an explosion is inevitable. A special type of politics emerges, and focuses on the suburb: the "politics of the particularists," a pattern isolated and divorced from other local public duties. Since education is of such unparalleled importance in making money, in the achievement of success, and especially in the well-being of a democratic society, it is a "unique" function. If it is unique, it has priority above all other governmental responsibilities. If it has such priority, it deserves special institutional arrangements and a special decision-making process. So the major public activity of suburbia is carefully set apart from the rest of suburban political life and wrapped in a shell peculiarly its own.

The politics of the schools, rooted essentially in the educator's assertion of primacy, intensifies and exaggerates — almost to the point of burlesque — the features of suburban political behavior that have been described.

Because the function is of such importance, it should demand the special attention of every resident in town. Further, it is not enough that school systems be local public institutions; they must be a particular type of local government. Since education is so vital a public activity, ordinary officialdom cannot be trusted with its management, and a special form of grassroots administration must be installed to isolate education from the more humdrum problems of land use, welfare, highways, police and fire protection.

Therefore, except in New England, an entirely separate government is provided for school management; and even in New England, the school board shares the limelight with the selectmen. Independent, popularly elected school boards and, quite frequently, elected school superintendents, take their places alongside — but apart from — other local officials. A separate tax levy is set aside for the school; generally, independent control of the budget is granted to the school government. Separate qualifications for the recruitment and advancement of the school bureaucracy are established; special arrangements are made with the state for financial aid.

Not only is the government divided once again but the political man of suburbia is himself subdivided. He is already partly partisan and partly nonpartisan. Now the suburbanite must become a "school nonpartisan" as well. Education is too important to be left to ordinary political attitudes and actions; it must be "taken out of politics," and the last vestiges of group dissension and compromise must be erased. The all-wise, objective citizen assumes another burden. Responsibility and objective inquisitiveness are no longer sufficient for good citizenship; for the schools, positive support, open dedication and unquestioned allegiance are required. Patronage and favoritism cannot be allowed to enter the classroom in the way in which they are acceptable in granting highway contracts. No real debate can take place about the comparative needs of schools and other functions for no one can seriously argue that the building of a new fire station should be made possible by cutting the school budget. The essence of politics — compromise among competing needs, majority decisions between competing values — is ruled out. The school citizen must talk only about school.

Yet if politics is barred, who makes the decisions? Here an important shift in the relationship between expert and interest group takes place. In the case of the city manager, the professional might actively solicit support, but when he crossed over the line from administration to policy, he still had to convince his audience of the correctness of his views. In the schools, the expert looms even larger; the interest group exists to support the professional, almost without regard to his policies. The Parent-Teachers Association unites bureaucracy and the school public to work continually — if vaguely — for school "betterment," and in rapidly growing, predominantly Protestant suburbs, the PTA quite frequently can deliver a majority of the electorate.

The critical figure is the school superintendent. He has, in the words of Herold Hunt, the obligation not to defend his policies, as is the case with other professionals, but to "explain" them. Standards of administration and personnel performance have become the almost exclusive prerogative of the professional along with the substance of the school program, the curriculum. Even the school construction program may be put into the hands of the educators instead of into those of architects or builders, since each physical detail of the classroom intimately affects the attitude of the child. The "lobby of the good," the professional leaders mobilized to defend the basic principle of American education and their lay disciples, frequently becomes the most powerful force operative in the public affairs of the locality.

Of course, the declaration that schools must be above politics and that the professional's judgment must be accepted as the determining one is not an accurate summary of the actual state of affairs. It is too much to expect a public activity, equipped with a popular decision-making process that includes elections, to operate without politics. The school board and the superintendent are subjected, as numerous case studies testify, to all kinds of pressures and demands. Some are of the ordinary, garden-variety type of political action: petty intrigue on the part of school architects, connivance in the adoption of textbooks, building and equipment awards. More frequently the focus is on the philosophy of education adopted by the given school system. Is the program excessively "modern" or too old-fashioned? Should progressive techniques be encouraged or would a return to the discipline of vocational training be more appropriate?

On the critical issue of philosophy — of what the schools should do — the school officials are often curiously silent, except for defending the development of the curriculum as a professional matter. Generally, they concentrate solely on the quantitative aspects of the problem. They make a "bricks and mortar" defense: more buildings, more teachers and more money. When pressed, they exhibit the uncertainty in beliefs and the capacity to change dogmas in midstream which the investigators of Crestwood Heights discovered when they studied the objectives of school experts. As a rule, however, the educators strive either to keep the problem to themselves or to avoid participating in its public debate.

In terms of political realism, this position makes more sense than the Crestwood Heights analysis supposed. It is not so much a commentary on the unsettled doctrines of the educational profession as it is a tribute to that profession's recognition of the Pandora's box which is unlocked when the bricks-and-mortar position is abandoned. For when the slogan "betterment of schools" is directly examined, it becomes nothing less than a debate on fundamental principles — on the validity of the underlying assumption which makes education a prerequisite not just for democracy but, in modern dress, for the reform of society itself. There is nothing else really left to debate since the divorce of school government from other government removes the opportunity to compare the values received from other public services. The demands for school expenditures become insatiable, for the goal of the school system is as unspecific as the citizen's individual prescription for the ills of all mankind.

Thus the school electorate finds itself at the extreme end of the road that the logic of nonpartisanship has built. The conscientious citizen is called upon to determine not only ways and means, to decide not just between competing priorities in functions. He is required to define, year after year, the goals of government itself, and to resolve persistent philosophical disputes. School politics take on the color of a constitutional convention that is continually in session, always discussing the fundamentals of its political order. It operates, moreover, in the open atmosphere that prevailed in France after the Revolution rather than in the closeted, protected circumstances in which the American Constitution was prepared. The participants are asked to dig up their first premises by the roots and examine them anew, while constantly under public scrutiny. When debate of this nature occurs, it is violent; ardent Deweyites are asked to defend their prophet, and sometimes they may be forced to read him. The "Americanist" strand of liberalism thunders that current school philosophy is nothing less than subversion. The dwindling ranks of Horatio Algers call out for a return to practical education without frills and fads. Lay Catholics are brought again to the question of defining the boundaries between Church and State, in an atmosphere in which even Jesuits find an orderly discussion difficult.

Once the politics of the school particularists become really politics, one of Jefferson's least promising injunctions is pushed to an extreme that even he never intended. There is no longer just a revolution every generation, there is a revolution going on constantly. Divorced from the rest of the political process, suburban school government may avoid some of the unpalatable by-products of partisan politics, but it exposes itself to the dangers of ideological politics where no holds are barred, common beliefs rarely recognized, and where opponents can constantly hurl charges of infidelity to basic principles. In school politics, grassroots democracy attains its ultimate promise: the citizens not only fully participate as individuals, but participate by laying bare their most fundamental convictions. And, since the goals of prevailing educational philosophy are open-ended, even agreement reached at one time in any one locality is unrewarding. The schools remain unsatisfactory, and the constitutional convention goes on unendingly.

The Grassroots of Suburbia

From this general discussion an impression of highly individualistic political behavior emerges. It is doubtful that any one suburb fits exactly the pattern that has been described and it is quite certain that some suburbs do not fit it at all. The possibilities of different combinations of forces, exceptions, and aberrations approach infinity. Suburbs composed of developments and commuters may largely abjure political activity; others, more settled and better off, may have routinized it; still others may have such a homogeneity that even in their school debates they are languid. Meanwhile, the industrial or slum jurisdiction may have a political process indistinguishable from its urban neighbors. Unquestionably, the most significant point to be made is how little systematic and reliable knowledge we have about suburban politics.

The evidence that is available, however, suggests that the distinguishing mark of suburban politics is not a difference in partisan attitudes between suburbanites and other Americans. If any conclusion is possible in this respect, it is that the suburbs, as such, have no significant influence on the fortunes of the two parties. The real point appears, rather, to be the way in which they intensify and exaggerate the traditional politics of small localities. More completely nonpartisan than one-party small towns in rural areas, and with the activities of the party leader more severely limited, the suburban municipalities represent the principle of direct popular political participation in a mode theoretically workable under modern circumstances. Paradoxically, although the tenets of modern municipal reform have been rejected as an adequate basis for city or metropolitan government, they have been embraced as a political creed for suburban communities. Each suburbanite is expected to undertake the responsibilities of citizenship on his own initiative and determine the common good by himself. He is called upon to rise above personal interest and avarice so far as the affairs of the suburb are concerned, and, largely unorganized and unled, to manage his local government in company with his neighbor. Whatever conflict in interest exists in the suburb must express itself informally, secretly, and without the sanction of law.

Under these circumstances, the importance of the professional public servant — the expert and the bureaucrat — obviously increases. The new positive role of local government makes his existence necessary. The nonpartisan vacuum places him in a strategic position to assume a role as community leader, especially since political leaders are suspect. Social investigators are quite right in emphasizing the importance of the suburban expert, with his groups of civic associations gathered around him, but their belief that his prominence arises from a new American character is more questionable. It is more likely that his influence stems from the abdication of the citizen, weary of the number of responsibilities his concept of good government has imposed upon him, and unskilled in the art of politics. With the professional politician and the party organization banished from the scene, systematic full-time supervision and criticism of local officialdom tends to disappear too. The bureaucracy makes the key decisions by default.

Under the circumstances, the expert should not be blamed for assuming a portion of community leadership. If he did not, the public business might well become unmanageable. The "bricks and mortar" approach in the schools may evade the central problem of school politics, but at least it keeps the schools open. The city manager's ideal of the way his suburb should develop may be quite different from the public's, but at least some sort of development goes on. Under modern conditions, the power of the expert is the price the suburbanite pays for maintaining order in his home town.

In the final analysis, the suburban man may become apolitical altogether. He has escaped from the divisive conflicts and hostilities of the great city in search of peace and fellowship among his own kind. The theory is that he has created a democratic haven in which a consensus of right-thinking men replaces a compromise among partisan-thinking men. This theory wraps him in a cloak of nonpartisanship and no politics, which makes active expression of political views socially unacceptable, if not immoral. If faithfully followed, the theory would demand so much of his time, so great a communion with his neighbors, so high a competence in public affairs, as to be nearly all-consuming. For most suburbanites, the feasible way out is indifference, as revealed by apathy in local elections. If the expert is entrusted with the really tough problems, the suburbanite has the best of all possible worlds: grassroots government run by automation. Under these circumstances, the purest theory of democracy requires no democratic action or responsibility at all.

CHAPTER 6

The Public Problems of Suburbia

The Struggle for Survival

Regardless of the difficulties and deficiencies inherent in suburban politics, it is quite clear that the symbol of the small community appeals mightily to many Americans. Both mentally and emotionally, in social intercourse and political behavior, they approximate, in certain important respects, the mores of their ancestors. The approximation becomes all the more impressive because of the sweeping changes that technology and modern organization have made in their way of life and their environment.

Extraordinary as the renaissance may be, however, there is a final test of reality involved in judging the potential and permanence of the suburban miniature. The vision that moves suburbia may be laudable, but is it feasible? Can we possibly imagine, in an era of urbanism, of large-scale organization, of automobiles, of dwindling natural resources, that small communities can endure, let alone flourish? The demands of modern life, the pressures, tensions and attractions are, after all, quite real. The physical conditions of vast distances and abundant material, and the social and political outlooks that supported the small community in earlier times are gone. Can an anachronism, by definition, ever have a chance for survival?

The answer to this question depends upon an estimate of the pressures that push the suburbs into the larger world weighed against the resources they possess in their fight for independence. In this tug-of-war the maintenance of political autonomy becomes all important for the small communities if they are to survive. If they are absorbed politically into large cities, they will be only neighborhoods, subcategories of larger communities, and the miniature can be only a nostalgic recollection.

In taking odds on the suburbs' chances, then, a judgment must be made on the capacity of their governments to function reasonably well. In this context, the pressures on the suburb are essentially three: it faces sizable new responsibilities of modern positive government; it has an apparent shortage of financial resources, made all the more severe by an antiquated tax system; and it is experiencing increasing difficulty in obtaining the natural resources on which the existence of its inhabitants depends.

It is this dilemma of mismatched supply and demand that has led experts to prophesy catastrophe for the urban fringe, to argue for consolidation not on the grounds of desirability but on the grounds of necessity. The imbalance between needs and resources has seemed so great that disaster has, for at least a generation, appeared to be just around the corner. It is by understanding the nature of this dilemma, and the complex strategy suburbia consciously and unconsciously has devised to resolve it that we can best estimate its prospects for success.

The Burdens of the Welfare State

The pressures on suburban governments cannot be wished

away; they are sizable and they are increasing. They arise, moreover, from apparently inescapable forces of technology rather than conscious political programs. The automobile, medical advances that extend life expectancy and raise new problems in geriatrics, and industrial requirements for a more literate and more skilled labor force are the culprits in the growing suburban budgets. It is in these demands for public services imposed by an urban industrial society that the first stresses on suburbia appear.

The quantitative pressures of the welfare state on local governments are frequently overlooked in public finance today. Because the federal government initiated many of the expensive social programs publicly performed at the present time, and contributes so heavily to their financial support, the federal budget has been for a long time the center of our attention. Increasing thirty times since 1932, expanding almost geometrically in the number of programs and activities, the expenditures of the national government have seemed to dwarf those of the states and localities. Swollen by the costs of wars and foreign aid, the figures have become astronomical and almost incomprehensible. Washington and the welfare state seem to many Americans to be one and the same phenomenon.

Washington taken alone, however, tells only part of the story of peaceful revolution through which the United States has passed. The trends of local expenditures and revenues illustrate a second phase of that upheaval in public service function, and it, too, is spectacular. In 1902, total local government expenditures were 700 million dollars; in 1932 they were 3 billion; in 1956 they exceeded 27 billion. Even when these figures are corrected for inflation and population growth, they are more than double what they were at the beginning of the depression of the 1930's. Since the war, local

expenditures for domestic civilian needs have increased at a
faster rate than federal expenditures.

This increase has been matched by an increase in local
revenue. Although the federal government now collects the
major share of taxes, the largest share of funds is devoted to
defense activities. When these are deducted, each level of
government raises about 12 to 14 million dollars on its own.
The accomplishments of local tax collectors are all the more
impressive because they are unabe to resort to monetary
policy to make borrowing easier and because they operate
under severe tax and debt limitations imposed by state constitutions.

The sharp upward trend in expenditures and revenues is
an indication — but not an explanation — of the expanded
responsibilities of local governments, the suburbs included.
In considerable measure, the increase is due to population
growth and price increases, but the most important explanation lies in the array of new functions local governments have
come to perform, and the rising standards of expectation
that have been attached to old functions.

This expansion in public services that were not considered
necessary in local governments before this century was partly
stimulated by the New Deal and is partly explicable in terms
of growing density and growing wealth. Regardless of the
reasons, the proliferation of new duties is extraordinary. A
survey of one city's experience reports that between 1900 and
1940 alone the number of municipal functions increased
from 140 to 256. The types of activity identified in the study
were not particularly unusual, for they included duties familiar across the country: high-pressure water systems for fire
protection, clinics, traffic signals, employment bureaus, am-
bulance service, air-pollution control, classes for handicapped
children, and branch libraries. Perhaps not all cities, let

alone suburbs, provide such an array of modern amenities, but almost all have come to accept recreational programs, building and health inspections, special school classes, and parking lots as necessary and proper additions to their budgets.

Even more important than the addition of new functions have been the vastly higher standards of performance expected of customary services by the public at large, again induced by wealth and population growth. These rising expectations combine with technological innovations and the increasing professionalization of local bureaucracy to double or treble the benefits or effectiveness of the service, but also to increase the cost. The net result is a steady upgrading in the standards of local government activities.

Some of these criteria for "acceptable services" are elaborate, such as those in modern schools, where pupil-teacher ratios, expenditures per pupil, and space per pupil figures are combined with long checklists of "enriched" school programs to develop minimum standards of quality. Some of them are crude: rough estimates of the number of policemen and firemen required per thousand population and the number of cases a social worker can effectively handle. Some are qualitatively sophisticated, as in installations required for water and sewerage systems, and some are only wistful, as the standards librarians and recreational leaders would like to see to ensure their citizenry's enlightenment and commitment to the vigorous life. Yet every function of local government now has "objective" standards for the adequate provision of a given service, and almost all of them call for increased expenditures.

In addition, the overhead costs of local government go up as general administration grows more effective. Merit systems and career programs in government service have their costs, whether determined by the knowledge and capacities of the specialists or the strength of government unions. While the patronage-ridden bureaucracies of the boss did not begin to approach the efficiency of modern municipal governments, they were not necessarily as expensive.

A final dimension of public demand should not be overlooked: local governments not only have new programs of their own, but they bear the brunt of administrative responsibility for many national social programs. Although they are generally compensated for these activities, they are not always completely reimbursed, and even when they are, the complexity of their job is magnified. It is true that some major activities have moved upstairs: welfare programs have become increasingly a federal responsibility, the construction of major highways has been taken over by the states, and on both of these higher levels there is a renewed interest in the schools. Yet none of these programs have been removed from the local scene in their entirety; the logic of federalism has a built-in preference for devolving operating responsibility to the local level regardless of the source of financing.

Thus, while local governments collected revenue during recent years at an annual rate of between ten and fourteen billion dollars, they spent between twenty and twenty-two billion each year. The difference between income and expenses was made up by grants-in-aid and borrowing, the federal government contributing, in 1953, for example, over three hundred million dollars directly, and the states almost six billion. Federal and state supervision, personnel requirements, and planning to some extent went along with the money, but as a general rule, local government had both the responsibility for keeping the program operating, and a measure of discretion as to how these duties were to be carried out. The net effect is another pressure on the time and energy of local officials.

There are no reliable statistics to show precisely how sub-

urban governments as a class have reacted to the general pressures for more and better local government. Expenditures
are reported according to the legal type of government involved, by cities, towns, school districts, counties, special districts and townships, not according to geographical location.
Moreover, even if separate financial reports were available
for suburban units of local government, the total tax burden
for any one suburbanite would be difficult to calculate. He
lives typically in the midst of such a welter of districts, villages, cities and authorities, that the problem of peeling off
the layers of local government in any given geographical location to discover the taxpayer who supports it is almost insoluble.

Yet it is fairly certain that the suburbs have felt the demands of modernity at least as strongly as the typical local
unit, and probably more strongly. Municipal expenditures
are not determined solely by population growth or even by
population densities, but they are clearly affected by these
forces, and suburbs have borne the brunt of migration in the
last twenty years. They have, moreover, entered their period
of greatest activity directly from a state of rural somnolence,
ill prepared to handle the demands that were thrust upon
them. Most suburbs experience "get going" costs, initial
outlays for public water systems and sewage disposal plants,
for schools and roads, for fire stations and police headquarters
that never existed before. In many cases, they start from
scratch and face, therefore, the necessity of long-run capital
improvements at the first influx of new residents. Typically,
the facilities are overtaxed almost as fast as they are completed, and even where population pressures are contained,
suburbs have been built at the high points of the inflationary
tide. Finally, costly physical facilities, erected in costly times,
are only part of the get-going costs: bureaucracies have to be

assembled as well. Even volunteer fire departments require training, even suburban police need to know how to clean a gun, and when the pig farms disappear, some sort of organization has to be assembled to collect garbage.

It is also likely that suburbanites want at least as high a general level of services as other Americans. They may be able to forego recreational facilities for a time by using the backyards of their quarter-acre lots. They may, if the local building inspector has been alert, get along with cesspools and septic tanks in place of a sewage system. Police and fire services can be handled, in predominantly residential areas, less expensively than in large cities. But schools must be built and operated, streets constructed or maintained after the developer has disappeared, and water supplies assured. These functions account for 50 per cent of the budget for the typical American municipality. They are necessarily higher in the suburbs if for no other reason than population growth, and they are likely to be pushed even higher, given the attitudes and disposition of the suburbanite.

It is probably a conservative estimate, then, that equates the per capita expenditures of suburban government to the 1955 national average of $67.59. The functions on which the suburbs can save, given the relative youth and prosperity of their citizens, are by and large a smaller part of the municipal budget than those on which they have to spend disproportionately. The burdens of initial investments required to subdue the hinterland, the large number of school children, the provision of basic public utilities, make suburban governments potentially the most expensive of all local governments in the next twenty-five years. The central cities face financial crisis because of the costs of obsolescence, the proportion of tax-exempt property, and the daytime demands that suburbia imposes. But the suburbs' problems are just beginning, and, in the end, building new communities is likely to be at least as expensive as restoring old ones. The suburbs may approximate the small town of old in size and politics, but in the nature and extent of their duties they are not likely to avoid the responsibilities of modern life.

The Supply of Resources

How do these apparently unslackening demands for public services compare with the resources suburban governments have to fulfill them? If we paint with a broad brush, the situation does not appear to be especially serious. When the general trend of government expenditures is measured against the trend of personal income, state and local governments take about the same percentage of our earnings as they did thirty years ago and claim about the same share of the gross national product.

From this perspective, many suburbanites have viewed the general trend of public finance with equanimity. They believe that by leaving the metropolis they escape the spreading blight of deteriorating neighborhoods, the crushing taxes imposed by welfare programs and corrupt bosses, and the rising per capita costs of every function as the costliness of congestion becomes apparent. To counterbalance the growing costs of local government, they look forward to the tax revenues that the higher assessments of new residential construction should yield. If population growth could be kept in reasonable bounds for any given suburb, the additions to the tax rolls, coupled with economies of size and scale made possible by expanded service loads, might serve to counteract the costs of more and better local programs. After all, the argument has run, it is the hard-working, thrifty, relatively prosperous members of the middle class who are mostly on the move, and they carry their income with them and invest it in their homes.

But this broad-brush picture becomes increasingly inaccurate, especially as suburbia comes to include all sorts and sizes of people and property. In Charles Adrian's words, "taxes may start at what appears to be a much lower level than those of the core city, but the suburban buyer can be assured that they will increase at a rapid pace." Specifically, two conditions have put the suburbs, as a class, in an unfavorable position: they have been more dependent than larger municipalities on the real property tax as their major source of revenue, and, within the framework of the property tax, they have, again as a class, suffered a comparative decline in the value of property resources.

The reliance of local governments on the property tax is well known, as are the deficiencies of that revenue source. Eighty-seven per cent of local taxes in the United States were raised from this source in 1953 and 43 per cent of all local expenditures were financed by it. For at least a quarter of a century, its inequities and inadequacies have been highlighted. Critics have long emphasized the fact that the ownership of land is no longer a measure of wealth, as it was in colonial days, and consequently that a tax on such ownership is unlikely to be directly related to the ability to pay. They have described the arbitrary calculation, the difficulty in administration and the depressive effects on business activity in general that characterize the tax. In the words of Seligman's classic indictment, "there is nothing the matter with the property tax except that it is wrong in theory and does not work in practice." When coupled with state limitations on the tax rates for any given assessment, and with national and state pre-emptions of other tax sources, the local property tax has been identified as the major culprit responsible for the financial crisis of all local units in the United States, suburban, urban, and rural.

Granted all the traditional arguments against the property

tax, however — its failure to capture incomes, the political capriciousness of its administration, its obvious inequalities in incidence — its injurious effects on local government in general, or on suburban governments, can be overstated. It is doubtful that the tax itself imposes crushingly unfair burdens so far as equity is concerned, or is alone responsible for local financial crises. The primary services that local governments provide — utilities, roads, schools, and inspections — often confer more direct benefits upon the property owners and enhance their investments more clearly than for any other citizens in the locality. As to adequacy, the President's Commission on Intergovernmental Relations underscored the potential still existent in the tax when it reported, "The nine billion dollars produced in 1953 by local general property taxes probably represents little more than 1 per cent of the current value of privately owned land, structures, and equipment — the elements in tangible national wealth that comprise the bulk of property assessed for local taxation. While the effective rates of these taxes vary widely, they are equal to substantially less than one per cent of appraised values in many parts of the country in most pressing need of additional local revenues." If the property tax were vigorously and impartially administered it would provide considerably more revenue than it now does, and the relationship of those who pay it to the benefits received from public services would be much closer.

For the suburbs as a whole, the problem involved in their tax system is less the evils of the property tax as such than the inflexibility of their general tax structure implied by the heavy reliance on property taxes. While other local governments, particularly large cities and independent cities with a rural hinterland, have been able to broaden their tax base considerably, suburbs, with notable exceptions, have not.

Municipal income taxes, sales and gross taxes, tobacco and admission taxes, levies on earnings, are not well suited to suburban governments. For one thing, they are difficult to administer, requiring a bureaucratic sophistication, an array of financial power, an assurance that their residents cannot shop elsewhere, and a variety of land uses that few suburbs possess. For another, they often place a suburb at a competitive disadvantage with its neighbors so far as the attraction of presumably desirable business and commercial activity is concerned. Although, as we will see later, suburbs have shown great ingenuity in discovering and inventing new sources of revenue, by and large they are excluded from the big money earners. While nonproperty taxes accounted for 27 per cent of all local revenues in the 481 cities over 25,000 population in 1956, and multiplied six times in the years between 1950 and 1955, it is doubtful that suburban governments — municipalities, school districts, and towns — figured prominently in the increase.

The heavy reliance on property taxation is the first fiscal liability of the suburbs. The second is the fact that, contrary to popular opinion, the property to be taxed is becoming less lucrative. The comfortable assumption that residential property values are almost always higher in outlying districts of the metropolitan areas — and, therefore, the suburban tax base is proportionately larger than that of the core city — justified many family migrations to the metropolitan fringe. In prewar years this was to a considerable degree correct, but for the last fifteen years suburban real estate has lost a great deal of its comparative advantage over that in the central city.

Almost 50 per cent of the dwelling units constructed between 1940 and 1950 were in the suburbs, and, typically, the values of the new residences were higher than the values of residences built before 1940. But the differences between old and new values are not nearly as great as they were fifteen years ago, and so far as the more expensive residential construction is concerned — houses costing over $15,000 — two important developments have taken place. First, in this category there is no significant difference between old and new suburban houses, and second, median values for new housing in the central cities are almost 30 per cent higher than in the suburbs. Moreover, the faster a metropolitan area grows, the lower the median value of residential housing constructed. In short, when housing values new or old are compared, there is a persistent tendency for the central city to have higher residential values and to retain them, and the faster the suburb grows, the lower is the average residential value. Suburbs are not attracting the high value development of our decade.

Even more important, general averages are likely to be misleading in suburbia, where land uses tend to cluster in the same way different occupations bunch together. Unlike the median values of a large city that encompasses all types of property, the limited jurisdiction of each suburb means that usually only one type of property value predominates. The search for homogeneity carries its inevitable corollary in property values, and suburbs differentiate themselves sharply in their financial resources when they segregate themselves by social status. For the suburbs taken collectively, this range has great significance, for it means that the cheaper construction now underway, especially in rapidly growing areas, is not spread throughout each suburb. Instead, it is concentrated in particular suburbs, heightening their fiscal crises while others take the lion's share of the more expensive residential property to provide the base for their public services.

The continuing dispersion of industrial and service activity may well tend to supply additional resources for the suburbs as a class and provide a welcome cushion to the tax base. But here again the question of variations among suburbs arises. Despite the newly favorable attitude many fringe communities are exhibiting toward light industry, there is, as yet, little evidence that industry locates where it is most needed in terms of tax resources. Most observers believe a contrary pattern is at work, in which "industries tend to locate in one suburban community and the workers locate in another community, with the result that the problem of financing services to the employees, and their families, of those industries, gets very serious indeed."

Nor are shopping centers likely to relieve the plight of low housing value suburbs. They tend to locate where incomes are higher and their aim is to draw together a number of businesses in a concentrated space. Thus their very success reduces the likelihood that neighborhood stores will scatter themselves throughout the suburbs, in physically unattractive but financially rewarding string developments along major streets. With the rich getting richer and the poor poorer, those suburbs with lower value housing and probably a greater need for services may have to depend more and more on residential property value to support their governments.

The continued shift in the labor force from agricultural and manufacturing occupations to "service" industries — and the consequent spread of trade establishments — may well alleviate the tight fiscal situation. And if the diffusion of industry accelerates in the next generation as many expect, more suburbs will find additional revenue sources. Stern reassessments, bringing tax valuations more in line with market price, may also increase the yield of present resources. But these trends are still in the making; at the present time, suburbs in general and in particular seem to face an uphill fight.

Yet the critical factor is not the present difficulties of suburbs as a class, the shortcomings of the property tax as such or the inability of most suburbs to develop other resources. Even the relative decline in suburban residential property value as compared to the central city may not be serious. Rather, it is the haphazard pattern of distribution of property resources among political jurisdictions, and the effect of the property tax upon that distribution, that spells real trouble.

Specifically, financial trouble lies ahead for the metropolitan regions because the property tax system works to encourage a further political fragmentation of the areas. It sets off a game of musical chairs which coincides with social and political proclivities for exclusiveness, and although the process carries with it the seeds of self-destruction, the logic of maintaining the separate status of each such suburb is inescapably reinforced. This is the real significance of the present financial pattern which, in the face of snowballing new demands, works to keep the suburbs divided.

The Scramble for Values

The internal workings of the property tax within suburbia are complicated, and it exists only because the region is already fragmented. But it is the policy induced by the financial system — not the tax itself, not the real wealth of the communities in relation to public expenditures — that is the key to understanding the so-called suburban financial crisis. George Duggar has provided the theoretical framework that explains the suburban maneuvers in their self-imposed battle for resources. He reasons that suburbanites tend to judge governmental expenditures according to whether or not the services they provide add to the land values, or, more specifically, whether their benefits for the individual land owner add to the total value of his property more than his taxes detract from it. Given this tendency, the logical tax policy for any local government is to maximize the benefits of public services and minimize their tax costs. Thus the objective it must seek is to entice high-value property within its borders and prevent the intrusion of low-value construction.

The rationale for this policy of "financial efficiency," so far as residential construction is concerned, is, of course, that expensive properties pay high taxes while they typically require the same level of public services as any other type of property of equal size. For high-value residences, the value of the land itself is proportionately higher and the share of private improvement value in the total value is lower than for low-value property. Thus the total taxable value is greater, compared to the services required, the higher a community climbs up the scale of residential quality. The suburban government of better-class neighborhoods finds itself in a happy position of being able to receive tax returns considerably in excess of the cost of services it must offer.

Moreover, because there is a monopolistic element involved in land prices, arising from the relative scarcity of good sites, the prestige value associated with exclusive neighborhoods, and the reduced importance of money for those who are able to live in them, the suburban government can exact higher prices for the services it provides. In actual practice, it can, of course, reduce the tax rate to the point where revenue equals expenditures, but in theory it behaves like a firm engaged in monopolistic competition — receiving revenues for each unit of service considerably higher than the cost of providing the service. By offering a special type of land advantages, it is able to extract taxes that are considerably larger than those received by other suburbs which do not have choice property but which have the same service needs.

On the other hand, suburbs in which very inexpensive development has taken place cannot hope to receive revenues commensurate with costs. In these municipalities, the value of a typical home is a much larger proportion of total real estate value — house and site taken together. Since the costs for government services are more closely related to the number of houses than the value of the land they are built upon, as construction becomes cheaper and cheaper, the capitalized costs of services per house or square foot of land come to exceed the capitalized taxable value, or even the market value per house or foot of land. Without the cushion which high site values give, the suburban government is forced to increase the tax rate to as high a level as possible, or to cut services. Even then, if total residential values are very low, it may not be able to make ends meet. Its financial position becomes progressively worse, for the ratio between tax burdens and benefits is reduced, each additional unit of service costing more on a capitalized basis than the corresponding unit of revenues the property produces, with the inevitable result of a rising tax rate. In these municipalities property values are not enhanced by government services; instead, they are adversely affected.

Thus, the overall policy implication of the property tax, as Duggar points out, is that suburban governments are led inevitably into an effort to achieve "financial efficiency" by a policy of "value differentiation" — that is, using local governmental powers to attract expensive improvements or to repel lower-cost improvements. This drive for high values may take the form of exclusive residential development or it may induce suburbs into the now fashionable search for "light industry," breaking down earlier attitudes antagonistic to industrial development. As these financial problems increase, as the amount of undeveloped land dwindles, many municipalities become actively engaged in enticing industry, regardless of the intrinsic economic value of their particular sites. Unwilling to trust the operation of market forces, they engage in "a sort of mercantilist interplay between municipalities, each fighting to keep its taxes down and its notables up."

Whether residentially or industrially inclined, however, from the point of view of any suburban government the sensible aim is to attract and maintain as large a concentration of high values as possible. Such a policy not only assures an excess of revenues over normal local government expenditures; in the end, it enhances property values even more, since the individual owner finds indirect benefits accruing from the "monopolist" position his government has attained — the value of "exclusive" neighborhoods, the provision of services that add to site value.

These value differentiation policies have obvious injurious effects on particular individuals. For the property owner the implication is, of course, that total property values are increased among expensive properties and reduced for less costly properties. The owner of a $10,000 Cape Cod house on a quarter acre lot has little economic incentive to build an extra room or add a garage. These "improvements" not only reduce the value of his site in a theoretical sense by distorting it from its "best and most economically desirable purpose" but they increase his taxes more than they increase the benefits he receives from local public services. While, from the municipality's point of view, his total tax burden does not exceed the cost of services rendered, the additional taxes on his new improvements reduce the total value of his property, for in effect they impose expenses greater than benefits. In extreme cases, the after-tax value of low-value property can even be reduced below the level of value of the improvements on the land alone, the market prices of the cheaper houses will fall, and expenditures for proper maintenance and further improvements will be discouraged.

In short, value-differentiation policies, when in full swing in a metropolitan area, work against the provision of reasonably inexpensive homes for the majority of Americans, handicap national policies designed to further home ownership, and encourage high-value construction rather than low for prudent investors. The further down the income scale a family is located, the less likely it is that a suburban house is a good investment. The more improvements made, the less the portion of investment which goes into land alone, the harsher are the tax burdens.

Individual inequities aside, an even more significant effect of these policies from the governmental perspective is the reinforcement of suburban autonomy. Inevitably, the drive for value-differentiation sets in motion a continued process of segregation of high-value property and continued depression of low-value property prices below the market price. Suburban governments, by any doctrine of prudent fiscal management, are forced to prefer expensive construction; such property returns more than it costs in services. The owners of high-value property are then rationally inclined to encourage their governments to resist invasion by owners of lower-value property. Even though the latter pay more than their proportionate share, the presence of cheaper homes may depress prices of the older, more expensive residences, and certainly it will increase overall municipal costs. A process is triggered off by which the suburb initially seeks high value because of the financial advantages accruing to the government and then is led into restrictive practices because these appear to be the only way to preserve the initial investments in the area.

Some authorities find the scramble for resources that goes on in metropolitan areas ethically questionable. Henry Fagin, for example, complains that "the very cities that can most easily afford to carry the burdens of inexpensive homes are the ones which most vigorously resist such homes and are the most successful in avoiding them." Certainly the drive for high-value and only high-value property buttresses the social and ethnic exclusiveness which suburbanites display in their search for small town homogeneity.

Yet, given the nature of the property tax, it is difficult to criticize suburban officials who are fortunate enough to have desirable locations for exploiting their position. To do otherwise when government costs are rising steadily — to be liberal in their attitude toward lower-income newcomers, to strive for heterogeneous neighborhoods, to welcome citizens regardless of race, creed or color — is to invite financial disaster. If the town fathers are to be faithful to their economic trust, they must practice discrimination. Having forsworn association with the metropolis, which might possess the variety of land uses to hold the injurious effects of the property tax to a minimum, there is now no stopping point. Ethically, segregation may be intolerable, but from the individual perspective of any given suburb, the continued splintering of the metropolitan region is now a financial necessity.

Strategy of the Anointed

The upshot of this inquiry into the implications of property taxation in suburbia is that, so far as the question of financial adequacy is concerned, the answer is, "It all depends." Some suburbs have ample resources to meet the demands of modern government; others are obviously inadequately equipped to stand on their own. As long as the property tax is the bulwark of their defense, the capacity of the suburbs to survive breaks down into at least two different issues, with a broad twilight zone in between. The answers to these questions require a study of the strategy of two types of suburbs as they go about resolving their quite different financial problems.

For the suburbs blessed with natural advantages, where big mansions are in existence and Levittowns have not appeared, the strategy of "high value" dictates a constant surveillance of the changing metropolitan scene to make sure no unwelcome intruders are admitted. A whole series of tactics are usually employed: the judicious use of regulatory powers, special requirements and restrictions demanded of builders, discrimination in taxation and in the quality of services extended to particular neighborhoods, selective annexations, imaginative employment of eminent domain, are all standard weapons in the battle. Collectively, they attest to the strength of will and stubbornness of suburban officials and citizens in preserving their land values and their communities.

The most spectacular weapon, of course, is the use of regulatory powers — zoning and subdivision control — for here the potency of the value-differentiation policy is most clearly seen. Henry Fagin has documented for the New York region the extent to which suburbs will go to preserve high values and exclude low ones. Among his investigations there appears the case of the New Jersey township which imposed an informal building permit moratorium "until 'the law' finally caught up with it"; the instance of the suburb which prevented mass development by requiring that each house differ in certain design characteristics from five of its neighbors; the town which set a five-acre minimum lot size; and the New Jersey borough which owns one third of the land in its jurisdiction and sells lots at the rate of a dozen a year to purchasers of its own choosing. Throughout the cases he studied, Fagin found a consistent policy, in towns which were financially able to support a growing population, to resist new residents and inexpensive construction. His extreme instance was the town which cheapened the existing school program while advocating, as an alternative, policies to encourage birth control.

In more detail, Charles Harr has reviewed the type of zoning program, popularized by the Wayne Township, New Jersey, case. Here, not only did the suburb establish a minimum house size, but it required a larger living space for those houses without an attached garage than for those with such an appendage, on the dubious rationale that the proper care of the automobile affected the health and safety of the family. Acting to halt suburban expansion, Wayne established stringent zoning regulations and set the minimum price of new residences above that of older comparable buildings. In the end, the New Jersey Supreme Court upheld the township, and neither Wayne nor New Jersey are unique. Around San Francisco, St. Louis, and Boston, and in almost every metropolitan area, zoning restrictions have come into effect which can only be designed to require high-cost construction or none at all.

Coincidentally with zoning regulations, communities frequently use a second tactic: they establish, as part of the building regulations or as prerequisite to construction permits, a series of requirements for builders — supplemental taxes, fees, land dedications for schools, parks, donations of facilities. These requirements often serve good purposes, but they also direct special discrimination against lower-value homes, for the charges are almost always passed on to the buyer, and sometimes they serve outright to prohibit development.

A third device — employed in low-value as well as high-value communities — is the creation of special districts within parts of a suburb to offset the financial drain of lower-value houses where they occur. The supplemental taxes which these districts impose result in a higher total tax burden than the suburb could otherwise legally levy and allow a discriminatory tax burden to be imposed on lower-income residents. So the consultants from the University of Pennsylvania could blandly assure the supervisors of Middletown Township that permitting a Levittown within their borders would not lead to financial difficulties; the "three expensive services" of street lighting, fire hydrants and refuse collection, the consultants suggested, "can be financed through special district taxes or assessments, paid for by residents of the Levittown area only." The greater the proliferation of districts, the greater the probability of taxing similar property values at different rates.

Discrimination may also take place in the provision of services, to help assure that tax returns cover costs and to penalize — if they cannot exclude — lower income residents in the more expensive parts of suburbia. Suburban governments commonly differentiate today in the type of fire-fighting facilities and police services required in certain areas, and, significantly enough, these differences do not correlate with need but rather with taxable value. In the words of one commentator, "Them what has taxable value gets," and exclusive residential streets are usually better cleaned and repaired, high-pressure fire systems first installed there, and the neighboring school newer and better staffed. It is only in the slum areas of the large cities, where high expenditures are required to maintain law and order and overcome the hazards of congestion, that per capita expenditures are likely to be higher than in the better parts of the better suburbs.

These weapons — zoning, building requirements, tax and service differentiation — are part of every planning kit, and, as tools, there is nothing reprehensible about them. It is also clearly legitimate for every community to shape its land-use pattern, to use foresight, to prevent blight, and to develop as its citizens desire. The ethical issue, if there is one, is not the propriety of these stratagems, but rather the extreme forms which they may take. Ethics aside, a factual evaluation of the policies of well-to-do municipalities in terms of their capacity to protect their own seems to lead to one conclusion: given the reluctance of the courts to intervene and the number of methods available to suburban officials for the practice of discrimination, the high-value suburbs can remain high-value if they wish. In their response to the welfare state, they can do more than survive; they can flourish.

Strategy of the Unwashed: (1) Up by the Bootstraps
While the exclusive residential suburb, and perhaps the well-planned industrial enclave, can take care of themselves, relatively few suburbs can succeed in enticing only expensive real estate inside their borders. The bleak fact remains that most new suburban construction is of an inexpensive character and that, despite unparallelled prosperity and all the innovations in residential financing, private or public, suburban property values are declining relative to the central city. Moreover, some suburbs incorporate only after the developers' bulldozers have come and gone, leaving a pent-up demand for municipal services that the property tax could not finance if every home in town were worth fifty thousand dollars. In other cases, the political bulwarks against invasion prove weak, and even in settled communities zoning standards crumble and hundred-foot frontages are authorized. Finally, there are limits, legal and moral, to the extent of

segregation that is permissible. The courts may ultimately strike down the most outrageous regulations and restrictions. Here and there, community ethics forbid the self-imposition of a ghetto philosophy. The new migrants are settling somewhere in suburbia, and as they do, municipal costs rise, property values become depressed and financial adversity becomes the rule, not the exception.

For the unwanted, kept out of the exclusive suburbs, a policy of value differentiation will not help, for they cannot zone themselves away. New strategies and tactics are required, both within the local finance system and from outside. One common method is to dispense with all but the most rudimentary of public services, and sometimes even with those. John Scott reports on Whyte's suburban Park Forest that the salvation of its government is that its citizens are fortunately unaware of the array of services its big city neighbors offer. "It is an interesting fact," he writes, "that if you have an honest police department and one that takes good care of lost kids, you can get a lot of credit for giving a high level of police service when, in fact, you may actually not be giving as good police service as at least is potentially possible within the police force of a large city."

The taint of poorer services and amateurism, regardless of the financial effort the new suburbanite is willing to make, spreads beyond the maintenance of law and order. Sewer systems are frequently not available even when the density of population clearly requires them, and often there are neither storm sewers nor water distribution systems. Streets may not be paved, street signs and lights not available. Fire protection is almost always provided by volunteer departments, and though the firemen may be enthusiastic, they are not likely to be as competent or efficient as professionals.

Even for the schools, the public function suburbanites

treasure most fondly and for which they will spend most willingly, compromises are made. The desire to escape big city schools, to secure for their children the advantages of better teachers, newer buildings, smaller classes and higher instructional standards, becomes ultimately self-defeating. Precisely because the school is the heart of the community and its independence consequently most jealously guarded, the pooling of its financial support among jurisdictions is generally a last, desperate resort. Suburbanites frequently prefer overcrowding, inexperienced teachers, double sessions, and the deterioration of standards rather than to relinquish their personal supervision, however ineffective, over their schools. So, while the *New York Times'* survey of contemporary metropolitan problems could find public school systems in expensive suburbs that epitomized the suburban ideal, it found two other types as well: one in the mass development suburb in which the schools had been overwhelmed by the influx of new residents, and the other in the older suburb in which the new residents were not a majority and their demands for better education were ignored by the old-timers who wanted above all to keep the tax rate down.

Yet even the poorer suburbs cannot push the quality of public services below the minimum for urban life, and where the suburban government has municipal powers and effective representation in the state legislature, a second tactic for self-survival is frequently employed. Every effort is made to broaden the local tax base by whatever means are available. Rarely can the suburbs impose lucrative new levies on income or general sales, or establish municipal businesses. But they can, in company with rich suburbs, require subdividers to finance streets, curbs, gutters, sewers and street lights, and they can join other municipalities in imposing a whole series of clumsy and expensive nuisance taxes.

The discovery and exploitation of these new sources of revenue varies from state to state according to legislative authorization, but it does not, in the last analysis, bail the suburbs out. Despite increased yield from these revenues, the new funds come nowhere near to "replacing" the property tax; they merely slow down the rise in property tax rates which follows the increased demand for public services. The new revenues are, moreover, typically available only to municipalities. Suburban counties and school districts must rely far more on the property tax than do other units of local government, while financial pressures may be heaviest on them.

Given the limited jurisdictions suburbia imposes upon itself, no single municipality can go far in developing a balanced tax system. For all their valiant efforts — the rows and rows of parking meters installed, the special licenses invented, the hidden charges inserted in the sale prices of "immoral" luxuries — suburban governments do little more than add nuisance burdens to the total tax bill. If the array of special taxes they have devised in the last decade were applied vigorously and enforced rigorously, the whole system of local nonproperty taxation would fall of its own weight. And it would fall because, given the intense financial competition among metropolitan jurisdictions, any suburb moving too far out of line would experience economic decline and abandonment. It would deserve to fall, for when the crazy-quilt of extra levies came to replace the property tax, it would be even more regressive than that tax has proven.

By striving to emulate the manners of the exclusive suburbs, then, the poorer jurisdictions push their analogy to the grassroots image to an extreme they may not desire: they recreate, for their governments at any rate, the conditions of frontier scarcity and poverty, the struggle for community existence that characterized the new settlements on a new continent. Left to themselves — as suburban municipalities were in Florida after the boom and bust of the twenties, and throughout the nation in the early years of the depression — these suburbs move inexorably to bankruptcy. Fractured urban government can recreate social and political conditions of small town life, but in a fundamental sense the reformers were right in emphasizing the economic base for community existence. No government is an island, if that island cannot have the means for its basic self-support.

Strategy of the Unwashed: (2) The New "New Federalism"
Of course, neither the suburbs nor local governments in general have been left to themselves. The margin for their survival, the necessary addition to their resources, has been supplied by the federal government and the states in the grants-in-aid programs, which blossomed forth in earnest during the New Deal and which have grown steadily ever since. In piecemeal fashion, as local governments hovered near bankruptcy, their big brothers have bailed them out, function by function. They have done so by transforming the traditional pattern of American federalism from one in which each level of government stood on its own financial feet to one in which the governments with the more flexible tax systems raise the money and those with the least flexible systems spend it. In academic language, the years 1930 to 1957 witnessed the rise of a "New Federalism," in which the antagonism and inherent conflict supposedly inherent in the geographical division of powers across the United States was replaced by a cooperative system of interrelationships and a recognition of mutual interdependence.

The sums supplied to localities are sizable and they come through many channels. The most typical source of funds is the states, whose own coffers are then replenished from Washington. In 1932 the states allocated 800 million dollars to the localities, and received in turn 228 million from the national government. In 1952 state aid to localities reached the 5 billion mark, and federal aid to the states and localities was almost 2½ billion dollars, about 10 per cent of total state and local expenditures. Thus, although federal grants in recent years average only 5 per cent of total national expenditures, they supply 20 per cent of the total revenue of the states. In turn, 30 per cent of state expenditures now take the form of grants and other allocations to local governments.

This federal-to-state-to-local fiscal double play now operates in so many important service areas that V. O. Key characterizes the modern role of the states as one of a conduit, in which the states become "governments that spend money they do not raise and raise money they do not spend." For the localities, the end result of these complicated transfers of funds is that 27 per cent of their total revenue now comes from sources outside their own taxing jurisdictions.

In addition to joining hands in financing the majority of aid programs, the state and federal governments also help localities on their own. The latter, for example, takes the lead in activating urban renewal and redevelopment programs, in the public health field, the school lunch program, and the provision of community facilities and services for areas with defense activities. It also appropriates funds directly for local activities to the tune of a half billion dollars annually. The states provide sizable grants, unmatched by federal funds, for education and highways. They have also assumed more and more of the responsibility for providing institutional care for the incapacitated, especially in the mental health and communicable disease fields. In these instances, where Washington bypasses the states and the states undertake responsibilities on their own initiative, the aid they provide jointly is supplemented to no mean extent.

The net result of the complex web of intergovernmental relations today is that in one way or another local governments are relieved of full fiscal responsibility for many of the most important activities of the modern welfare state. Pragmatically, the federal government and the states have arrived at a rough and ready division of labor in supplying the needs of an urban, industrialized population. The six great grant programs which account for 92 per cent of all federal assistance funds — public welfare, highway construction, school lunches, employment security, school operations in defense areas, and hospital construction — either give the federal government the role of predominant leadership or buttress the states in some of their new activities. The states' participation in education and institutional care effectively relieves localities of the burdens of the other costly innovations in public service. Local government stands on its own feet largely in the fields of public safety, the provision of public utilities, and such fringe activities as recreation or libraries.

This system of support to localities now seems a permanent part of the American scene, and there is every indication that it will increase in importance. State and federal financial assistance has risen steadily as a share of the local budget over the past twenty years, largely unaffected by changes in the political complexion of state or national administrations. Special study commissions, legislative committees of inquiry, state and national, are established in weary repetition to review assistance programs, often with explicit instructions to eliminate or prune categories of grants. Almost invariably, these bodies become converts to the system in the process of their investigations. Administrations dedicated to a fight against big government, which have campaigned on a platform "to keep as much of the government as close to the people as possible," end up by putting more and more tainted money into local coffers. In highways, in mental health, in sanitation, in housing, in social security, and probably, ultimately, in education, additions to and expansions in existing programs go on year by year. For local governments, the question is not whether grants will continue, but how many fields they will come to embrace and how rapidly they will rise.

This steady supply of federal and state money does not mean, of course, that outside assistance is channeled to either the localities or the functions most in need of help. There is no outright guarantee that the poor suburbs on the urban fringe will receive their due. Grants are usually based on a crude population measure of need, and their amount may have little correspondence to other factors — age, density, income, professional requirements — which determine demand for a public service. They are often calculated without regard to the fiscal capacity of the jurisdiction involved, either in terms of taxes paid, or income.

Investigating the Federal Assistance program only, James Maxwell found a haphazard pattern of benefits and burdens arising out of the present programs, with high-income states frequently having a record of high per capita grants and poorer states often receiving considerably less, especially in relation to their ability to pay. While he discovered that the relatively progressive federal tax system had an equalizing effect so far as tax contributions of rich and poor states were concerned, the grant payments produced an opposite tendency, and the result was one in which no clear relation obtained between assistance, need, or local financial ability. Since state tax systems are even less progressive, the divergence between need and capacity is increased, and, in aggregate terms, the present system does not — nor is it intended to — equalize financial resources of states or local governments.

Other factors also reduce the effectiveness of grant porgrams in dealing with local fiscal adversity. For one thing, they have been developed piecemeal, function by function, for specialized purposes and objectives. They are viewed as "stimulating" certain activities, which, for one reason or another, should receive priority from the national or state point of view. General-purpose grants are rarities, and only as a given situation becomes critical — or pressure groups in support of a specific program powerful — is money forthcoming. Consequently, while certain functions are well-assisted, others are ignored, and what may seem to a given locality as a top priority problem, for which money is needed, very often finds no recognition at all in a grant program.

Moreover, at both the state and national level the effects of the American system of legislative representation — a preference to count acres as well as people — show up in the grant programs. Because rural communities trade most effectively on the grassroots symbol and are overrepresented in Congress and state legislatures, grant formulas are often rigged to give preference to the hinterlands. There may be minimum levels fixed, which every local unit must receive, or disproportionate weights attached to low density factors in the calculation of awards, or outright favoritism shown to the rural over the urban population. However devised, the effect is almost always to penalize a municipality as it grows larger, and, on a per capita basis, to give more money to the institutional vestiges of rural life.

This compassion for the suffering of country folk shows up sharply in the statistics of state aid broken down by types of local government. School districts fare best, with 43 per cent of their revenue derived from outside sources, on a national average. Counties follow closely with 38 per cent. Township receive 25 per cent of their total funds from grants and shared taxes, while cities must be content with less than 13 per cent, and the larger the city, the smaller its share within this average.

Yet cumbersome, unscientific and biased as the aid programs may be, suburbia, even in its poorer sections, does not come off too badly in the final awards. A combination of circumstances operates to turn the uncoordinated array of specific assistance programs to the suburbs' advantage, and once again to deter efforts toward metropolitan consolidation. And in much the same way as the property tax encourages the independence of the richer suburbs, the grant program enjoins the poorer suburbs to remain free.

One reason for this is that the grant program most important to most suburbs is an exception to the general rule. The professional educators have developed and put into effect, in many states, grant formulas that *are* related to need and fiscal capacity. While state educational aid programs pay due regard to the needs of rural schools, they generally apportion aid according to the number of pupils and the taxable wealth of the district. In the service for which the suburbs need more help than any other, state assistance is forthcoming according to the most equitable practices authorized today.

Second, suburbs, as presently constituted, fall within the medium-to-small population ranges of municipalities. Thus they frequently receive special treatment, which the legislature may have intended primarily for the rural areas. Statutory discrimination can be carried only so far, and so long as a suburb retains legal characteristics and a size comparable to a village or hamlet, it receives comparable benefits. If a suburb were to join a central city, it would immediately forfeit the privileges that its independent status confers and become a part of a jurisdiction which, "in the eyes of state officials, commonly wears neither the badge of virtue nor that of poverty."

Finally, the very proliferation of governmental jurisdictions in the suburbs allows a more complete exploitation of the various uncoordinated sources of federal and state assistance than would otherwise be possible. Even when no consolidation with the central city is contemplated, it behooves suburbia to follow the example of the amoeba and continue to divide. A small school district will, even under the most scientific formula, receive a larger grant per pupil than a large one, since the ratio of capital to operating expenditures must necessarily be greater in the smaller district. Other special districts, although they do not receive a high proportion of state aid, receive some assistance that would not be forthcoming if they were not in existence. If the county and township agreed to combine certain functions, the possibility would arise that grants formerly received by both would be reduced. In short, any movement to reduce the number of local units of government or to place more people in a single legal jurisdiction runs the risk of diminishing — or at least making uncertain — the flow of funds from the state capitol and from Washington.

The present grant-in-aid shared tax program, then, patchwork though it may be, is large enough in amount to keep the suburbs going and to stave off disaster. Its form and formulas give preference to the smaller, less efficient, and less financially resourceful local government, and although suburbia does not come off top dog in the allocations, it fares above the average. Like the property tax, the aid programs make little theoretical sense, but they add another powerful economic incentive for the suburb to resist reform. To capitulate to the call of reason, to return to the metropolis, not only implies an abandonment of grassroots ideals and grass-roots politics; it means also a loss in the revenues that provide the difference between survival and catastrophe. Integration penalizes the well-to-do for the benefit of the poor, but even for the poor, reform would go against enlightened self-interest — which in this pragmatic nation is as powerful a guiding principle as any other standard we have.

The Separation of Purse and Power

The succor the suburbs receive from their big brothers has made it possible — so far — for them to meet the new demands of modern government. But does increasing reliance on outside aid square with the suburban desire for independence? The strategy of grants-in-aid on which most suburbs — and most local governments — rely so heavily may be self-defeating, for as the flow of federal and state funds increases, so does the possibility that local governments may be "left hollow shells, operating primarily as field districts," with the form but not the substance of autonomy.

The specter of the New Federalism as a Trojan horse filled with officious bureaucrats from Washington and the State House, who are intent on bringing duly elected local leaders to heel, is a powerful — and perhaps the prevalent — interpretation of intergovernmental relations today. Many find this thesis of entrapment persuasive. They warn that the assistance programs mean only that a Machiavellian Washington chooses seduction instead of rape as the most effective way to violate meaningful local powers.

The ancient political adage that power inescapably follows the purse leads distinguished scholars and public leaders to believe that once beleaguered local governments accept assistance they slide down the primrose path to permanent domination from above. They hear overtones of a coolly calculated plot, a deliberate intention by the national government to commandeer the most productive revenue sources, to cut off the supply of funds "naturally" available to the localities, and finally to reduce lower level governments to a state of impoverished subservience. As the programs go on, Americans are less inclined to look upon them as blessings and become more obsessed with their subversive potentialities.

The eloquence of this interpretation reaches great heights, often persuasive enough to hide the flaws in the argument. We are presented with a picture of federal encroachment contrary to the aims of the "Founding Fathers," a vision of "subsidies, doles, paternalism and an irresistible rush to centralization — then state socialism — then dictatorship." We are told that "the grassroots level is gradually being vitiated by the constant reaching out for power by the Federal Government." We are advised that the only salvation is to "unscramble the prodigious omelet of federal-state relations," to "eliminate the paternalistic pressures which the grant system has enabled the federal bureaucracy to exercise," and to return to the era in which each level of government stood on its own feet.

Some of the exaggeration and emotionalism in the devil theory of federalism can be quickly exposed. The founding fathers were not, as William Anderson has demonstrated, concerned with the encouragement of local prerogatives; they were intent on the establishment of national supremacy. The federal government does not have a predominant role in domestic expenditures, and its share in these costs is not increasing. The Federal tax system does not "exhaust" revenue supplies, for all taxes are paid ultimately from personal income.

Yet the logic that power follows the purse is not so easy to dispose of, and few defenders of the present system of intergovernmental relations have tackled it head on. They prefer to refute the more outrageous claim of conspiracy behind the grants-in-aid, pointing out that the national government and the states are also representative in character and responsible to the people. In brief, the defense of the present system is usually a plea to recognize the interdependence of the modern world, the necessity of big government, and the requirements of progress.

It is possible, however, that even the advocates of grants-in-aid overemphasize the decline in the power of local government which the age of cooperation is supposed to bring. The more the power-purse proposition is examined, the more qualified the generalization becomes, at least in the field of federalism. Obviously a whole new pattern of administrative collaboration has arisen, but whether this is accompanied by a diminution of local authority is much less certain. Program by program, in schools, highways, public health, the localities continue to show a sturdy independence as to what should be done, when and how. They retain the choice of content, personnel and procedure, and commissions of inquiry search in vain for instances of spectacular surrender of local power.

If control means to apply a consistent philosophy about the nature of a public activity, to determine the ends of the policy to be adopted and to direct the resources employed, then local governments are far from controlled. On the contrary, the grant system seems to "have underwritten the continuance of archaic local governmental jurisdictions and irresponsible local administrative structures and procedures." Local governments, suburbia included, seem well on the way to having and eating their grant-supported cakes.

The belief that American localities have in fact accomplished the separation of power and purse rests first on an examination of the so-called strings attached to the grants and appropriations. By and large, these directives are not dictatorial decrees. They are little more than minimum standards for professional administration, relating essentially not to the aims and substance of a program, but to the honesty and competence with which it is executed. On paper, federal and sometimes state regulations in assistance programs may appear formidable, but their scope is narrow and their sanctions are weak. "Controls" in a grant system usually consist of requiring the government that receives funds to initiate a "plan" of proposed action in accordance with some broad and, usually, permissive set of regulations, and then to submit to occasional inspections by field representatives, resulting in audits and reports that are retrospective in nature. The details of the plan are rarely questioned by the grantor agency, unless they violate the broad generalities by which the policy was authorized. Inspections and audits are likely to be perfunctory and a good deal less than meticulous, and the reports are usually filed away. Given a recognition by all levels of government that a particular function should be a public one, there is rarely a substantive issue between the grantor and the grantee on the general outline of the program.

Over a length of time, the dispensing agency may bring about a good deal of improvement in administrative, personnel and professional practices. It is likely to make progress, however, by assuming the role of collaborator, suggesting better ways of operating, advising and consulting but almost never directing. Even in the heyday of the New Deal, when men from Washington ventured forth borne on visions of radical reform, federal agencies rarely undertook to coerce their counterparts in the states. When they did, the results were disastrous. State officials are usually even more considerate of local opinion. The literature of public administration reports many instances of federal and state agencies failing to provide guidance and advice when needed or solicited; it documents a reluctance of those on the higher levels to interfere in an unsatisfactory local situation. It contains little, if any, evidence of high-handed direction or supervision from above, even when conditions obviously called for it.

This pattern of passive, ingratiating, collaborative relationships in grant programs is only what should be expected in a country traditionally contemptuous of its public servants. Any administrator, charged with carrying out a program he believes in and dependent upon operating personnel whom he can neither hire nor fire, must rely chiefly on techniques of persuasion, discussion, and exhortation. If he resorts to the ultimate sanction — withholding funds — he disrupts the program he is committed to carry out; he makes impossible the realization of the goals he seeks, and he forfeits the gains of the past. Since the assistance programs operate through a complicated maze of institutions and procedures, which violate every dogma of control and executive management, passivity is the natural characteristic of the administrators involved. Personnel standards may be raised slowly, local corruption reduced, instances of incompetence eliminated. These improvements come about, however, by a process of voluntary conversion, appeals to the better nature of the local bureaucracy, and spontaneous, uncoerced agreement. Pressures and maneuvers to force local acceptance of unpopular actions are not unknown; but these tactics are borrowed from the world of diplomacy, not from the office of the model executive.

In the final analysis, local governments may experience irritation and frustration in the multitude of forms and regulations with which the red-tape of modern federalism surrounds them, and they cannot always violate administrative procedures as they might wish. Yet, typically, they emerge with their virtue intact. Successful administration of grant programs begins with the recognition that local autonomy is real and it goes forward on the basis of respect for that independence.

There is an even stronger line of defense for local autonomy than the innate sensitivity to local attitudes and the nicety of administrative manners engendered by the structure of assistance programs. More fundamentally, the political and policy-making processes of state and national government provide such ample opportunity for the representation of local interests and for the exercise of local power that it is difficult to conceive of parochial autonomy being seriously threatened. Built into the pattern of legislative apportionment and procedure, the executive institutions and the party organizations of our federal system is a series of arrangements which suggest that, when the chips are down, the localities emerge from their quest for funds not weakened but renewed in their capacity to act.

The most obvious and formal source of protection against federal tyranny is the geographical pattern of legislative representation. This pattern fuses the apparently separate levels of government and destroys the semantical fiction that the three tiers of American government are rigidly compartmentalized, self-contained units of power, totally divorced in their source of authority from each other, poised to oppose and compete.

The geographical plus population formulas for representation in Congress and state legislatures buttress local prerogatives in an important way. Congressmen quickly discover that taking care of local interests and problems that bear on the activities of federal agencies may be a sufficient guarantee of reelection. Once his own people are protected the Congressman can, if he wishes, be active or inactive on issues of great national moment, regard or disregard the wishes of the party, accept or reject the pleas of national groups. The limited territorial base on which a congressman depends provides him with considerable freedom of movement; it also allows fidelity to his local constituency to absolve him automatically from any claim of higher loyalty to party, president or nation. Similarly, state legislatures rarely express state-wide interest, and the apportionment of state legislatures, even more than that of Congress, adds potency to the influence of grassroots interests.

Not only the legislatures but also the executive institutions of the Federal system are directly affected by considerations of localism. Even the Presidency, the single office of national responsibility, is not isolated from the practical pressures generated by the lower levels of government. Archaic as it may be, the electoral college still injects arithmetical considerations based on localism into the process of selecting a President. A popular majority is not enough to ensure election; the majority must be so distributed as to encompass adequate representation from widely diverse regions, if the electoral vote is to be sufficient. The cabinet is still chosen by an informal process that represents each major area of the country, whether its occupational composition is predominantly millionaire or plumber. Further down the Executive hierarchy, agencies and departments continually display loyalties to particular Congressional committees and particular outside associations, which in turn reflect the interests of localities.

Governors face local pressures even more directly, for their executive prerogatives are far more limited and circumscribed than the President's. They may strive to advance a state-wide point of view in highways, education, or institutional care, but usually they find their powers employed as a bargaining weapon, exchanging highway projects in one area for support of a general program in another. And, in the large states, the governor frequently finds himself a representative of local interests as well, stating the case for the cities, on whose support he depends in his state-wide elections, against the rural-minded legislature.

The orientation of the representative, legislative or executive toward localism is powerfully supported by a party structure similarly inclined. The combination virtually guarantees the protection and promotion of local interests. American parties are frequently described as "temporary alliances of local leaders held together by the hope of winning elections," and they are notorious for their lack of discipline and absence of a national point of view. The reasons for the development of our two parties into loose, nonideological, lackadaisically organized confederations are complex; the lack of deep and divisive issues among the American people, our extraordinary agreement on fundamentals, the structure of federalism, which encourages the building of our parties from the lowest level of government upward, are all contributing factors. But the net result is a party process in which localism finds sturdy defenders.

The typical party leader works up from the bottom, building his support on his original constituency. State party leaders and governors find their control of delegations powerful factors in Presidential nominations, and resist any tendency toward a national party organization. As party leader, every President deals with the mosaic of state organizations, big city leaders, and rural machines, and faces an array of mayors, governors and legislators who represent constituencies smaller than his own.

Governors and state legislators, in their turn, are not unconcerned with the problems — and the power — of local party chieftains and officials. State associations of sheriffs are almost always strong enough to circumscribe severely the powers of the state police. Selectmen in New England, mayors in the country generally, clerks of the circuit courts, assessors and county supervisors are frequently as powerful at the State House as in their own home town. These party pressures from the influential people back home encourage legislators and executives to do what the formal basis of their election already makes natural: they consider and protect the local interest.

Rowland Eggers sums up the triumph of grassroots government when he describes how legislatures "sweeten the pots" of local finances, giving money but abstaining from control, providing resources in a policy framework so broad as to fit any conceivable local attitude. And he marks the pressures on the executive when the nomination is at stake and governarships "are now more likely to be openly and unashamedly bargained for at the counter of state-local relations, with wampum made up of intricate old plans and imaginative new programs for pumping more and more state dollars in local coffers."

There is nothing new, of course, in this emphasis upon the geographical basis of American representation and parties and its consequences for elected officials, legislative or executive. The fragmented nature of our political process, and the potency of the local constituency are textbook material for any course in state and national government. Still, it is surprising how frequently these features of American government are overlooked when grants-in-aid programs are discussed. It is as if the influence of the legislator in setting the basic standards for assistance policy were nonexistent, his readiness to question energetic administrators a fiction, his awareness of the political capital to be gained by securing benefits for his home town quite lost in his admiration for the larger society he serves.

Assistance programs quite possibly change the relationships between municipal officials and the legislators who represent the town. They enhance and strengthen the influence of those who sit at the capitols in local party organizations and increase the stature of Congressmen in the eyes of the members of the local chamber of commerce. Yet it is doubtful that these new relationships do anything to diminish the Congressman's dependence on his own limited constituency and it is doubtful that they encourage him to push for an extension of control from above. In financial terms, the states and the nation may have assumed superiority over the localities. In terms of political power, the channels of influence may have become more complicated, but it is unlikely that the grassroots have either withered or been trampled on.

Stripped of the oratory and prophecies of doom, then, the process of sustained intergovernmental relations has produced, on the one hand, extraordinarily tame and docile administrators whose primary allegiance is to the professional program they carry out and not to the government they serve. On the other hand, it has developed extraordinarily aggressive legislators bent on securing the maximum benefits for their localities, with minimum controls. Boiled down to its essence, the definition of cooperative federalism becomes one of assistance programs devised in institutions composed of local governments for the benefit of local governments and ultimately executed by local governments. These programs are prepared by politicians who depend on local constituencies and a locally oriented party for support.

They are supervised by administrators in an organizational structure that vitiates every principle of effective management in order that local autonomy may not be impaired. At every state in the development and implementation of these programs, elaborate safeguards — constitutional, procedural and informal — exist to ensure the protection of local interests. When issues in the program arise, they are almost always resolved in favor of the local unit involved.

The American system of grants-in-aid has many problems. Its separate programs could be far better coordinated than they are; its formulas for allocation could be rationalized; the professional specialists working in each program could be more carefully supervised. But the threat to local autonomy and independence is not a genuine problem; it is a straw man in the political debate.

More than anything else, modern American federalism represents an ingenious political innovation which flaunts the maxim of purse and power. Symbols, not money, talk. Power expresses itself through other than financial channels. If the climate of opinion is carefully prepared, if alarms are sounded frequently and loudly enough, the wolf never appears at all. In the intergovernmental world of today, it is the receiver and not the giver who dictates how the bequest should be spent. And, because of the special potency of the grassroots ideal, the donor will be forever apologetic that he had to give at all.

Securing the Suburban Habitat

So far as a supply of money to meet modern public demands is concerned, then, the suburbs seem likely to pull through. Over all, their expenditures impose no crushing burdens on present levels of personal income and wealth; their access to financial resources seems secure. For the fortunate high-value suburbs, the property tax is sufficient;

for their poorer neighbors, although individual circumstances may dictate individual temporary crises, over the long run the states and the nation seem disposed to support them without jeopardizing their independence. Moreover, the logic of both the property tax and the pattern of grants-in-aid dictates fragmentation into small units. Going it alone is not only virtuous; it pays off in dollars and cents.

Money, however, is not the only necessity of suburban life. Over and beyond the matching of governmental demand and financial supply, there remains the question of whether or not the suburbs can be provided with access to the basic physical resources. They need not only funds but water, food, fuel, lumber, metal, bricks, equipment, furnishings, and the whole array of processed and unprocessed material on which organized, civilized life depends. The issue of providing a reasonable, sustained balance between man and nature is the last and perhaps the most important part of the suburban dilemma. It goes to the heart of the capacity of the suburbs as discrete entities to assure that, in their present disorganized state, they can properly tap the economic and resource system of the great metropolitan areas.

In essence, this challenge breaks down into two parts: an adequate water supply and a transportation system that brings all the other materials to the suburban door. An adequate supply of money can help in solving these problems; wise land-use policies can curb the quantity of demand; the ingenuity of technology can provide new methods for securing probable water and building transportation systems. But, more and more experts have warned that the dwindling resource base of metropolitan regions as a whole and the increasing difficulty of assuring an efficient, rapid movement of goods and people is the real basis of possible suburban catastrophe.

The water problem, in recent years, has been pointed up

as a major impetus for metropolitan reform. Suburbanites typically consume one hundred and fifty gallons per resident per day — two and a half times more water per resident than the rural population. Urban industrial and domestic water consumption now account for about eighty billion gallons per day and the greatest industrial water consumers are those plants concentrated most densely in metropolitan areas.

Years ago, central cities found surface and ground water supplies within their own boundaries inadequate, and reached out to the hinterlands for additional reservoirs. Suburban municipalities tended generally to rely on wells or to establish their own waterwork systems. Now the staggering requirements for water, its increased use in cooling systems, industrial processes and for suburban lawns, have, throughout the country, outstripped supply. Around New York and Chicago, in the newer metropolitan areas of the Southwest and the Far West, suburban wells are drying up, the water table falling, and rationing measures have become common. Bitter conflicts over access to regional rivers and lakes and over the apportionment of existing supplies rage in courts across the land.

While individual water systems are being overtaxed and the 15,000 separate municipal waterworks are competing with one another and with industrial and irrigation uses for the remaining water sources, the companion problem of pollution strikes at the suburbs. Partly, the problem results from inadequate building requirements and inspection standards. Suburbs seem to learn only slowly and painfully that cesspools and septic tanks cannot take the place of sewer systems in quarter-acre lot developments. But the most serious aspect of pollution is the damage done to the streams and rivers of America — the raw sewage of one and a half million persons dumped annually into the Connecticut, the fouling of bathing beaches along the Delaware and the Potomac, the transformation of the Rio Grande into an open sewer for at least thirty miles of its length. Half of all the municipalities in urban areas discharge untreated waste into their waters; in the East, nearly two thirds of all cities and factories are guilty of this practice. The absence of adequate abatement and treatment measures intensifies the natural water shortages in urban areas. It forces the abandonment of local sources years before their time, increases the cost of water facilities, and reduces the number of available sources, even when reservoirs are located hundreds of miles away. Rivers become more than ugly and dangerous; they become barren and useless.

Serious as the suburban water problem has become, it is no more grave than the crisis in the suburban circulatory system, the breakdowns in its channels of commerce and communication with the outside world. Probably no aspect of metropolitan life has received so much attention; none seems to bulk larger as a continuing basic problem in the future. Disruption of the circulatory system for a matter of hours causes inconvenience and complaint; serious disruption for more than a few days would mean the loss of the essentials of human existence.

The circulatory problem comes in three parts: the plight of mass transit systems, the inadequacy of terminal facilities, and the undisciplined use of the automobile. The first two fall primarily but not exclusively within the province of the central city. Suburbanites are also affected by the congestion in the downtown areas; they pay added freight and handling costs when truck and rail terminals are poorly planned and located or inadequate. Many of them suffer the indignities heaped on the railroad commuter and the subway rider, and the financial straits of the mass transportation system are reflected in the higher fares that suburbanites have been paying since the end of World War II.

But by moving to the suburbs, more and more middle-class citizens declare their independence from rail and bus transportation. Given car pools, willingness to use an older car in rush-hour travel, and the means to finance car purchases over time, the suburbanite frequently finds that the automobile is not only the most convenient way to travel; it can be the cheapest. Even when he travels alone and when parking costs push his expenditures above nine cents a mile, the American love affair with the internal combustion engine is an extraordinarily durable romance. The central city may be forced to continue mass transportation for that dwindling minority that cannot afford a car, and the railroads may be constrained to maintain at least a facsimile of adequate short-haul service, but for suburb dwellers, the private automobile and the truck loom as the major channels of access to the outside world.

If the trend toward increased reliance on automobile transportation continues at anything like the rate of the past ten years, the present traffic-jams, bottlenecks, and tie-ups are only a mild portent of things to come. Left unbridled, the automobile may function, not as the servant of the urban age but as its master, to dominate and frustrate modern life and ultimately to make it impossible. In 1958, according to some estimates, it takes longer to cross Manhattan Island by car than it did to make the journey by horse and buggy in 1890. Already city planners report a migration back to the central city of many who are disillusioned by the money and physical effort involved in their return to the pastoral scene. Express highways designed to reach maximum levels of use in 1985 exceeded the goals set for them within two or three years after they were put in use. The thirty-billion-dollar federal aid program that went into effect in 1956 is, according to many experts, grossly inadequate.

The expedients that local traffic engineers devise with such ingenuity — one-way streets, restricted lanes, reversible flow patterns, a ban on left turns — are barely capable of keeping traffic moving at the present time. Congestion is not confined to the central city; it spreads throughout the suburbs and towns, and it is frequently worse where the downtown expressways end and antiquated suburban arteries begin. The disorderly mixture of land uses, the continuing dispersion of people and industry, which suburban growth implies, add to the loads on the already overstrained highways and roads. With 84 per cent of all suburbanites owning cars and with a projected gain in motor vehicle registration of 51 per cent in the next eight years, Wilfred Owen's prophecy that "only trouble lies ahead" may well go down as the understatement of the generation.

In grappling with these basic problems, the provision of water and the maintenance of a semblance of access to the outside world, no suburb can be expected to find a tolerable solution by itself. The best available water supplies have long since been spoken for, and no small municipality is likely to be able either to find a new source or to run the legal gauntlet established by legislation and the courts to block exclusive access to it. Clearly, no single municipality can, on its own, deal effectively with pollution problems created by actions occurring miles from its borders. Certainly, no suburb alone will untangle the traffic jams that result from uncoordinated highway construction and a failure to plan transportation facilities according to the regional traffic flow. It is these obvious suburban inadequacies which, for many, have pointed in the direction of metropolitan-wide governments.

Yet to these most obvious centrifugal pulls the suburbs have replied with a dogged stubbornness and imaginative ingenuity, and rarely have they admitted defeat. Here and there, as in Los Angeles, suburbs capitulate when faced with lack of water and exchange their legal birthright for access to the water supply that the central city foresightedly or fortuitiously acquired earlier. Far more typically, however, suburbs prevail on the central city simply to sell water on a contractual basis, as Chicago does for 54 suburbs, Cleveland for 62, and New York for 50. Attempts to emulate Los Angeles frequently result in mounting suburban political pressures operating through the state government to force the central city to abandon its bargaining position. Milwaukee, for example, felt the wrath of a Governor's study commission in 1956 as suburban water tables dropped and the city continued its policy of annexation as the price of obtaining city water. Milwaukee, the Commission reported, had put the provision of a basic utility to a political use, and it echoed traditional suburban sentiments when it stated, "In America, we have deep-seated objections to economic coercion of this type, particularly by a public utility."

When ad hoc contractual arrangements and cooperative endeavors among a few suburbs are not available, the common solution is to rely on the traditional ally of suburban independence, the nonpolitical Authority. For water, the Authority takes the form of a metropolitan water district, operating under the aegis of the state or as an independent commission formed by the municipalities themselves. Inaugurated in 1895, the Massachusetts Metropolitan Water District represents one variety of this institutional makeshift. A quasi-state agency, it furnishes water at wholesale to twenty-three member cities and towns with a population of well over a million and a half, and provides 200 million gallons per day. The North Jersey District Water Supply Commission typifies the second organizational alternative; established by eight municipalities, it now serves twenty. Pennsylvania, Maryland and California have passed authority acts and in each of these states special districts have come into being for metropolitan areas. As a final resort, suburbs can encourage, as they have in parts of New Jersey, the formation of private waterworks companies, thus making certain that even though their citizens pay higher water bills, their governments are secure in their independence.

Metropolitan Authorities play their part in whatever solutions have been forthcoming in the transportation field as well, but here the pattern of challenge and response is more complex. In a few large areas, autonomous government corporations labor separately to break highway bottlenecks, construct expressways and lure passengers back to the mass transit systems. In New York, the Port Authority and the Transit Authority vie, sometimes spectacularly, with Robert Moses (in his several institutional capacities) to provide for the fast circulation of goods and people throughout the region. More generally, the states and the federal government have come to provide the basic plans, personnel and money to keep the automobiles moving. The 1944 Federal Aid Highway Act gave serious attention to the cities for the first time, allocating one fourth of assistance funds to construction within the jurisdictions of sizable municipalities, and since then federal aid has increased rapidly. State aid for local roads also has almost tripled in the last fifteen years and is now approaching the one-billion-dollar mark, and more and more states have assumed responsibility for major arterial routes in metropolitan areas.

Thus, though local governments control almost eighty per cent of the roads in the United States, crash programs for new expressways are likely to be carried out either by Authority direction or by joint financial schemes in which the states participate heavily. Rarely does this complex pattern of Authorities and state and federal aid add up to a coordinated attack on the transportation problem; the respective potential of highways and mass transit are not usually considered together, and a rational regional solution obtained. "Something" is done, however — poorly perhaps, but well enough to permit survival as long as the nation is cushioned by a prosperous economy.

At first glance the rise of the Authority in these fields may seem to pose a threat to suburbia; indeed, some observers look forward to a general government emerging from the corporate cocoon. Surveying the Authorities, state and local, that have sprung up in increasing number over the country, and the expanded duties they were assuming, John. C. Bollens could speculate that perhaps the multipurpose special district was the forerunner of genuine metropolitan government.

Certainly, as Authorities come into being, there is a strong tendency for their responsibilities to expand. The Massachusetts Metropolitan District began by simply supplying water; it then was combined with an earlier Metropolitan Sewer Commission. Next, it assumed the work of the Metropolitan Park Commission in acquiring land and constructing parkways; and finally, as a logical development, it added the establishment and maintenance of parks. The New York Port Authority was first conceived to have the primary job of rationalizing railroad terminal facilities on the Jersey side of the Hudson. Unable to make progress in its negotiations with the railroads, it abandoned this controversial effort and concentrated on the building of bridges and tunnels. Then it entered the airport and bus terminal field, the construction of truck loading and distribution facilities, until its last final report listed eight separate activities, ranging from the operation of nineteen terminal and transportation facilities to pleadings before the Interstate Commerce Commission in the interests of port developments.

Despite the obvious popularity of corporate devices and reasonably autonomous districts as means for securing the basic resources for the suburban environment, it is doubtful that suburbia is threatened by their development. There is a built-in limitation in the Authority: its activities have to produce revenue. Its greatest practical advantage is that, by being financially independent, it escapes the debt and assessment limitations which the ordinary units of local government face. Thus, though occasionally Authorities may flirt with providing amenities of urban life that do not return profits, they cannot stray too far from a self-supporting budget. Hence, many municipal activities — public safety, health, and education — are beyond their reach. They may leave municipalities poorer by removing revenue-producing activities from their jurisdictions, but they are not likely to displace the municipality as a general form of government. Their function will remain that of offering a nongovernmental solution to the resource problems the suburbs face.

So far as the resource problems themselves are concerned, the ad hoc and haphazard employment of Authorities, state highway departments and assistance programs has one major implication. The solutions found for water scarcity, river pollution and transportation congestion will be predominantly engineering ones. When several separate authorities and agencies become involved in dealing with the metropol-

itan resource complex, the possibility that the different
needs and demands will be dealt with on an integrated rational basis diminishes sharply. Few opportunities exist.
under present arrangements, for really effective planning
on a regional basis, and few of the commissioners, directors
and department heads can afford to take time to look at the
forest instead of their particular trees. In transportation
especially, there is no structure that can relate the highway
and parking programs either to each other or to the mass
transit system. In water districts, the emphasis is necessarily
on the acquisition of water supplies and their distribution
to industrial and domestic users. Some attention is paid to
pollution control, but securing other related benefits — in
recreation, reforestation and soil conservation — which are
an integral part of river basin development, cannot be expected. A good quality of construction and sturdy honesty
are the hallmark of the Authorities, and few states have to
apologize for the material accomplishments of their highway
departments. But imagination, foresight, the capacity to
relate different resource needs and to look to the region as
a whole, are not characteristics produced by the special district approach.

As in the case of finances, in facing up to the conditions
of their environment the suburbs have found ways and
means to maintain acceptable standards of existence. They
by no means realize their ecological potential: rivers remain dirty, air fouled with grit and fumes, streets over-
crowded and parking scarce. Nor are they by any means safe
and secure so far as the future is concerned. The automobile
alone will challenge urban policy-making for years to come.
But no suburb as yet has disappeared because its residents
died of thirst or starvation, or succumbed to disease borne
on polluted waters, or were unable to receive the necessaries

of life or go to work in the outside world. The often ingenious and always intriguing innovations in public institutions, with which the metropolitan areas abound, work well enough to provide a livable environment. They do so without threatening the autonomy of suburban governments, and they encourage suburbanites to continue their flight from the city. They provide what Charles Cherington, in speaking of the Boston experience, has called the "modicum of integration . . . a quarter loaf," which forestalls more radical changes. Again in Cherington's words, "The agitation for further integration continues, but at the moment we can say with united smugness: We Keep House."

The Suburbs Persevere

The longer the public problems of suburbia are studied, the more impressive become the qualities of suburban tenacity and inventiveness which preserve the grassroots in the face of the continuing challenges of modern life. The winds of the welfare state beat persistently and sometimes at gale force upon suburban governments. Here the technological impact of the automobile, society's requirements for technically skilled and managerially trained personnel, and the welfare costs which modern medicine fosters are revealed most clearly. Here the problems of population growth, of building new communities, of handling the volume of residential construction engendered by sustained prosperity are focused. Here exist the unprecedented challenges in political organization, public administration and the provision of public services, since no other migration has so swiftly and with such force disrupted the balance of human organization and nature.

To these challenges, the suburbs have brought a weak and unbalanced tax structure, no longer representative of the

wealth the community has at its disposal, poorly administered, and with built-in pressures to continue the process of
metropolitan fragmentation even further. Their political
institutions and processes have typically been inadequate
and ill equipped; their bureaucracy amateurish and untutored. By every test with which we judge the vigor, strength
and staying power of modern government, most suburbs
seem to fail miserably.

Yet suburbia perseveres. Some suburbs alertly seal themselves off from the onrush of the new middle class and, by
shrewd employment of their local prerogatives and powers,
avoid most of the challenges. Others capitulate, but find
sanctuary in the protective programs that state and nation
have extended to them. All employ the new political inventions of the twentieth century, the government corporation
or the intensified use of the special district device of earlier
times, to meet special crises in special ways, even though
sometimes this involves nothing more than fictitious double-
counting of the resources that are available.

Each of these stratagems has one principle in common:
independence, the capacity to decide, to have an option, is
preserved. Frequently, fidelity to this principle means doing
without a service or continuing it on a minimum basis. Sometimes it means an outright transfer of a specific responsibility
to a higher level of government, without surrender of the
capacity to govern generally. Often, it means the abandonment of democratic government in the sense of popular control, as the citizen becomes bewildered at the number of
units that have jurisdiction over him and relinquishes authority to the expert.

But in any given suburban territory, small governments,
truly local governments, remain to enhance the feeling of
the small community in the modern world, to cling to the

ideal of the republic in miniature, and to prevent the encroachment of the metropolis. Suburbia is brave to the point of rashness in its struggle for existence; it is resourceful, aggressive and so far successful. Only one question of importance remains: is it right in its decision to remain free?

PART III

CHAPTER 7

The Miniature Re-examined

Defenders of the Faith

The values of the small government and the small town are not usually considered proper subjects for debate in America. As Roscoe Martin observes, "the Grassroots concept is invoked with confidence in support of manifold causes . . . treated almost universally with a respect bordering on reverence . . . one who rejects or ignores a grassroot incantation does so at his peril, for the public mind does not entertain the alternative of grassroots fallibility. *In hoc signo vinces* was not devised for the grassroots talisman, but it might have been."

Thus, if by the miracle of technology the modern suburb seems to be a reasonable reconstruction of our heritage, our instinctive reaction is to welcome the renaissance with open arms. Here is at least a partial answer to the threat of the great organization, a reassuring sign that the nation has not abandoned completely its fundamental principles. The working life of the commuter may be subsumed within the soulless corridors of big business, his daily ordeal of travel may be impersonal and faceless, but at home and in his local government he has a life that has an elemental appeal.

Yet if suburbia is — as a matter of demonstrable fact — the modern carrier of a time-honored and respected ideology, there is literally no alternative but to question the values it represents. There is no other way of understanding the difficulties suburbia presents: its clear indifference to the metropolitan world about it, and on which it clearly depends, its obvious failure to solve effectively the social and political problems of its own people, and its irresponsibility toward the circumstances of its next-door neighbors. It is at least possible that it is these very traits that are ultimately responsible for the deficiencies in life and politics that observers have chronicled. Ultimately, a decision must be made as to whether the qualities suburbia brings are more desirable than the ones it destroys.

This is quite a different problem from the question as to how the residential suburb comes to have the essential properties of small town life and government. It goes beyond the issue as to what factors account for the qualities of propinquity, interdependence, the sense of equality and the time to participate in communal affairs, and produce a special pattern of politics. The problem is not one of fact but of values, and it is concerned primarily with examining the benefits which the small town supposedly bestows. Thus, the problem is not limited to the present suburb and the present generation. It extends to Tocqueville's Northwest town and Jefferson's ward, to the English parish and the European village before America. The question is universal and timeless, and, simply put, it is: why believe that the small community produces the best life, and more especially, the best government?

Since antiquity the answers to this question have been overwhelmingly on the side of the ideology and, as Martin indicates, the consensus is so great that any criticism begins with poor prospects of success. Classical Greece appears as the first defender of the values of the modern suburb, for there the small community was originally presented as the center of the good life and there philosophers first insisted that an ideally satisfactory state must be limited in size.

Plato provided the basic rationale by making personal acquaintance among all members of a society a necessity for civilized existence. To him, once a community numbered more than 30,000 inhabitants it could not preserve the intimate mingling of home, family, government, economic pursuit and social custom essential to its moral health. Aristotle was even more explicit in his convictions. His picture of the ideal state was one of small area, with a population large enough "to the fulfillment of its work" but never exceeding the limits of personal acquaintance. "If the citizens of a state," he reasoned, "are to judge and distribute offices according to merit, then they must know each others' characters."

To the Greeks, size was never to be confused with greatness; the goal they sought was a social and political unit representing the perfection of human development, "an organic sense of structural difference," a corporate whole. And their firm conviction that the good life could only flourish in the small community was not the least of the reasons why their civilization was chronically incapable of organizing itself on a national basis.

The picture of the ideal state that Plato and Aristotle first presented and which their people practiced reappears again and again in history, defended by distinguished thinkers of every age. St. Thomas, Botero, Bodin, Montesquieu, each in turn emphasized that a state must remain small if it were to be well governed. Rousseau gave this ideology its neo-classic expression when he named the Swiss canton the

purest representative of democracy and liberty, and endowed
the small community with a purpose and a morality quite
apart from the individuals who composed it. Burke, however much concerned with presenting the entirety of England as a commonwealth, based the existence of society in
general upon the instinctive feelings, customs and traditions
of the neighborhood. Of all the vicious follies he saw in the
French Revolution, none seemed more ill advised than the
violent demand for national rather than local allegiance,
the increase of the strength of Paris against the strength of
Gascony, Normandy, and Brittany.

"We begin our public affections," he wrote, "in our families. No cold relation is a zealous citizen. We pass on to
our neighborhoods and our habitual resting-places. Such
divisions of our country as have been formed by habit, and
not by a sudden jerk of authority, were so many little images
of the great country in which the heart found something
which it could fill . . . To be attached to the subdivision,
to love the little platoon we belong to in society, is the first
principle (the germ as it were) of public affections. It is the
first link in the series by which we proceed towards a love
for our country and mankind."

But it is not essential to believe with Burke, Rousseau,
or Plato, in "the massiveness of communal life" and their
emphasis on the innate disposition of humans to live together
in order to defend the small community. Even if a man
legalizes his relationships with his fellows and is more an
individual coolly pursuing self-interest than a social animal
searching for companionship, the most obvious and most
direct source of legitimate political association and authority
seems to be the jurisdiction of limited size. The small society
may not be ideally a union of family, neighborhood, church
and town hall, with a morality and corporate identity of its

own, and its social and economic bonds may be only contrived. But it seems still — purely as a matter of scale — a most convenient place in which to order the relations of man to man. The fundamental duties of government, the protection of person and property, the defense of natural law are discharged there, and the private rights of the individual are there best protected.

Thus philosophies that emphasize the individual rather than the community and that see the state as an artificial structure contrived for the private benefit of each citizen share the small town ideology. Ever since Althusius showed how a series of social contracts could be employed to construct a large state from an association of small ones, most political thinkers in this tradition have preferred to retain local autonomy. John Stuart Mill made representative government his ideal only on the grounds of practicality. To him, since "nothing less can be ultimately desirable than the admission of all to a share in the sovereign power of the state," representative government was acceptable only because "all cannot, in a community exceeding a single small town, participate personally in any but some very minor portions of the public business." Lord Bryce echoed Mill's sentiments, calling small communities "tiny fountain-heads of democracy, rising among the rocks, sometimes lost altogether in their course, sometimes running underground to reappear at last in fuller volume."

For the twentieth century, John Dewey remained convinced that "democracy must begin at home and its home is the neighborhood community." Additional support in the modern contractual tradition comes from as sturdy an individualist as Louis Brandeis, who underscored the importance of "neighborly affection" and insisted that personal acquaintance was essential for the rational conduct of public affairs.

Today Learned Hand has sounded the alarm that "the herd is regaining its ancient and evil primacy," arguing that "the tiny city utopias of Plato and Aristotle; or of Jefferson . . . living in proud, honorable isolation" must somehow be preserved against the onrush of Leviathan.

Thus the onrush of the large organization does not diminish the value assigned by many advocates of the contractual theory of society and government to the small town. Instead the changes modernity demands from political theory, the construction of empires and nation-states, the problems of social welfare and social justice that industrialism raises, have intensified this belief. The "Great Society" of national and international relationships places a strain upon governmental structures and on the political inventiveness and ingenuity of the citizen, however rational, to exercise proper supervision. With so many demands on his attention, with so many complex and almost inscrutable developments taking place on the larger stage of human affairs, men need more than ever, it seems, a place where problems are concrete and familiar, where abstractions are unnecessary and where "people take what they can use without surrendering their way of life."

In the modern world, the small town still appears to provide an opportunity for people to participate in public affairs, to have a "sense of personal competence to make a difference," to make mistakes and not bear catastrophe as a consequence. For the most part, technology and the disparate elements of industrial life appear to confirm rather than destroy the ideology. To many scholars the job of modern political thought is to preserve the intimate contact of the neighborhood, to reconcile large-scale operations with small-scale independence and to make the small community a living one for twentieth century man.

Of course, those who see human relations essentially as a matter of deliberate contrivance differ importantly from those of the body politic school of thought in the values they ascribe to small government. Especially in the United States, we have not accepted the Greek concept of a society of order, class and structural balance. Our sense of community emphasizes individual equality, and, since the beginning, Americans have been "held together not by the knowledge that they were different parts of a corporate whole, but by the knowledge that they were similar participants in a uniform way of life." Where Plato and Aristotle sought civilization as the supreme objective of the self-sufficient community, where Burke appealed to the continuity of history, the philosophy of reason emphasizes individual freedom and democratic participation as more important end-products.

Nevertheless, whether man arrives pure and undefiled on the political scene or finds his true birthright only in political association; whether he is rational in the eighteenth century sense or psychologically encircled by twentieth century emotions; whether there is a natural law or the expressions of Locke are only fiction, there has always been, in every general scheme, a place for the small community and the small government. Its origins may be utilitarian or ordained by supernatural prescription, individualistic or pluralistic, but the result is almost always a recognition of the locality and a reaffirmation of its right to separate existence, wherever possible. The construct of community remains the highest purpose of political science, and though the Great Society may offer more security and wealth, few have argued that it is as happy or as kindly as the small. In the final judgments the great thinkers concerned with the problem of legitimate government unite in defense of the grassroots ideal.

The Logic of the Faith

Testimonials — the conclusions of important philosophers — are one way to defend the small community; logical argument is another. To buttress the case in the modern world, the insights and judgments of every age can be put together into a simple, apparently commonsense chain of reasoning that runs essentially like this: Small towns offer certain indigenous qualities which, taken collectively, create a milieu in which the American aims of equality and liberty are best secured. They promise the development of individual initiative, operate as a bulwark against concentrated political power, provide the most effective union of the collective and private disposition of mankind that we can hope to find. Destroy these qualities, embrace completely the gargantuan world in which we live, and the traditional goals of American society are also in peril.

But what specifically do the qualities of small town life contribute to a harmonious relation of man to man and to good government? In the logic of the faith, each characteristic has its own beneficial effect which can be recognized and defended. Whether found in the small town of other centuries or in the modern suburb, propinquity, interdependence, common beliefs and backgrounds, some measure of leisure time are thought to encourage political acitivity which almost guarantees effective democratic government. And when their separate contributions are added together, the case for the small locality seems sturdy indeed.

Propinquity, for example, apparently provides the familiarity and experience, the intimacy of personal relations, that Plato and Aristotle stressed so heavily and that helps ensure the sense of integration so sought after today. In a small town, individual identity is never a problem; people can know whomever it is important to know. There are fewer secrets and fewer idols than in the large cities; flaws and strengths of character are quickly recognized; the good are separated from the bad. In the small government, the public program and the official who carries it out are known, judged, understood directly; they can be experienced, they are visible. Life does not impose impossible demands on rationality and character; community organization is attuned to the reality of human nature. The situation is of manageable proportions, and, because the boundaries are fixed, it can stay within manageable proportions.

To the concreteness of life that propinquity provides, the condition of interdependence is thought to add a healthy motive of good will. Men want to cooperate in the small town; they cannot tolerate the troublemaker, for his existence threatens the existence of all. Since they are bound together in their common fortunes, the solution to communal problems affects directly each man's personal future. Since total resources are limited, all members are encouraged to pull together, to be good neighbors. Sickness, adversity, natural disaster visited on one member are known to all, and since all recognize that an act of God may come again, the urge to help is reinforced by the knowledge that everyone "is in the same boat."

The bonds of fellowship that propinquity and interdependence encourage seem further strengthened by the common goals and common values inherent in the equality of a small town. The locality may be, relatively speaking, better off or less fortunate than its neighbors, or than similar communities elsewhere, but its very size fixes limits on the extremes within its own social order. There can be, it is argued, only a few who live on the Hill, if there is only one hill in town; only a few who are socially unacceptable if there is only one shanty town. Opposing values, different ambitions, sharply divergent beliefs are rarities in such a situation.

Even where differences in wealth and position exist, the variation seems acceptable. The successful succeed not through any mystique, but by working harder or being more excellent in the pursuits in which the majority are engaged. In these circumstances it is difficult to infect recognition of ability with envy and spite, for the means of accomplishment are open to all. Sharp dealings, to be countenanced, must be the established rules of the game, part of the mores of the entire community. A vast common ground of shared beliefs and customs makes cooperation comfortable and intimacy pleasurable.

Under these conditions, so the rationale runs, each member is likely to participate fully and freely in public affairs. A citizen speaks his piece in the small town first of all because what goes on is vital to his own ambitions. It concerns property, education, and the provision of utilities basic to existence. Wars, diplomacy, the fluctuations of the national economy, these matters are both difficult for the average man to understand and difficult for him to influence, but the land use of his neighborhood, the proper recording of his property, zoning, water rights, the protection of his person, the education of his children, the construction of a new highway at the right place and at the right time, affect his everyday life. Whether or not they are provided, how they are provided, the use made of the limited resources to which the citizen contributes directly and not by the accounting sleight-of-hand of the withholding tax, are matters he understands and cares deeply about.

And even if a small town resident did not care, if his stake were slight and his status low in the narrow scale of the social order, he would still participate in public affairs, for that participation expresses, asserts, and guarantees his political equality. Only the eccentric, the hermit, the deviate, remains aloof; the proof of citizenship is by association with your neighbor, and a man establishes himself when he stands up and is counted.

In such a context, the defenders of the small town insist, leadership partakes of special qualities, at once removed from the patrician and the rabble-rouser. A leader in the small community supposedly can be neither, for in an equal society he can neither assume that his fellows are inferior nor can he raise the standard of the underdog and cannily set slave against master. The leader expresses the sense of the community and he helps formulate and crystallize it. But he can never "deliver" the majority opinion and he cannot be above it. Bounded by the conditions of equality and participation, known intimately by his fellows, the leader cannot rely on oratory or adulation, nor can he exhibit only driving ambition. Typically, he operates almost invisibly, knotting together one personal association with another until he has secured sufficient respect and support to put his measures through.

The respect may be misplaced; the leader may simply have cultivated a familiarity which his neighbors mistake for fellowship. On the other hand, he may have a genuine, lively interest in the work which must be done, and a willingness to accept responsibility. But, regardless of motives, his leadership is never flamboyant. Small town leadership is in town moderator style, unassuming, calm, equitable and knowledgeable, without frills or airs. Accessibility is the key condition, whether the leader operates as a petty tyrant or a devoted trustee to the community spirit, and being accessible, his success depends on his own sensitivity to the moods and aspirations of his fellows.

Finally, it is argued, the activities of the small community are likely to take place in an atmosphere of leisure, in the sense that vocation does not consume all time and all attention. There is a limit to the number of things that must be done, and a limit to the number of events that demand attention. Each day or each week may bring a major problem to the fore, but it is likely that the problem is the only one for that period. The question of *choosing* the event is rarely an issue, for in the small town there is usually but one church social, one fire, one scandal, one television program, one public emergency at a time, and men shift attention successively from one event to another and are not — indeed cannot be — confused by competing spectacles.

So advocates of the ideology point out that there is time for reflection, for contemplation, for second thoughts, for deliberation, for the cooling of emotions, for rational appraisals, which permit a sense of direction and rational decisions. To many, this quality of time is the most precious blessing the small community can offer. More than propinquity, equality, the opportunity for active participation and passive leadership, the slower rhythm ensures the manageability of the small community. It encourages the expression of the communal nature of man in an orderly, regular fashion; it removes the tensions of self-seeking and provides the requisites for sensible common action.

The elaboration and description of these qualities, collectively and individually, is the reasoned argument that supports the authority of the philosopher and the instinct of the laymen who defend the small government. Its appeal seems universal, because the traits seem common to all men of all times. Good will, neighborliness, courage, fair play, tolerance, patience, open-minded inquiry — since Plato, these are the human qualities that are to be idealized. And they can exist, if one follows the logic, only in small settings. They are not, in Arthur Morgan's words, "the fruits of civilization, but rather its roots." Since they can apparently be found only on a small scale, great civilization paradoxically can be constructed only from small societies where government and neighborhood commingle and political and social reality become one.

It is little wonder that men wax sentimental when they write of the grassroots, speak of "plain citizens and humble leaders," and find poetry in the Town Meeting. The spirit of communion affects each quality observed, and reason confirms instinct in approving the Miniature. Individuality tempered by neighborliness, equality used to promote cooperation, community which tolerates eccentricity — this would seem to represent the best of America.

Probing the Lines

A faith so long established, so closely reasoned and so universally acclaimed has the aspect of a phalanx on the battlefield of philosophy. Yet the very unanimity of opinion is suspicious, for the two broad schools of thought that collectively supply the arguments for the small community have contradictory basic assumptions and seek widely divergent ends. Given this fact, evidently one of them is mistaken when it embraces the faith. Either the men who view society and politics as principally corporate affairs with collective goals beyond those of the individuals err when they applaud the ideology, or those who regard the state as a contrivance serving only private purposes are deceived. If the desirability of the Miniature is the issue, one question to ask is which philosophy was right and which wrong when it sided with the small town?

The most accurate answer to this question is that both of

the philosophical camps we have been describing deluded themselves. The ultimate aim of those who see man essentially as a social animal is to create a body politic of such dimensions that the richness and variety of human experience can be encompassed. Their vision is a mosaic of intricate design, in which each individual makes his contribution to a purpose higher than his own aims, and the grandeur of that vision is used to justify the gradations in rank and status, the obligations of duty and discipline, the array of mutual responsibilities and social controls that are required to produce the splendid work of art.

But the small community, in and of itself, never realizes that end — it never comprehends the variety of life; at best, it can serve only as an intermediate grouping within the greater whole. In Greece, the golden age was not associated with the city-state; it arrived with the Athenian Empire. The medieval city had meaning only within the Kingdom of God; Burke's parish was but a connection between the family and the commonwealth. In short, civilization has never existed within village boundaries, and the small community is nothing more than a segment in the larger pattern, expressive of only one element in the universe, and by itself quite meaningless.

Yet if corporate philosophers can use the small community only as a stepping stone for its greater purpose, the advocates of individualism have even greater difficulty in fitting it into their scheme of values. Particularly, the American version of the ideology, with its emphasis on equality as a means for liberating the individual, errs grievously when it embraces the small community. Participation in communal affairs is a simple matter in the small towns, but this expression of equality does not lead necessarily to freedom in the personal sense. More often than not, the common standard of the

small community, its proudly displayed principle of equality, its suspicion of "social airs," operates in a profoundly
anti-individualistic way. In Louis Hartz's words, "The man
who is as good as his neighbors is in a tough spot when he
confronts all his neighbors combined."

Precisely because the small town represents the most radical application of the democratic theory, it raises the greatest
problem for individualism. Here is the extreme expression
of popular sovereignty against which Madison strove: popular control unchecked by a notion of minority rights; a principle derived from natural rights which destroys natural
rights, with all the ethical and impersonal inconsistencies
and deficiencies that Robert Dahl has detailed. Here is no
conscious agreement freely developed through debate and
discussion but rather passive acquiescence, an irrational
expression of uniformity of attitude and outlook, a certainty
of the rightness of the majority which amounts to compulsion.

It may be true, as Dahl suggests, that theoretically the
respective roles of majority and minority are never neatly
balanced in the search for freedom, but certainly, in the
small communities, the scale is weighed heavily in favor of
the majority. "You have to go on living with people," Sherwood Anderson reflects, "day after day, week after week.
You can't just ignore your brother-in-law, forget him as you
might in a city. Tomorrow you will meet him in the street.
You will be meeting him in the stores and in the post-office.
Better make it up, start over again." Equality of this kind
liberates only when the individual is part of the majority.
When he dissents, equality is as likely to display as intol-
erant a disdain for private opinion as does an autocratic state.

When the lines are probed far enough the small community stands as representative of the worst of both philos-

ophies: the requirement that man subordinate his individual aims to that of the group, without the group possessing any quality of greatness; the prescription that a man begins on the basis of equality with his neighbor, with no guarantee that he can go forward on his own. The respectable values that both interpretations hold out as perennially valid, the insights into human nature that they contribute, are lost. What is left over are the dregs of their speculation, the flaws of their grand analysis, the unacceptable portions of their doctrine. Order without purpose; equality without liberty; these become the hallmarks of the ideology.

The essence of this residue can be summed up in a single concept: fraternity. Grassroots life is "the test of man's ability to adjust himself. It tells the story of his skill in living with others." This is the heart of the small town, the reason it is acclaimed and the reason why it may be defective. It is not surprising that the descriptions of "democracy at work," town meeting style, become invariably anecdotal: instance after instance of informality, good will, the triumph of personality over procedure, the potency of the wisecrack at the proper time, the decision tailored to the person involved, the horseback judgment overriding the expert opinion. In the rosy glow of the fellowship which propinquity and equality produce, the pattern dissolves into a series of character sketches, each actor classified and typed, each reading his lines in the comfortable assurance that the script has been agreed upon by all.

Quite certainly, fraternity is a persistent inclination of mankind; it fills some needs of human nature. It promises security in a group of like persuasion; it bolsters faltering egoes, it banishes an awful sense of loneliness, it fosters togetherness and belongingness. To the degree that these qualities reinforce the individual, soothe nerves, banish discord, promote harmony, they are doubtless useful. Lodges, clubs, fraternities have their function, for when a man is free to choose his associates the choice can be both a bulwark against the world and an expression of himself. No one doubts the beneficial values of neighborhood, where the lessons of getting along with the outsiders are first learned in the company of friends, where a knowledge of the common traits of human nature is gained, and where the drift of affairs is, above all, predictable. In these circumstances, the uses of fraternity are sometimes admirable.

At other times, however, fraternity may be less than admirable, with overtones of exclusiveness, narrowness, provinciality and clannishness. Privacy cannot be countenanced in a brotherhood; personal ambitions bow necessarily to group aims; unanimity becomes essential, for how else can a fraternity survive? When the fraternal order is the only order of life, it seems unsatisfactory as a way of organizing society-at-large or establishing a government. When neighborhoods are equipped with political boundary lines, when the fraternal club becomes not an informal part of life but instead its formal expression, when individual purposes can be achieved only through the fraternal process, then the less attractive elements of conformity — compulsion and suspicion — come to the fore.

Yet the concept of fraternity as *the* way of life is, of course, the inescapable implication of grassroots autonomy: an ideal of a self-contained whole to which all members belong and from which none can exit without a violent wrench, a vision of a government which "institutionalizes the neighborliness of the village." But this neighborliness is no universal brotherhood with a higher purpose of a greater civilization, nor is it a voluntary brotherhood, where the common bonds of every man are freely recognized and freely defined.

The fraternity of the small community is a union without ambition and without competition. It may be comfortable; it may be forgiving; but it cannot promise the excellence that civilization itself or the individual alone can possibly achieve. "It is," in Sherwood Anderson's words, "a case of love," justified because "Life can never be intimate enough."

Checklist of Operative Democracy: (1) The Rule of Law
The conflict between democracy and fraternity can be set forth in abstract terms; it can also be documented specifically. Once the spirit of the small community is equated with the spirit of fraternity, the violence the suburban image wreaks upon other operative ideals of American society becomes clear in three important ways. A nation committed essentially to the concept of contractual relations as the legitimate method to order human associations has embraced a doctrine of personal relations. A nation that has constructed sophisticated and highly complex restrictions on popular participation in the actual operation of government has accepted the doctrine of direct democracy in its most extreme form. A nation that establishes individuality as the prime goal for its society has deprived itself on the local level of the means to secure that end.

The inconsistency most immediately apparent is between the concept of fraternity and the theory of contractual relations. American life is built on the Lockian proposition of "the reality of atomistic social freedom," a view of the state as an association of free men and an insistence that there be a clear distinction between society and government. The classical expression of this view of legitimate government has always been constitutionalism — the application of systematic regularized restraints on the political power, the guarantee that certain aspects of living are beyond the reach of organized community power, that the government is both something less than, and different from, society.

As Carl Friedrich describes the constitutional process, it rests fundamentally on law — on rules that organize a government, limit the exercise of its authority, and provide the means by which the community and its political organization are distinguished. Government, restrained in action by a bill of rights, by the separation or geographical division of powers, by judicial review, remains apart from the community it governs, and the supreme power of the community comes into play only when the political process fails to function.

There is, of course, no place for such a systematic distinction between the social and political spheres within the meaning of fraternity. Although men are bound together in the American small town not as a hierarchy but as a brotherhood, their bonds remain tightly drawn. They are simply members of a larger family, and intimacy and intercourse are so inevitable that public and private affairs are difficult to separate. The proud boast so often repeated that "the town meeting *is* the town" is true, and the entire community is the government, not on the rare occasions of catastrophe but whenever public affairs are carried out.

One result, of course, is the special environment in which local government tries to carry out its duties. A public agency operates not so much according to law or under the collective supervision of the community assembled formally as its governing body; instead, it functions under the constant, haphazard, and sometimes suffocating scrutiny of whichever members of the town decide to busy themselves with the agency's affairs. The outstanding example is the public school, for here the line between public function and social institution becomes almost impossible to draw. Lane Lancaster captured the blending of the professional obligations and personal characteristics of the small town teacher in a memorable passage when he wrote: "Not only does the teacher live under the constant espionage of her charges, but she is seldom free from the feeling of utter dependence upon the community which controls her 'job.' From the moment she arrives in the community her goings and comings become matters of general interest and in every real sense her life ceases to be her own. Where she shall 'board and room,' do her banking, attend church, seek diversion and recreation, the charities she supports, the books she reads, where she will make her personal purchases, the choice of her associates and her clothes, the use of her weekends — all these are matters for gossip in the village which has 'hired' her and which exacts a rigid conformity to the lowest common denominator of village mores."

More serious, perhaps, is the intrusion government can make upon society under these circumstances. The concept of constitutionalism, of law, of impersonal relations between the individual and the group, becomes difficult to maintain. The notion of systematic, regularized restraints filters down from higher levels of government; statutes, regulations, Robert's rules of order become the departure point for public action. But the most significant feature of small town politics is the frequency with which legal and procedural requirements are overlooked and ignored. They are always to be adjusted according to the "common sense, down-to-earth judgment" of the participants, to take account of unique conditions and provincial peculiarities. Tickets can be fixed, favors granted, contracts awarded, not because these irregularities will remain hidden but because they are acceptable on the basis of personal esteem. The successful town moderator is the one who moderates between the rules of the game

and the disposition of the meeting. Government indistinguishable from society, when no country gentry is permitted,
no lord of the manor allowed, is personalized government.
Men come to take on, as Granville Hicks notes, a profound
cynicism toward the law. "Every predatory pioneer instinct
goes into operation when the average native is confronted
with his government — town, state or federal. Governmental
bodies apparently exist to be cheated and regulations were
made to be evaded."

Personalized government can be both effective and beneficial. It can adjust abstract legal generalizations to the actual
state of affairs, make regulations tolerable, and bring them
into line with informal mores and customs. But it can also
be offensive, as were the personalized duchies which Huey
Long created out of the Louisiana parishes, the tight domin-
ions of courthouse gangs, the one-man sovereigns of the rural
county whose rule was no less arbitrary because it was accepted.

It is no accident that the folk hero of local America is the
law-enforcement agent who interprets the law according to
his own lights. The archetype of the Western sheriff substitutes his concept of justice for the statute book; he does his
duty, as in *High Noon,* and then grinds his badge underfoot;
he operates as often as a vigilante outside the law as within
it. And he is applauded, approved, even today, because his
concept of justice seems so direct, without frills, legalism, or
delays. In short, his law ignored the processes of restraint
and orderly procedure on which order is built.

So in the small community, power depends on personal
qualities, on the "fit" of the individual to his neighbor,
whether or not the official and the citizen are on good terms.
Tocqueville identified this grassroots tendency precisely
when he wrote, "In general, the American functionaries are
far more independent than the French civil officers within the

sphere which is prescribed to them. Sometimes, even, they are allowed by the popular authority to exceed those bounds; and as they are protected by the opinion, and backed by the cooperation, of the majority, they venture upon such manifestations of their power as astonish a European. By this means habits are formed in the heart of a free country which may someday prove fatal to its liberties."

Grassroots government may or may not be good government then; it is difficult to say. It depends on whether the town is good or not. The smaller the town, the more justice is a matter of personal opinion in the community itself, rarely formalized, rarely examined, rarely permanently established, depending on the sentiment of the moment. It is little wonder that the local justice of the peace is the laughing-stock of the legal profession. Even if he knows his duties, how can he possibly impartially administer justice in an atmosphere of overwhelming intimacy?

In this way personalized government, the only form acceptable to fraternity, moves counter to the tradition of law and constitutionalism, confident that familiarity makes it possible to rule by direct knowledge of the neighborhood in place of abstract principle. In such a context, the notion of contractual relations is replaced by the reality of personal relations, who belongs and who does not. The individual depends on the sanction of the group and remains uncertain of his rights and prerogatives. In the end, he has no fixed standard to indicate how he stands in the face and the eyes of his neighbors.

Checklist of Operative Democracy: (2) The Role of Controversy

An innate tendency toward personalized government is one way in which the small community goes against the grain

of the broader American creed. An undiluted acceptance of
the principle of direct democracy is another. Woven into the
institutions and procedures of the nation and the states is an
array of formal and informal provisions designed to limit
direct popular participation in government, to check and to
balance it. Partly, of course, these strictures arose as necessities for managing a popular government over a wide ex-
panse of territory. Partly, they result from prejudices of the
founding fathers, long since abandoned. But in good measure, these complicated arrangements are the product of considered judgment and experience as to how a popularly supported government can work effectively. They are rooted
in both a realistic view of human nature and a thoughtful ap-
praisal of the limits of popular sovereignty if left to function
on its own.

The fundamental premise of American democratic politics, as of Western politics generally, is that men view the
public good in different ways, from different perspectives.
Factions and parties are regarded as part of the political process, however regretfully men may have accepted their existence and hesitated to sanction their operation. Given this
recognition of conflicting opinions and judgments, it has followed, in the logic of constitutional government, that a public policy is hammered out in an arena of discussion and debate until some acceptable compromise develops. It follows
also that in order to make the discussion meaningful and reasonably effective, "opposition," in V. O. Key's words, "should
be institutionalized"; in short, that it be expected in the normal course of affairs.

In a sense, this expectation of disagreement provides the
saving grace of humility to stand against the inherent arrogance of a belief in popular sovereignty and righteousness.
The normal democratic political process becomes not a gilt-

edge guarantee of responsible, able government, but instead, as Dahl explains, "one in which there is a high probability that an active and legitimate group in the population can make itself heard effectively at some crucial state in the process of decision." A pair of competing party hierarchies, a polyarchal political structure in which many minorities participate, a pattern of interest groups and pressure politics appear as the most effective ways in which modern democracies can operate.

By these standards, the small community is singularly ill-equipped to construct a working democratic process. Its spirit of fraternity proceeds on an assumption quite contrary to disagreement and opposition: it expects essential unanimity. This unanimity is not just an agreement on fundamentals, a consensus about profound beliefs; it is a characteristic supposedly operative on every major public problem. The ideal of the town-meeting citizen is a man capable of divining the public good as a thing apart from his personal attitudes, prejudices, and beliefs. It is a notion of public discussion that has all the aspects of a conference, not a debate. Provide the facts, set forth the problem, and all right-thinking men will arrive at the same decision; or, in the rationale of suburban nonpartisanship today, "there is no Republican or Democratic way to pave a street, all the citizens want is 'good' government."

It is no accident that Madison, perhaps the most realistic of the early American statesmen, after his statement on the inevitability of divisions within the body politic, looked sourly on the direct democracy of the small town. To him, "The smaller the society, the fewer probably will be the distinct parties and interests composing it; the fewer the distinct parties and interests the more frequently will a majority be found of the same party; and the smaller the number of individuals composing a majority, and the smaller the compass within which they are placed, the more easily will they concert and execute their plans of expression." Madison saw clearly that the grassroots ideology had no expectation of serious divisions within its constituency and consequently made no effective provision for the protection of the minority. Instead, it embraced the principle of popular sovereignty to its limits, certain that the majority would always be right.

It is not the possible deprivation of the theoretical natural rights of a minority that is the central issue, however. It is doubtful whether a convincing case for natural rights, demonstrably defined by God, can be established in modern times. In any event, the popular sovereignty of small town and suburb will seldom produce persecution, or even the conditions of oppression that Madison hypothesized. The personalized aspect of local government, rather than its majority principle, is more likely to be the villain in this respect.

What is significant, however, in the direct democracy of the idealized small town is its ineffectiveness in providing a practical operating popular government. The highly optimistic conviction that reason will prevail fails to provide contrasting poles of opinion for meaningful discussion, and most of all, for effective opposition. Here is no spectacle of competing minorities, of parties appealing to the voters while always sensitive to the strategy of the opposition, of organizations sophisticated in political strategy, of seasoned leaders, of professional politicians ready to play the broker between the governed and the governing. Here is only the annual town meeting, the occasional popular referendum, the mass of citizens face to face with the complex public problem, expected to operate always at the peak of civic virtue. It is quite natural that Carl Friedrich, for all his sympathetic concern and respect for the grassroots tradition, could warn of the danger of the manipulation of mass psychology, and point out that too strong a dose of direct democracy destroys the balance of constitutional government. An excessive reliance on direct popular action can lead, as the discussion of suburban politics has suggested, to no popular action at all with the citizen baffled and perplexed and the expert and the small clique in charge.

Tested against the working standards of modern democratic theory, the small town version, with its reliance on citizens instead of institutions, thus operates under major handicaps. To begin with, its very scale makes it unlikely that a reasonable variety of attitudes and opinions will be brought to bear on a problem and that the process of discussion will provide information, knowledge and understanding. A minority that is hopelessly outnumbered can be forgiven for declining to make its case with vigor and completeness. In this way the prime function of minority rights — to provide an opportunity to persuade, to enlighten, to require the majority to defend its position more adequately, to amend and qualify — often goes by default. Sensible men hesitate to stick their necks out when the prospects of success are dim.

Even given a determined minority, however, the opportunity for that minority to organize itself and to operate as a going concern runs into severe institutional handicaps in an atmosphere of nonpartisanship and direct participation. The town meeting is not an effective arena for continuing debate or persuasive argument; it may "ventilate grievances" but it rarely settles them. A dissenter may make a noise, but he rarely can make the kind of noise Dahl defines as an effective voice: one that officials not only listen to "but expect to suffer [from] in some significant way if they do not placate the group, its leaders or its most vociferous members." No wonder Lancaster discovered "New England querulousness institutionalized in the Town Meeting." An opposition, despairing of being effective and accustomed to unrelieved defeat, has a right to be peevish. Rousseau's judgment was even more succinct: "So perfect a government does not suit human beings."

Checklist of Operative Democracy: (3) The Quest for Freedom

The final defect in the grassroots model, and its most fundamental one when judged by operative democratic standards, is the limitations it places on individual development, or, more directly, on freedom. The most obvious of these restrictions applies to the isolated minority and arises out of the internal contradiction in the notion of equality when applied in too intimate circumstances. This limitation, as we have seen, is the fatal inconsistency in the liberal philosophical argument for the small democratic unit, the theoretical flaw in the doctrine of majority rule that has never been erased.

Yet, even if the individual in a small town belongs to the majority, believes in its values, and plays the part of a favored son, a second limitation comes to bear. Unless one believes "the local is the ultimate universal, and as near an absolute as exists," unless the outside world is only an endless repetition of experiences found within the village, then small size diminishes the prospects for individualism. Individualism can only be defined as the special way a man responds to an elemental and recurrent cycle of experiences — birth, courtship, marriage, family and death; spring, summer, fall, and winter. A spectacle arises of man inexorably facing the rhythm of nature, testing himself against a fixed number of temptations and a fixed number of challenges.

Ideologically, Americans have, of course, never accepted this view of individualism, in spite of the fact that in the context of the small town it is a true one. Opportunity, limitless, boundless, unfettered, has been the key concept — the notion that one could never tell what one would become, what experiences and what adventures one might have. The almost moral obligation of an individual to rise, to get up in the world, has been a fixed constant in our faith. "Energy, self-reliance, and independence, a strong conviction that a man's fate should depend upon his own character and conduct, are qualities without which no nation can be great."

This type of individualism has had its crass side, of course, in the roughshod climb of an Horatio Alger scrambling for undreamed-of heights. And it has its idealistically optimistic side, the dream of perfectibility, as each generation moves another step along the road of progress. Its essence remains, however, a conviction that on his own initiative, a man selects from a number of alternatives instead of simply reacting to one; that growth is unlimited, and that as the number of alternatives expands, freedom expands as well.

The spirit of fraternity directly contradicts this American concept. It cannot rise above the commonness of experience. In place of a promise of progress, of many rainbows and many pots of gold, there is only the routine of the provincial life: the work week, the Saturday night revelry, the schooldays, the church service, the hours spent on the bench on the courthouse square. The village never stirs itself; it is moved only by exits and entrances from the outside world. And so, in place of incentive, of growth, of development, are the characteristics of parochialism: somnolence, lethargy and resignation, "the buried life," "cornpone opinions," the "mill-bound world." Or, as R. A. Woods has described it, "The country village is made up of those who are out of the fight because they never tried. Life runs in a narrow circuit; there is little to stir the blood or stimulate the imagination."

Of course, under modern circumstances, the issue of individuality is cast in a different context. When suburbia becomes the carrier of the grassroots image, there is no physical isolation between the town and the city, and the variety among suburbs presents a spectacle of many ways of living. Thus Edward C. Banfield and Morton Grodzins see the existence of suburbs in the metropolitan area as enhancing the prospects for individuality when defined as a choice among alternatives. They liken the small town suburbanite to a consumer faced with an array of cultural islands, each representing a special brand of homogeneity. The individual can live in the area that best represents the social status he desires, and "spheres of free choice for individuals and community groups" are maintained. "Wide options, including the option to be exclusive and expensive, prevail," and, in modern suburbia, "the consumer is in a position to know what combination of goods and services — trees and sidewalks as against food and clothing, for example — will give him the greatest satisfaction."

Two comments are in order about the individualism fostered by the modern suburb. First, though a system which ensures "that the widest possible range of choice will be open to the consumer" is clearly within the American tradition, it is doubtful that it represents the best of that tradition. As the ideal of equality can result in conformity, so the ideal of personal enterprise can border on selfishness. The analogy of the "consumer" used by Banfield and Grodzins is revealing, for the individuality the modern suburb offers is of the laissez-faire variety. The man who chooses his community in the metropolitan free market in the same way in which he buys his car has embraced the theory of contractual relations in its most extreme form. Self-interest, unmitigated even by the notion of obligations freely entered into, becomes the definition of freedom, and issues of equity and humanitarianism are muted. The sense of responsibility of free men to one another and the recognition of common purposes that constitute a persuasive part of the American creed are lost, and the spectacle ensues of a simple scramble to the top for the best market baskets of local government services.

A second observation to make about the streamlined suburban version of the small town is that the rampant individualism it espouses by no means dampens the spirit of fraternity. Paradoxically, an attempt to rediscover fraternity becomes the overriding goal of suburban free choice. Freedom is sought in order to return to some facsimile of the elemental world; men struggle to succeed for the purpose of residing in a community peopled exclusively by their own kind. The growing homogeneity of these cultural islands, and the restrictive practices that bar the unsuitable, become little more than a reassertion of the fraternal spirit.

In this context, modern observers sometimes speak approvingly of the reappearance of clusters of suburban small towns as a means "for the effective management of conflict, especially of conflict arising from the growing cleavages of race and class." Yet, even the desire to "manage" conflict, to promote harmony by the ghetto system of society, remains basically a fraternal drive — and an anti-individualistic one. An individual exercises options among a series of fraternities but once he makes his choice, he reenters a world where individuality is suspect. Discussion, debate, disagreement thus have no role either in building a community on the basis of recognizing common interests, or in the expression and articulation of individuality. A man is freed to follow his immediate desires but forfeits his individuality by the very process.

Meanwhile, the carefully preserved boundary lines, the meticulously drawn building regulations, the informally applied restrictive practices, ensure that the fraternal spirit predominates; that harmony, once natural in the small town, is now contrived; that conflict, out of which understanding and individual growth conceivably could come, is carefully avoided. Unless one reconciles himself to a series of moves as his values grow and change, freedom of choice is exercised only once or twice. As an everyday proposition, it becomes unworkable.

Other Roads

What emerges from a comparison of grassroots values and democratic values is a single major conclusion: in this vision of the "good American" life, there has always been a fundamental confusion between the concepts of fraternity and of democracy. It cannot be said too often that the fraternal spirit has a crucial role to play in the organization of human affairs. Neighborhoods, clubs, associations are the means by which men come to recognize that they have common traits and common goals. The happy savage, Eden before redemption, are perhaps indications of man's potentiality, but they are far from accurate descriptions of the reality of human nature.

Yet it also cannot be said too often that democracy, as commonly understood, is something much more than and much different from fraternity. It must begin with an understanding of things men hold in common, but it must proceed to a recognition of their uncommon qualities as well. The trademark of democracy is a process by which men decide and accept responsibility for the interests they hold in common while retaining the option to exercise individual choices. And in that process, in the American tradition, the recognition of "things in common" does not appear automatically or easily but is painfully put together by compromise, by adjustments, by trial and error. It is an aggregate of a series of choices by a series of minorities temporarily coming together. To move in an opposite direction, as the modern suburb now does, to identify the uncommon qualities, segregate them, and place them with their own kind, is an effort to avoid the process of democracy entirely.

Beyond this basic misapprehension of the requirements of democracy, still another factor makes the suburban renaissance less than laudable. The small town ideal not only embodies basic flaws within its own dominion, but it mirrors with peculiar intensity the deficiencies of the larger American system. The pressures for conformity represented by super-Americanism on the national scene stem from the same excessive application of equality that reveals itself in the suburban drive for unanimity. The extreme individualism (almost indistinguishable from sheer exploitation) that marred the rise of American capitalism is identical with the suburban consumer's "shopping" for his exclusive home. It is ironical, in the exact sense of the word, that the ideology most revered in the United States is the one that does the greatest disservice to our broader vision. In the grassroots world, our vices stand the most completely exposed; our virtues are almost totally ignored.

Perhaps an even deeper irony in the suburban attachment to the old dream is that it is no longer necessary today. The historical confusion between democracy and fraternity in the United States is understandable because there was, in the beginning, no alternative to small town life. Men were forced to live with the internal contradictions of equality and individualism at the grassroots level. In the mid-twentieth century, this necessity no longer exists; the technology that has given us the wealth to reconstruct the republic in miniature has also given us other choices. We are free to choose; we can accept other ways for organizing metropolitan life, if we will.

We can examine again, for example, the proposals of Geddes and Howard, their ideal greenbelts and "balanced communities," their orderly constellations of small towns geometrically placed around the outskirts of a metropolis that itself would be devoted to cultural and civic achievement. Within this scheme, every part has its purpose; a glittering mosaic springs forth; space and form are blended into an appropriate setting for man; land use is rationalized; industry and commerce are located with precision; "life values" are carefully cultivated. If, in David Riesman's words, "Planners and prophets are heeded," the metropolitan area might reappear as a splendid work of art, a civilization produced by those blessed with vision.

Stated in such grandiose forms, of course, the whole concept of greenbelts runs against the grain of the contractual tradition. The controls implied, the government regulation that would be required, the blurring of social, economic and political aspects of society involved — these fit more neatly with the Platonic and Aristotelian tradition than with our own. The stubborn issues of who defines the shape and substance of beauty, who determines the balance of each community, who arbitrates good taste, who decides the value of life, remain as unresolved in their modern context as they did in their ancient one. The essentially alien quality of the master planner in American values explains much of the difficulty the advocates of this vision have had — and have — in modern life.

Yet, if the greenbelt appears to be too abrupt a departure from our value scheme, at least one other choice remains. It is contained, though not always recognized, in the proposals for metropolitan reform, for the single government of a new community, of the gargantuan city. This alternative needs to be sketched not in its traditional form as an attempt to apply the small town picture to a larger stage, nor as a reluctant compromise between the goals of securing administrative efficiency and preserving grassroots autonomy. Its case, in value terms, is stronger than its advocates have ever made it. It deserves to be analyzed, as suburbia was, by the standards of a democratic society.

By such a test, the gargantuan city, the great organization applied to local government, does not come off too badly. For one thing, though neighborhoods are possible in a city, a single neighborhood coincident with city boundaries is not. Personalized government, therefore, takes on quite a different form than it does in the small town. It can exist, of course; the political bosses rose on the basis of personal ties and personal favors. They grafted the intimacy of a neighborhood onto the organization of a political party. But personalized government, big city style, is always government by a minority, not a majority, and the difference is crucial. Let political behavior become too outrageous, let the dominance of a single figure extend too far, and the opposition is always forthcoming with reasonable prospects of success. A city is composed of too many elements, presents too diverse a pattern, for its government ever to absorb the range of its activities or for acquaintanceship to be the bond that ties men together.

These limits on the extent of personalized government make a rule of law, at most times and in most cases, a necessity. It is not a completely satisfactory rule of law; there are flagrant miscarriages of justice. There are accessible police and accessible judges, and the "fix" can operate on a grander scale than a small town can conceive. Yet the fix cannot operate in the majority of cases, and it cannot operate in the sense that the community as a whole flaunts its own regulations. The majority of relations between the individual and the government, as a simple mathematical proposition, must be conducted on an impersonal basis, formally, without the parties involved having a speaking acquaintance. So the big city network of the influential, the insiders, the favor-seekers and the favor-granters, operates always covertly, without sanction, with the possibility of exposure. The rule of law is certainly not perfect, but it is likely to be as perfect as generally is found, and it is far more firmly established in the city than in the hinterlands.

In the same way, no notion of popular sovereignty by a miracle of unanimity and consensus can long be entertained in the city. The classes, creeds and races are too numerous for anyone to expect harmony as a way of life. Conflict is not to be avoided; it is to be maintained within reasonable bounds. Even when a single party presents a monolithic face to the outside world, beneath its serene façade, factions and splinter groups, and disenchanted followers abound. The leader of a city party never possesses the comfortable overwhelming support that the courthouse ring enjoys. He cannot afford to dismiss the opposition contemptuously and he lacks the capacity to banish dissenters from his jurisdiction. The balance in a large city is too precarious, even when one party apparently holds undisputed sway. New York Democrats must always take a Republican or Independent challenge seriously; the scales can swing too swiftly the other way.

In this way, big city politics come to approximate the concept of government by a series of minorities functioning through reasonably well-identified organizations and interest groups — the modern norm of acceptable democratic practice. The constituency is not expected to participate in every public action, or to do much more than indicate the broad direction of public policy. Major responsibility rests upon public officials and party leaders, operating in the light of publicity; their actions are "spectacularized," in Morris Lambie's word, by the institutional position they occupy. Even cities operating on a supposedly nonpartisan basis find it necessary to develop party organizations, to face determined oppositions and to exist in a world of controversy. Political campaigns, pressure group tactics, deliberations on important questions of policy come to be institutionalized, made visible, and accepted as necessary instruments of government.

Of course, this polyarchal pattern of politics remains offensive to many, and a government controllable only by "sporadic outbursts of popular indignation" seems far removed from the democratic ideal. A position in favor of partisanship, as V. O. Key has noted, is still a rather lonely outpost at the present time. Yet the recent history of city government in the United States, despite the obvious absence of "a direct and easy channel through which public opinion can function," presents solid evidence of the existence of responsible leadership and of alternative challenges, of constructive, informed criticism.

In Philadelphia, New York, Chicago and Baltimore, partisan organizations in command of the municipal government have demonstrated their capacity to carry out public duties responsibly, effectively and honestly. The election of energetic, able men to the office of mayor, and the continuing professionalization of the city bureaucracy has provided both the leadership and the competence on which constitutional government basically depends. Good government seems to be less the exception and more the rule in the large cities, as constituencies perfect the techniques of representation and as democratic theory moves to a more realistic view of the political capacities of the citizen.

If the big city offers a better environment than the grass-roots for the development of the political qualities of leadership, criticism, and constraint, it promises even more so far as individualism is concerned. A great metropolis can be characterized as a bundle of constant, never ending choices for the individual. There are choices, first, in the political arena just described: the endless parade of associations, groups, and parties-in-interest, at the center of the process, each capable of "energizing the government when the group cares deeply enough on the issue in question." There are choices in the economic realms on a scale the small town cannot imagine: the specialty shops, the department stores, and the discount houses, in contrast to the general store and the Sears Roebuck catalogue; the one hundred and one used-car lots versus the exclusive Ford franchise in town; the medical clinics and the medical specialists versus the general practitioner. In the great city, the pattern of local monopolies inevitably breaks down, and even the suburban shopping center cannot begin to match the variety which "downtown" offers. And certainly choices abound in the realm of leisure activities and culture, for the city remains the symbol of civilization: the Boston Symphony instead of the First Baptist choir, the legitimate stage in place of the Little Theater, the museums in contrast to the culture section of *Life* Magazine.

This multiplicity of choice has two simultaneous effects: it liberates the individual from his fellows, while it instills an inescapable recognition of their presence. "New York," writes E. B. White, "blends the gift of privacy with the excitement of participation; and better than most dense communities it succeeds in insulating the individual (if he wants it, and almost everybody wants or needs it) against all the enormous and violent and wonderful events that are taking place every minute . . . Every event is, in a sense, optional, and the inhabitant is in the happy position of being able to choose his spectacle and so conserve his soul." Yet at the same time, "the citizens of New York are tolerant not only from disposition but from necessity. The city has to be tolerant, otherwise it would explode in a radioactive cloud of hate and rancor and bigotry. If the people were to depart even briefly from the peace of cosmopolitan intercourse, the town would blow higher than a kite."

The individualism of the city thus comes to have three distinguishing characteristics. One is that any individual, capable or incapable, successful or unsuccessful, may wrap a blanket of precious anonymity around himself. No one climbs high enough to be conspicuously alone on the top of the Hill, and when one falls, his degradation can be his own affair. He may be placed in an institution, but he need not, unless he wishes, become a poor relation. A second quality is that for those who choose, life can be lived at the top of their potential. Tensions, neuroses, and stresses are obvious companions in such a drive, but so is a sense of accomplishment, a purpose for energy, rewards commensurate with effort. Finally, the tolerance of necessity begets the condition of civility. The fact that the city "compresses all life, all races and breeds," inevitably implies individual growth through a recognition of others. It is this characteristic that most sharply distinguishes the urban resident from the suburbanite, for although the latter has much the same range of economic and cultural choices before him, he has foresworn political and social responsibility for his associations. Instead he has undertaken to escape and evade them.

It is undoubtedly true that the urbanite pays a price for his freedom. In his private life, the price is usually in terms of loneliness and anonymity, when that condition is not desired. In his public life, the toll exacted is in concentrated effort and sustained work, for group support does not come "naturally" in large enterprises. The channels that exist between constituent and official are more complex than in the small town, even while they are more effective when properly applied. Competence, sophistication, and professionalization are required in all phases of big city life, political as well as others. Yet these are conditions that must be expected by a person or a nation committed to a contractual theory of government and to an individualistic theory of society. Individuality in this context has the inescapable annotation of self-reliance. People claiming independence must, in the end, demonstrate competence.

Moreover, even this picture of effort and anxiety should not be drawn too starkly as a sketch of Darwinian struggle. In the city the option to abstain from tumult and confusion is always present; a man can decline to participate and he can exercise this prerogative without censure. He can also do so with far more personal safety than in the small community, since someone else of similar outlook and persuasion is always available to speak for him. Moreover, if he wishes, the individual who retreats can still find in the city the blessings offered by grassroots fraternity; he can go back to his own neighborhood. For this neighborhood is still a part of urban life, and the city is a collection of thousands of neighborhood units, each reasonably self-sufficient in a social sense, each exhibiting the condition of fraternity within the boundaries of propriety. A man can have "over the fence" living, if he wishes. It is his choice to make.

These conditions of urbanity are the basic reasons for supporting the ideal of a single metropolitan government, and they seem more logically persuasive than the customary arguments of efficiency and administrative tidiness. A single local government comprehending an entire metropolitan area is likely not only to be better managed in the professional sense but more democratically managed as well. Quite clearly, the quality of partisanship, debate, discussion and compromise through institutional channels would be strengthened in comparison to what exists in our large central cities today. The preponderantly Democratic city and the Republican-oriented suburb would have to vie at almost equal strength in the provision of alternatives for public policy. The handicaps the city operates under, the loss of its middle-class citizens, the poverty of public finances, the absence of space and of solid residential sections, would be removed. Finally, though neighborhoods would remain to provide the beneficial functions of fraternity, and to be represented in the government-at-large, they would no longer themselves be the government. By making the metropolis a true metropolitan political entity, a different type of blending of urban and suburban becomes possible. It would be less comfortable, perhaps, than the present organization, but it would be more defensible in terms of the values the nation has accepted.

Probability and Potentiality

An argument for the values of the big city should not be mistaken for a forecast that metropolitan reform is just around the corner. One of the gifts political philosophy bestows is the capacity to speculate on what might be as well as to describe and evaluate what is. The arguments here have been conducted in this framework, measuring the gap between potentiality and actuality. This type of analysis has its uses, so long as it keeps in touch with human capacities, but the power of prediction is not one of them. To criticize present arrangements, to show the unpalatable consequences that flow from them, to condemn the suburbs for the values they represent, is not to prophesy suburban defeat.

Indeed, if on a different level of political analysis an estimate of the odds that suburbia will redeem itself is undertaken, the chances seem slight. There are few inexorable
trends that seem likely to make a radical reorganization of
the metropolitan area necessary. The evidence of the last
chapter pointed in the opposite direction, so far as the economic base and the public problems of suburbia are concerned. The distribution of industry and commerce, the
growing wealth of metropolitan areas, indicate that suburbs
can continue on their autonomous ways if they wish. Even
the most serious of present problems, transportation and land
use, seem capable of tolerable (though not particularly effective) solution under present governmental and social arrangements. As a nation, we are rich enough to indulge ourselves in the luxury of recreating small towns over and over
again.

Nor are there any really powerful political forces on the
scene to agitate for metropolitan reform for reasons of their
own. Neither city Democrats nor suburban Republicans are
likely to relish exchanging their comfortable local majorities
in those parts of the metropolitan area over which they preside for a situation in which a tight two-party fight is almost
guaranteed. There are few business leaders who are so adversely affected by the present state of affairs and so uncom-
mitted in their personal life to the suburban ideology as to
be interested in pushing for reform. Though they may grum-
ble about rising taxes, conflicting regulations, and public
programs, they generally prefer to live with the present situation by personal negotiation than to risk the unknown —
the possibility of an effective, area-wide government where
individual bargains may not be so easily accomplished.

Most of all, there is no solid institutional base from which
to launch an attack. The city government is suspect, the sub-

urbs are suspicious, and the state legislatures are wary of creating a new and more powerful urban unit. Although the prospects for a new tier of offices and a new vehicle for the exercise of leadership may be appealing to some public figures, many more are likely to see reform as a threat to their present positions. A host of suburban mayors, country clerks, police chiefs and other public officers fidget nervously whenever metropolitan integration is mentioned.

So the banner for reform is for the most part carried by a thin rank of largely ineffective agitators — editorial writers in the metropolitan dailies, planners, professors, a few executives who are genuinely appalled at horror stories of administrative inefficiency and financial irrationality, the "public spirited" presidents of voluntary civic associations, a scattering of businessmen whose interests in landholdings and retail investments are seriously affected, perhaps the mayor of the central city, possibly the governor. This is an ill-assorted collection of interests and personalities unlikely to be strongly motivated, rarely possessing sufficient influence to carry the public with their ways, and always ready to snatch at any plan that might take a half step forward.

Sometimes, as in Atlanta and Miami, a partial solution is accepted, in a form carefully devised to maintain the grassroots ideology, using the appeal of efficiency and economy as a cover for advance. Even the Atlanta and Miami reforms are surprising accomplishments for such an interest group. Obviously no direct advocacy of the critical issue — of the true alternatives in political and social organization — could be expected. In a tactical sense, such a campaign would be disastrous, for the ranks of reform itself would become irreparably divided. Considered dispassionately, according to the votes the competing ideologies can muster, the conclusion is that genuine metropolitan reform is not a likely prospect in our metropolitan areas for some time to come.

The fact that the odds are impossibly slim, however, is a
genuine unpleasant fact. It is too bad that there is little inclination to consider rationally the benefits that a gargantuan metropolitan government and social order might offer.
It is too bad that on the local scene, the worst and not the
best of the American political tradition is emphasized, that
all our contradictions and inconsistencies are brought to the
fore. It is too bad that we continue to cling to a grassroots
legacy, begun as a necessity and of less and less usefulness as
time goes on.

This commitment is regrettable not only for the reasons detailed in the last pages. It is also regrettable because, by rejecting the vision of the metropolis, the American faith loses
its best opportunity to defeat the corporate philosophy at its
own game. By clinging to the grassroots, we forfeit the
chance to provide variety, to offer the full spectrum of human
experience — always the appeal of those who seek to impose
a civilization — and to offer that variety under arrangements
consonant with freedom. When we reject the metropolis we
reject the possibility of securing a cosmopolitan pattern of
living created by a free people and maintained by a free government.

In a final way, the persistence of the image of the suburb as
the all-American small town is unfortunate in our times. It
represents another symbolic protest against the great organization and the large society, and this is the most disastrous
consequence of all. The American great organization and
the American large society are after all man-made. They are
the expression of a commitment to the proposition that man
is more rational than irrational, more confident in progress
than fearful of change. That the great organization presents
problems and challenges is not to be doubted for a moment.
But that something created by the energy, wit, and morality
of man should be fundamentally feared, fled from, and re-

jected as unmanageable is essentially inconceivable. It is inconceivable, at least, in a nation in which energy, wit and morality have been prized attributes, and whose history has always shown a commitment to the proposition that growth and change are beneficial. That such a nation should cherish the legacy of the grassroots is the final irony of suburbia.

Notes

CHAPTER 1. *The Image of Suburbia*

SUBURBIA AS LOOKING GLASS

page
4. The definition and description of suburbia as "looking glass" is used here to group a number of contemporary interpretations, including those of David Riesman in *The Lonely Crowd* (New Haven, 1950), William H. Whyte, Jr., *The Organization Man* (New York, 1956), John Seeley, R. A. Sims, and E. W. Loosley, *Crestwood Heights: The Culture of Suburban Life* (New York, 1956), John Keats, *The Crack in the Picture Window* (Boston, 1957), A. C. Spectorsky, *The Exurbanites* (New York, 1955), and in fiction, Sloan Wilson, *The Man in the Gray Flannel Suit* (New York, 1955), Max Shulman, *Rally Round the Flag, Boys* (New York, 1957), and, in places, Eugene Burdick, *The Ninth Wave* (Boston, 1956). Origins of the interpretation can, of course, be found in H. G. Wells' provocative *Paper on Administrative Areas Read Before the Fabian Society* (1911), and Lewis Mumford, *The Culture of Cities* (New York, 1938). A provocative summary of recent thought is found in David Riesman's "The Suburban Dislocation," *Annals of the American Academy of Political and Social Science* (November, 1957). Two other valuable articles are Harry Henderson's "The Mass Produced Suburbs," *Harper's* (November and December, 1953), and Frederick Lewis Allen's "Crisis in Suburbia," *Harper's* (June and July, 1954).

Obviously an attempt to summarize a school of thought numbering disciples with such different backgrounds and perspectives does disservice to the views of each individually. I have tried, however, to select the common elements involved and to emphasize what I interpret to be their major conclusions, i.e., the "newness" of the modern American character, its basic orientation to group life, and the apparent disappearance of individuality variously defined.

4. The statistics of the suburban trend are taken from the U.S. Census, *General Characteristics of the Population,* of 1940 and 1950, and the Special Census Reports of the Government Division, U. S. Bureau of the Census, in particular C–35–35, "Local Government in Metropolitan Areas." For special interpretations in earlier periods, see Victor Jones, *Metropolitan Government* (New York, 1942), Chapters I and II. For a comprehensive analysis of the 1950 Census, see O. D. Duncan and A. J. Reiss, Jr., *Social Characteristics of Urban and Rural Communities, 1950* (New York, 1956), especially Chapters 11, 12, and 14.

5. The quotations "to knock down . . ." and following are taken from John Keats, *The Crack in the Picture Window,* p. xiv.

6. *Crestwood Heights* gives particular emphasis to the relentless time schedule of suburban life. William H. Whyte, Jr., in *The Organization Man,* also considers it important.

7. Again *Crestwood Heights* provides the most detailed observations of the function of the school in one modern suburb. It is the major professional study focused on the suburban scene exclusively.

HOLDOUTS IN SUBURBIA

9. The most authoritative sources on suburban governments, or more properly, metropolitan governments, are Victor Jones' classic, *Metropolitan Government,* previously cited, John C. Bollens, *The States and the Metropolitan Problem* (Chicago, 1956), and Jones' article in *The Future of Cities and Urban Redevelopment,* Coleman Woodbury, ed. (Chicago, 1953). Other important works include Betty Tableman, *Government Organization in Metropolitan Areas* (Ann Arbor, 1951), R. D. McKenzie, *The Metropolitan Community* (New York, 1933), Paul Studenski, *The Government of Metropolitan Areas,* National Municipal League (New York, 1930). Over 80 surveys of individual metropolitan areas exist or are underway. Outstanding examples are the *Boston Prize Contest,* C. J. Friedrich and associates (Boston, 1946); the Miami Study of the Public Administration Service; and the Metropolitan St. Louis Survey, *Path of Progress.* For an introduction to the problem see the *Proceedings* of the National Conference on Metropolitan Problems, held at East Lansing, Michigan, in 1956.

SUBURBIA AS RENAISSANCE

12. The suburban penchant for small government is documented in

almost every survey of specific metropolitan areas. The National Municipal League has completed a more general analysis, as yet unpublished, on the prevalent suburban attitude. See also the articles by Basil C. Zimmer and Amos H. Hawley on attitudes of fringe residents in the Flint metropolitan area in the *Public Administration Review* (Autumn, 1956) and *Land Economics* (November, 1956) including detailed statistical analysis of variations in suburban opinion according to place and time of arrival of residents, social and economic status and other factors.

13. William H. Whyte, Jr. in *The Organization Man,* Part VII, pays particular attention to the qualities of small town life, even though he does not specifically identify them as such. See also Riesman's perceptive comments on the egalitarian elements in suburbia in "The Suburban Dislocation."

15. John Keats' description of his ideal is found in Chapter 8 of *The Crack in the Picture Window.* For other examples of the goals of the "looking glass" observers, see the concluding chapters of Whyte, Riesman, and Seeley.

17. The quotation "so big that no one counts . . ." is from an editorial of the *Malden Evening News,* Malden, Massachusetts, January 29, 1958.

CHAPTER 2. *Roots for the Image*

THE AMERICAN MINIATURE

page
20. The brief sketch of the social and political characteristics of early American communities on this and the following pages is intended to emphasize the "fitness" of early American communities to the ideology of localism. Accordingly, it does not deal with the variety and complexity of colonial life or the factors which actually created community consciousness in those times that are considered more empirically in Chapter IV. Nonetheless I have tried to keep the generalizations in reasonable conformity with reputable historical judgments while presenting a picture of the way most Americans look back on the settlements of their ancestors. The basic sources are Carl Bridenbaugh, *Cities in the Wilderness* (New York, 1938) and *Cities in Revolt* (New York, 1954); John F. Sly, *Town Government in Massachusetts* (Cambridge, 1930); Lane W. Lancaster, *Government in Rural America* (New York, 1937); Edward P. Channing, "Town and County Government in the English Colonies of North America," *Johns Hopkins University Studies in Historical and Political Science,* II, No. 10; and general histories of the period.

21. The quotation "the exercise of English common sense . . ." is from Channing, "Town and Country Government," p. 5.

22. The quotation "the original government of the New England town . . ." is from Lancaster, *Government in Rural America*, p. 48. The comparison with English local governments of the same period is treated at greater length by Stanley Elkins and Eric McKitrick, "A Meaning for Turner's Frontier," *Political Science Quarterly*, September and December, 1954, Part II.

23. The quotation concerning selectmen is from Sly, *Town Government in Massachusetts*, p. 38.

24. Limitations on local governmental autonomy and the qualifications on the democratic process are reported by Bridenbaugh, *Cities in the Wilderness*, Chapters VIII and XII, and Lancaster, *Government in Rural America*, Chapter I. An effective summary is found in Charles Adrian, *Governing Urban America* (New York, 1956), Chapter III.

25. Jefferson's quotation is taken from *The Basic Writings of Thomas Jefferson*, P. S. Jones, ed. (New York, 1944), p. 749.

26. The quotations are from Alexis de Tocqueville, *Democracy in America* (Reeve translation, Colonial Press Revised Edition, New York, 1900), p. 66. See in general Volume I, Chapters V, IX, XIII.

27. With regard to the rationalization of local democracy, Lancaster, *Government in Rural America*, presents an especially attractive and persuasive elaboration of this general perspective in Chapter I.

THE MINIATURE UNDER PRESSURE

28. Arthur M. Schlesinger, Jr., *The Age of Jackson* (Boston, 1946), Chapters 2–4, 26, gives the background for this section. Sly, *Town Government in Massachusetts*, provides specific documentation regarding the development of New England town institutions.

30. The reference to Walsh is from Schlesinger, *Age of Jackson*, p. 508.

30. The quotation from Adams is found in Sly, *Town Government in Massachusetts*, p. 111.

31. Adrian, *Urban America*, Chapter 3, presents a general summary of changes in local government during the Jacksonian period.

32. Arthur M. Schlesinger, Jr., *Age of Jackson*, Chapter 2, describes the expansion of public services.

32. The quotation of Croly is found in Lancaster, *Government in Rural America*, p. 116.

THE MINIATURE CRACKS

33. Arthur Meier Schlesinger, Sr., *The Rise of the City, 1878–1898* (New York, 1933), provides the classic interpretation for the post-

Civil War urban development, and the first pages draw heavily
from this source.

36. The quotation from the *North American Review* is from R. Wer-
ner, *Tammany Hall* (New York, 1928), p. vi.; that of Plunkitt is
from William L. Riordon, *Plunkitt of Tammany Hall* (New York,
1948), p. 8. The Steffens quotation is from Lincoln Steffens, *Autobiography* (New York, 1931), p. 494. For other works on the boss,
see especially D. D. McKean, *The Boss* (New York, 1940), Edward
J. Flynn, *You're the Boss* (New York, 1947), Brand Whitlock,
Forty Years of It (New York, 1920), James Bryce, *The American
Commonwealth* (New York, 1910 ed.), H. Zink, *City Bosses in the
United States* (Chicago, 1930), S. Forthal, *Cogwheels of Democracy:
A Study of the Precinct Captain* (Chicago, 1946). Quotations and
characterizations in this section come from these sources, together
with Arthur Meier Schlesinger's *The Rise of the City*.

38. An extended account of the dislocation of the countryside is given
by Arthur Meier Schlesinger in Chapter II and III of *The Rise of
the City*.

39. The reassertion of state control is reviewed in Adrian, *Urban
America*, p. 17.

THE REJECTION OF REALITY

43. The quotation "the land of . . ." is from Steffens, *Autobiography*,
p. 574.

43. The quotation "vitality and depth . . ." is from Lancaster, *Government in Rural America*, p. 4.

44. The references to Patrick Geddes are from his *Cities in Evolution*
(revised edition, London, 1949). See especially Chapters 2–5 and
17. The specific quotation, "the great city . . ." is from p. 80.

45. For the contribution of Ebenezer Howard, see his *Tomorrow: A
Peaceful Path to Real Reform* (London, 1898).

THE MECHANIZATION OF REFORM

46. This history of municipal reform movements described generally
in this section is discussed in almost every textbook on urban
government. The most meticulous documentation of the most
important organization is Frank M. Stewart's *A Half Century of
Municipal Reform: The History of the National Municipal
League* (Berkeley and Los Angeles, 1950). For the essentials of the
reformer's faith, Richard S. Childs, long an outstanding leader in
municipal affairs, has presented the case most clearly in *Civic
Victories* (New York, 1952). See especially Chapters 5–7.

48. Stewart, *Half Century of Municipal Reform*, Chapter I, describes

the inadequacies of the "moral" revolts and the details of the Municipal Programs.

49. The quotations "we shall undertake . . ." and "the will of the people . . ." are from Childs, *Civic Victories*, p. 79.

50. Stewart, *Half Century of Municipal Reform*, Chapter IV, describes the city-manager philosophy. See also the publications of the International City Managers' Association and the National Municipal League.

50. The quotation "The minister who . . ." is from Childs, *Civic Victories*, p. 143.

51. The slogans concerning "good government" are taken from Stewart, *Half Century of Municipal Reform*, p. 17.

51. The quotation "Proportional representation takes the chess play . . ." is from Childs, *Civic Victories*, p. 141.

53. Munro's and Anderson's comments are quoted in Stewart, *Half Century of Municipal Reform*, p. 199.

CHAPTER 3. *The Rise of Metropolis*

TECHNOLOGY REDEEMS ITSELF

page

55. The quotations about the nineteenth century suburbs are from Victor Jones, *Metropolitan Government*, pp. 43–49. See also Studenski, *Government of Metropolitan Areas*, and H. P. Douglass, *The Suburban Trend* (New York, 1925).

56. The quotation "each city had its outlying residential area . . ." is from F. L. Allen, *The Big Change* (New York, 1952), pp. 15–16. A more scholarly account may be found in R. D. McKenzie, *The Metropolitan Community*, particularly in Chapters VII and XIII. See also Douglass, *Suburban Trend*.

57. Statistics respecting automobile production are taken from the *Economic Almanac* (New York, 1956) published by the National Industrial Conference Board.

57. The quotation "the motorized suburb became a reality . . ." is from Allen, *The Big Change*, p. 126.

58. The statistics respecting production, income, and wealth are from the *Economic Almanac*.

59. The account of mortgage transactions is described in F. L. Allen's account of the Florida boom in *Only Yesterday* (New York, 1931), Chapter XI, and the quotation "the four thousand a year salesman . . ." is found on p. 304.

59. Statistics respecting volume of home construction are from the *Economic Almanac*.

60. The scope of subdivision development is documented in Victor Jones, *Metropolitan Goverment*, Chapter I.

60. The earlier growth of suburban population is described by Jones, *Metropolitan Government*, Chapter I. See also Homer Hoyt, *One Hundred Years of Land Values in Chicago* (Washington, 1933).

60. The figures on specific suburbs are from Jones, *Metropolitan Government*, pp. 5 and 6.

62. The statistics of the volume of governmental housing activities are from the U.S. Government Housing and Home Finance Agency, *Annual Reports*, 1955, 1956.

63. Figures on suburban migration in the 1950's are from the *Proceedings of the National Conference on Metropolitan Problems*, 1956.

63. Data on shopping centers is found in *Financing Metropolitan Government*, a symposium conducted by the Tax Institute (Princeton, 1955).

64. The description of the industrial suburban trend is based on Woodbury (ed.), *Future of Cities*, Chapters 5 and 6.

64. Figures on value added by manufacturing and retail sales were compiled in a special analysis for the Bureau for Municipal Research, Harvard, prepared by Richard Caves, 1956.

65. For a statement of the "promise" of the new suburban communities, see Douglass, *Suburban Trends*, particularly his concluding chapter.

CRISIS IN AUTONOMY

67. The quotation "the rise of the suburb" is from A. F. Weber, *The Growth of Cities in the Nineteenth Century* (New York, 1899), p. 475.

68. The quotation "A crowded world . . ." is from Douglass, *Suburban Trends*, p. 163.

68. The quotation "so general in their scope . . ." is from Stewart, *Half Century of Municipal Reform*, p. 78.

69. The figures on number of governments in 1900 and 1920 are from Studenski, *The Government of Metropolitan Areas*, p. 26. The 1950 and 1957 figures are from the U.S. Census, *State and Local Government Special Studies*, G–55 36, April, 1954, and *Local Governments in Standard Metropolitan Areas*, Vol. I, No. 2, 1958.

70. The general description of metropolitan financial problems and the loss of fiscal autonomy are from Jones, *Metropolitan Government*, Chapter III, and the general references on metropolitan government cited earlier.

72. The Boston experience here summarized is extensively documented in the *Reports and Communications* of the Finance Commission of Boston and the *Bulletins* of the Boston Municipal Research

Bureau. See also the Tax Institute's *Financing Metropolitan Government,* 1955, for a general statement of the problem.

73. The statistics on tax rates in 1930 are from Studenski, *The Government of Metropolitan Areas.*

74. The quotation "the crazy quilt hodge podge . . ." is from Wells, *Administrative Areas,* p. 11.

74. The quotation "The need for servicing . . ." is from Jones, *Metropolitan Government,* p. 24.

74. The quotation "Sins of omission . . ." is from Tableman, *Government Organization,* p. 53.

74. The Gulick quotation is from *Proceedings of the National Conference on Metropolitan Problems,* p. 42.

SUBURBIA BESIEGED

76. The quotation "These local government areas of today . . ." is from Wells, *Administrative Areas,* p. 14.

77. The quotation "neither the intellectual penetration . . ." is from Lewis Mumford, *Culture of Cities,* p. 216.

77. The statistics on annexation are from Bollens, *States and the Metropolitan Problem,* pp. 25–52.

78. The quotation "annexation is no longer practicable . . ." is from McKenzie, *Metropolitan Community,* p. 306.

78. The quotation "annexations in the past half century . . ." is from Jones, *Metropolitan Government,* p. 129.

79. The best review of specific proposals can be found in the *Proceedings of the National Conference* previously cited and the *National Municipal Review,* the official publication of the National Municipal League.

81. The history of the Toronto Plan has had wide publicity. For a short summary, see the address of Frederick C. Gardiner before the National Conference, *Proceedings.* For additional information, note *U. S. News and World Report,* "Rush to the Suburbs Just Starting," March 2, 1956, the articles by Whyte in *Fortune* in 1955 and again in 1957, and the special metropolitan surveys of the *New York Times,* January 27 to February 3, 1957, and the *New York Herald Tribune,* May, 1955.

83. The quotation "Many better and wiser city planners . . ." is from Thomas H. Read, "Hope for Suburbanites," *National Municipal Review,* December, 1952.

SUBURBIA TRIUMPHANT

83. The statistics on number of governments are from U. S. Census

Special Studies C–55–36, p. 4, and *Local Governments in Standard Metropolitan Areas.*

84. The most comprehensive and authoritative study on the subject of special districts and authorities is John C. Bollens, *Special District Governments in the United States* (Chicago, 1957), Chapter 2.

84. The quotation "confuses the citizen . . ." is from Jones, *Metropolitan Government*, p. 99.

85. The quotation "all the people . . ." is from Arthur E. Morgan, *The Small Community* (New York, 1942), p. 175.

85. The quotation "I would feel . . ." is from Jones, *Metropolitan Government*, p. 297.

CHAPTER 4. *The Nature of Suburbia*

THE CASE OF THE DISAPPEARING COMMUNITY

page
91. Scott Greer, "Individual Participation in Mass Society," a paper prepared for Conference Study of the Community, Northwestern University, 1956, provides an extraordinarily able summary of the development of theories about communities in this century. See also Walter Firey, *Land Use in Central Boston* (Boston, 1947), Arthur E. Morgan, *The Small Community,* and the as yet unpublished proceedings of the Society for Political and Legal Philosophy, December, 1957, on the topic "Community."

92. The discussion of the primary community also relies on Albert J. Reiss, "Some Logical and Methodological Problems in Community Research," *Social Forces,* October, 1954. The article summarizes a larger memorandum prepared by Professor Reiss for the Social Science Research Council, which treats various analytical problems in approaching a study of community. I am indebted to Professor Reiss for the use of this memorandum; it provides a comprehensive summary of the literature in the field.

93. R. D. McKenzie in *The Metropolitan Community,* Parts II and IV, was among the first to offer a systematic case for "metropolitan dominance." For an able summary, see S. A. Queens and D. B. Carpenter, *The American City* (New York, 1953), Chapters 7 and 8. A. J. Vidich and Joseph Bensman in *Small Town in Mass Society* (Princeton, 1958) advance the thesis that even the country village is now overrun.

93. Greer, "Individual Participation," pp. 4–6, emphasizes the scattered pattern of association in metropolitan areas.

94. Queens and Carpenter, *American City,* Chapter 9, effectively trace the notion of suburban coalescence with the central city.

SECOND THOUGHTS ON THE VANISHING ACT

96. Reiss, "Logical and Methodological Problems," stresses the difficulties involved in developing a theoretical model for communities.

97. Conrad Arensberg, "American Communities," *The American Anthropologist*, December, 1955, provides a lucid description and comparison among community types, past and contemporary, in the United States, and the contrast among earlier American settlements is based upon his report.

98. The colonial involvement with the outside world is pointed out by Greer, "Individual Participation," p. 12.

99. Stanley Elkins and Eric McKitrick, "A Meaning for Turner's Frontier," *Political Science Quarterly*, September and December, 1954, Part I, make the most explicit comparison between old community and new. The quotations "the one from . . ." and "it has been chronically difficult . . ." are found on p. 340.

100. The quotation "The Americans never use the word . . ." is from Tocqueville, *Democracy in America*, p. 322.

100. The differences between New England, Northwest and Southern towns are described in Arensberg, "American Communities," pp. 44–58.

101. The quotation "political democracy evolves most quickly . . ." is from Elkins and McKitrick, "A Meaning for Turner's Frontier," p. 326, and the quotation "a period of trouble solving . . ." is from p. 325.

102. The quotation "while they have been born free . . ." is from Louis Hartz, *The Liberal Tradition in America* (New York, 1956), p. 3.

THE CASE FOR THE REAPPEARING COMMUNITY

103. The description of the Victorian City is based on Arensberg, "American Communities," p. 60. For descriptions of the plight of the rural communities in this period, see Arthur Meier Schlesinger, *The Rise of the City*, especially Chapter IV. Robert A. Woods, *The Neighborhood in Nation Building* (New York, 1923), Chapter I and V, also make provocative comparisons.

104. The conflicting trends in metropolitan social organization are set forth in an excellent summary in Chapter 8 of Queens and Carpenter, *American City*, although their conclusions are on the side of metropolitan dominance.

107. For an analysis stressing the local orientation of the suburbs, and particularly the influence of family structure, see Wendell Bell, "Social Choice, Life Styles, and Suburban Residence," *The Subur-*

ban Community, William Dobriner, ed. (New York, 1958). Other articles in this book provide additional support for the thesis, although available quantifiable data is both sketchy and subject to conflicting interpretations.

PROPER PEOPLE IN PROPER PLACES

109. The quotation "huge mosaic of . . ." is from Arensberg, "American Communities," p. 61.

111–114. The statistical descriptions presented on this and the following pages are derived from O. D. Duncan and A. J. Reiss, Jr., *Social Characteristics of Urban and Rural Communities — 1950.* In some instances, reference has been made directly to Census data; in others, intertable comparisons have been used. So far as Tables II–IV inclusive are concerned, it should be pointed out that different definitions of suburbs, according to Census usage, have been employed, one referring to urban places over 2500 and another to characteristics of the urban fringe areas. The characteristics available for comparison also vary slightly. For purposes of contrast with other urban communities, however, the comparisons seem justified and the definitions appropriate to their use.

TABLE I

COMPARATIVE STATUS: SUBURBS AND CENTRAL CITIES

	Suburbs	*Central Cities*
Median Age	30.9	32.7
Sex Ratio	95.1	93.5
% Population under 14	27.0	21.6
% Native White	86.2	75.9
% Married Males (White)	71.6	67.4
% Married Females (White)	67.8	62.3
% Population in Family Units	95.0	91.0
% Males in Labor Force	81.6	80.2
% Both Sexes in:		
White Collar	23.0	19.6
Skilled Labor	37.5	35.0
Clerical and Sales	23.9	25.6
Service	6.6	10.1
Median Income (Family)	2,499	2,249
Years Education	11.1	9.9

TABLE II

COMPARATIVE STATUS: SUBURBS AND INDEPENDENT CITIES

	Metropolitan Suburbs		Independent Cities	
	10–25,000	25–50,000	10–25,000	25–50,000
Per Cent 12 Years and Over	66.9	68.7	65.6	66.6
Sex Ratio	95.8	94.4	93.8	94.1
% Native White	4.5	4.3	9.0	10.1
% Married Males	72.5	70.2	69.2	67.6
% Males in the Labor Force	80.5	81.4	77.1	76.5
% Males in:				
White Collar	26.1	23.5	22.1	22.4
Skilled Labor	42.6	45.6	43.7	42.9
Clerical and Sales	16.2	16.0	14.6	15.7
Service	5.5	6.5	7.4	8.3
Median Income (Family)	3,458	3,389	2,593	2,682
Years Education	10.9	10.8	10.0	10.1
% Homeowners	63.5	56.3	55.7	53.8

TABLE III

COMPARATIVE STATUS: SUBURBS AND URBAN FRINGE (CHICAGO)

	Chicago Suburbs	Chicago Urban Fringe
Median Age	31.9	27.4
Sex Ratio	96.4	106.8
% Married Males	71.8	73.4
% Married Females	68.2	75.0
% Males in Labor Force	81.0	84.1
% Males in:		
White Collar	27.4	19.7
Skilled Labor	42.1	52.7
Clerical and Sales	16.2	11.7
Service	4.9	5.3
Median Income (Family)	4,532	4,054
Years Education	11.4	10.0

TABLE IV

COMPARATIVE STATUS: SUBURBS AND VILLAGES

	Suburbs	Rural Non-Farm Villages
Median Age	30.9	30.1
Sex Ratio	95.1	94.1
% Native White	86.2	88.9
% Married Males	71.6	69.4
% Separate Females	2.3	2.4
% New Residents	12.0	12.0
Fertility Ratio	534.0	610.0
Median Income	2,499	2,276
Years Education	11.1	9.1

SUBURBS AND SUBURBS

116. The broad descriptions of types of suburbs are taken from Queens and Carpenter, *American City*, Chapter 9; Adrian, *Governing Urban America*, Chapter 2. The emphasis on the role of cultural values is supplied by Firey, *Land Use in Central Boston*, Chapter IX. Classification of cities as to their relative "goodness" is found in E. L. Thorndike, *Your City* (New York, 1939), and Robert C. Angell, "The Moral Integration of American Cities," *The American Journal of Sociology*, July, 1951.

116. The economic classifications of suburbs are compiled from figures in the International Association of City Managers, *Municipal Yearbook*, 1956, and Duncan and Reiss, *Social Characteristics of Urban and Rural Communities*, Chapter 16.

120. The variations in St. Louis are reported in Metropolitan St. Louis Survey, *Background for Action*, 1957, Chapter 3.

SUBURBS COALESCING

121. The literature on spatial and social area analysis is extensive. Important work on metropolitan communities was undertaken by Ernest W. Burgess, "Urban Areas," in *Chicago: An Experiment in Social Science Research*, ed. T. V. Smith and L. D. White (Chicago, 1929); and Homer Hoyt, *The Structure and Growth of Residential Neighborhoods in American Cities* (Washington, 1939). More recently, Eshrel Shevky and Marilyn Williams developed a classification system designed to categorize population in terms of three factors — social rank, urbanization and segregation — in *The Social Areas of Los Angeles: Analysis and Typology* (Berkeley, 1949).

Wendell Bell and Otis and Beverly Duncan among others have developed and refined these indexes. Cf. Wendell Bell, "The Utility of the Shevky Typology for the Design of Urban Sub-Area Field Studies," *The Journal of Social Psychology*, 47: 71–83 (1959), and Otis and Beverly Duncan, "Residential Distribution and Occupation Stratification," *The American Journal of Sociology*, 60: 493–503 (1955). Queens and Carpenter, *American City*, pp. 95–104, provide a concise summary of the different theories of spatial organization.

122. The influence of historic landmarks and symbolic values are detailed in Firey, *Land Use in Central Boston*, Chapter I.

123. The thesis of occupational clustering is based on Otis and Beverly Duncan, "Residential Distribution and Occupational Stratification," *The American Journal of Sociology*, March, 1955. Preliminary findings of the New York Metropolitan Survey confirm this pattern for the New York Area.

NATURAL NEIGHBORHOODS PLUS POLITICS

126. William Whyte, *Street Corner Society* (Chicago, 1947) is a modern classic on urban neighborhoods and neighborhood groupings.

RE-ENTER THE METROPOLIS

128. The line of reasoning examined in this section is, of course, the major thesis of Riesman, William H. Whyte, Jr., and similar writers. As outlined in the first chapter, the suburbanite is used primarily as an example of the middle class American wherever he is found. According to this thesis, the suburb represents the purest illustration of the new American, offering differences in degree, but not in kind, from other American communities.

Vidich and Bensman, *The Small Town in Mass Society* advance the same thesis with respect to the small rural town, resting much of their analysis on the basis of economic interdependence considered in this chapter and political intrusions from the outside world, considered in Chapter VI. So far as the newness of the mass character is concerned, however, these authors conclude, "Basically, an historically indigenous local culture does not seem to exist. The cultural imports of each decade and generation and the successive waves of migration associated with each combine to produce a local culture consisting of layers or segments of the mass culture of successive historical eras . . . The conflict between 'spurious' and 'genuine' culture appears to be a conflict between two different ages of 'spurious' culture," p. 86.

129. The quotations referring to Hadley, Massachusetts, and Stark

County, Ohio, are from Elkins and McKitrick, "A Meaning for
Turner's Frontier," pp. 600 and 353, respectively.
132. The quotation " 'the wheel,' intelligent . . ." is from Henderson,
"The Mass Produced Suburbs," *Harper's*, November, 1953, p. 86.

SMALL COMMUNITIES EN MASSE

134. The quotations ". . . opportunity for companionship . . ." and
"focal point not only of our material activities . . ." are from
Adrian, *Governing Urban America*, pp. 31 and 32.

CHAPTER 5. *The Politics of Suburbia*

THE THEORY OF CONVERSION
page
136. The quotation "the strand of rural . . ." is from V. O. Key, *American State Politics: An Introduction* (New York, 1956), p. 227.
136. The citation of Louis Hartz, *The Liberal Tradition in America*
(New York, 1955), refers to his thesis that the major conflicts in
American political thought and action are contained within the
Lockian tradition. The implications of this uniquely American
philosophy for the grassroots ideology are considered more fully in
Chapter VII.
137. The description of the conservative temperament typical in small
towns is based on V. O. Key, *American State Politics*, pp. 230–36.
Almost every standard text on American political parties gives
some emphasis to this point.
138. The importance of home ownership and social status is emphasized
in Louis Harris, *Is There a Republican Majority?* (New York,
1954), Chapter VIII. Most of the works cited in Chapter I also
characterize suburban political behavior in this way. The quotation "everyone knows that the town . . ." is found on p. 122.
138. The quotation "put a Dewey sticker . . ." is from Eugene Burdick,
The Ninth Wave, p. 286.
139. The quotation "politically, during the war . . ." is from Harris,
Is There a Republican Majority?, p. 121.
139. Metropolitan voting returns are taken from the *New York Times*
and Richard M. Scammon, *American Votes* (New York, 1956). See
also Samuel Lubbell, *Revolt of the Moderates* (New York, 1956),
pp. 112–13, 275–76.
140. The analysis of future voting trends is from Edward C. Banfield,
"The Changing Political Environment of City Planning," paper
delivered at the American Political Science Convention, 1956.
140. The quotation "A sense of property rights . . ." is from the *New*

York Times, May 31, 1956. The citation from the *Chicago Daily News* is July 5 and 6, 1956.

THE THEORY OF TRANSPLANTATION

142. Samuel Lubell, *The Future of American Politics* (New York, 1952), Chapter 4, stresses the middle class drive for status. The same view with less emphasis is expressed in *The Revolt of the Moderates.* The quotation "I own a nice home . . ." is from p. 63.

142. The white collar analysis is detailed in Chapter VIII of Harris, *Is There a Republican Majority?*

143. Lubell's comments on suburban ghettos are from *The Future of American Politics,* Chapter 4.

144. The voting analyses are based on figures published in the *New York Times* immediately following the 1948, 1952, and 1956 elections, and from G. E. Janosik, "The New Suburbia," *Current History,* August, 1956.

144. The analysis of St. Louis suburban voting was made by Charles Edson in his senior thesis, "The Suburban Vote," at Harvard University, May, 1955.

145. The analysis of Bucks County, Pa., is reported by Janosik, "The New Suburbia," p. 93.

146. The Boston survey was undertaken as a graduate student project, and the analysis is still going on. The results reported here are taken principally from the investigations of David Bodner of the Harvard Graduate School of Public Administation. Findings of a more exhaustive study of two Boston suburbs, Wellesley and Natick, which involved the questioning of a sample of 225 newcomers, conducted by Professor Philip Sorotkin and Claire Zimmerman of Wellesley College, add confirmation to the straight statistical analysis so far as the thesis of transformation is concerned.

THE FRUITS OF ELECTORAL ANALYSIS

152. The lack of suburban interest and relative independence in party voting is stressed by Harris and Edson.

POLITICS AT THE LOCAL LEVEL: SYMBOLS AND BELIEFS

153. Suburban political proclivities toward respectability and civic duty are emphasized in Harris, *Is There a Republican Majority?* Chapter VIII and Henderson, "The Mass-Produced Surburb," *Harper's,* December, 1953.

154. The statistics compiled on nonpartisanship are from the International City Managers' Association, *Municipal Yearbook,* 1956.

Childs, *Civic Victories*, adds confirmatory evidence in Chapters XV and XXVI and also makes clear the close relationship between nonpartisanship and the city-manager form of government discussed in Chapter II. 84.6 per cent of all city-manager governments have nonpartisan elections according to Childs. The discussion of Washington, New York, and Connecticut experiences are based on the author's participation in the case of Washington and observations in connection with the New York Metropolitan Region Study.

155. For a statement of the ideology of nonpartisanship and the traditional nonpartisan view toward parties at all levels of government, see Childs, *Civic Victories*, Chapter VIII. Both Whyte, *The Organization Man*, and Henderson, "Mass-Produced Suburbs," provide illustrations of the suburban nonpartisan attitude toward party leaders and activities. Childs, *Civic Victories*, is especially suspicious of the local party in his discussion of "democratics" in the Introduction. His quote on p. 71 from *H.M.S. Pinafore* is also revealing: "I always voted at my party's call, and never thought of thinking for myself at all." Classical expressions are found of course in Washington's *Farewell Address*, Jefferson's *Inaugural*, and Lord Bryce's *The American Commonwealth*.

156. The quotation ". . . many suburbanites in the United States . . ." is from Janosik, "The New Suburbia," Current History, p. 92.

158. It should be made clear, particularly with respect to the New York suburbs, that Democratic and Republican activity exists at the local level and that local offices are regarded as important indices of party strength, as evidenced in the *New York Times* reports of the 1956 elections. The essential point, however, is that the local elections are considered "separable" from other campaigns, not simply in terms of issues and candidates, but in the ideological approach expected. A prime example comes from a Republican suburban leader in New Jersey, Richard D. Baker, who insists that local offices in his area be filled without the consideration of party affiliation which apply at the county and state level.

INSTITUTIONS FOR NONPARTISANSHIP

159. The literature, serious and popular, on the modern town meeting is fairly substantial. Good selections are found in Robert Morlan's *Capitol, Courthouse, and City Hall* (Boston, 1954). The written observations, in this instance, are buttressed by the author's experience in his own suburb, which has an unlimited town meeting.

160. For descriptions of arrangements encouraging direct participation outside of New England, Victor Jones, *Metropolitan Government*, offers several prime examples of this suburban pattern, p. 297 and

beyond. Alan K. Campbell and Wallace Sayre have supplied the author with specific examples in the New York suburban area.

THE MANAGEMENT OF ISSUES

162. So far as the direct contact between citizen and official is concerned, Edward C. Banfield and Morton Grodzins, in *Housing Policy and the Government of Metropolitan Areas,* a report prepared for ACTION, December, 1956, attach considerable importance to this condition of personal familiarity and seem to regard it as a generalized condition of suburban governments they have studied. Their theoretical evaluation of the benefits attained by this intimacy are considered more fully in Chapter VIII. The view that this intimacy rarely produces effective results is expressed by John W. Alexander and Monroe Berger, in Morlan, *Capitol, Courthouse, and City Hall,* pp. 207–12.

164. For a fuller discussion of the problem of corruption, see my article on "Ethics in Government as a Problem in Executive Management," *Public Administration Review,* Winter, 1955.

164. So far as the citizen's capacity to decide local fiscal matters is concerned, see Arthur C. Millspaugh's article in Morlan, *Capitol, Courthouse, and City Hall,* p. 12.

165. Charles M. Haar has provided a series of illuminating insights on the problems and complexities of suburban zoning and the difficulties in developing adequate means for equitable and effective application. See in particular, "Zoning for Minimum Standards: The Wayne Township Case," *Harvard Law Review,* April, 1953, and "In accordance with a Comprehensive Plan," *Harvard Law Review,* May, 1955. The fact that land law increasingly involves constitutional issues further suggests the difficulty of direct citizen action.

THE SUBURBAN BOSS

167. The function of the political leader in a large city is well treated in Wallace Sayre and Herbert Kaufman's forthcoming book, *The Government of New York City.* The same point has been made in more summary fashion in Joseph C. McLean, "Wedding Big-City Politics and Professional Management," *Public Administration Review,* Winter, 1954.

167. So far as suburban political leadership is concerned, published works, or even manuscript sources of suburban political organization are rare. Janosik, Henderson, Whyte, Lubbell, and Harris

discuss some aspects of the problem, and Charles Adrian, in *Governing Urban America* (New York, 1956), discusses the political leadership in an industrial suburb of Detroit. Richard F. Candell's *This Is Westchester* (Sterling, New York, 1954) gives a good account of the political history of Westchester County, New York, and the respective roles of William H. Robertson and William L. Ward, concluding that "there is scarcely a gaunt professional politician in Westchester today." Edward M. Abramson in "The Suburban Boss: A Typology of Suburban Political Leadership," Senior Thesis, Harvard University, March, 1957, presents additional information about the New York suburbs, particularly with respect to Nassau and Suffolk Counties. Otherwise, the material for this section was developed from interviews and observations in the Boston and New York areas and conversations with fellow political scientists in other areas. It may be inapplicable for some other regions of the country, and certainly, no inference should be drawn that suburban party organizations play no role in local affairs. The history of Westchester and Nassau Counties in New York illustrates the contrary, but it also demonstrates the special suburban tactics discussed here.

168. The quotation "traditional and flagrant types . . ." is from Janosik, "The New Suburbia," p. 96.

169. The description of rural political organization is elaborated on in Lancaster, *Government in Rural America,* p. 66.

170. One illustration of the suburban political leader who attains national recognition is, of course, Mr. Leonard Hall of Nassau County, New York, in his service as National Chairman of the Republican Party. Note, however, that Mr. Hall's previous service was as United States Congressman. It is also my impression that a sharp distinction exists in the Boston area between party and local activity even where local elections are conducted on a formal party basis.

172. Sayre and Kaufman, *Government of New York City,* stress the interrelation of party politics at state and local levels in urban centers as does V. O. Key in his chapter on Virginia in *Southern Politics* (New York, 1949) as far as rural areas are concerned.

172. The quotation "the independence of the voter is so fierce . . ." is from Janosik, "New Suburbia," p. 87.

SUBURBAN DECISION-MAKING

175. The quotation "A consolidation of electoral strength . . ." is from V. O. Key, *American State Politics,* p. 269.

176. For a general listing of published works on metropolitan politics, see the Continuing Conference on Metropolitan Government, *Bibliography*, 1956. Previous citations of Jones, Childs, Stewart, Adrian, and Whyte are also applicable. For a provocative construct for the analysis of community decision-making, suburban and otherwise, see James S. Coleman, *Community Conflict* (Glencoe, Ill., 1957).

178. The findings about Winchester, Mass., are reported in Charles Ball's, "Metropolitan Boston: A Critique of Pure Integration," Senior Thesis, Harvard University, 1956, Chapters I and III.

179. The findings about Brookline, Mass., are reported by Stanley Aronoff in "Rent Control in Brookline," Senior Thesis, Harvard University, 1954, and for Newton by Frank Mann, "Civil Defense in Newton: A Case Study in Administrative Frustration," Senior Thesis, Harvard University, 1955.

180. The Arlington, Va., Case is reported from personal observations extending over three years.

181. The quotation "Buried in the mud . . ." is from E. B. White, *Here Is New York* (New York, 1949), p. 19.

181. The quotation "men of middle age . . ." is from Ball, "Metropolitan Boston," Chapter III, pp. 66–74.

184. The discussion of the role of the suburban city managers is based on such books as Clarence Ridley and Orin Notting, *The City Manager Profession* (Chicago, 1934), Donald A. Stone, *City Manager Government in the U. S.* (Chicago, 1940). For a declaration of the new positive role of the city manager, see C. A. Harrell, "The City Manager as a Community Leader," *Public Management*, Vol. 30, 1948. For an effective criticism see Wallace Sayre, "The General Manager Idea for Large Cities," *Public Administration Review*, XV, 1955.

THE SPECIAL ISSUE OF THE PUBLIC SCHOOLS

186. The primary source of references for this section is the case studies compiled at the Harvard Graduate School of Education. Covering many sections of the country, and almost every aspect of educational politics, they have been invaluable references. The reports of the School's Center for Field Studies are also useful, as are the publications of the New York Metropolitan School Council, Columbia Teachers College. John C. Bollens, in *Special District Governments* (Berkeley and Los Angeles, 1957) Chapter VI, presents an able analysis of the structure of school district government and a particularly effective summary of pros and cons respect-

ing their separate identity. General references include the *National Education Association Journal,* The National Commission on School District Reorganization, *Your School District* (1948), The National Society for the Study of Education, *The Community School* (Chicago, 1953). The *New York Times Metropolitan Government Series,* January 27–February 3, 1957, also gives considerable attention to the problem.

187. A generalized summary of metropolitan school experience as well as an able argument of the educator's position is found in Walter Cocking, *The Regional Introduction of Education Practices in Urban School Systems of the United States,* 1951.

188. Alan K. Campbell, Chairman of the Department of Political Science at Hofstra College, has provided important information and guidance in detailing the experience in some suburbs of New York with respect to the influence of ethnic and religious factors.

189. Seeley, *Crestwood Heights,* and Whyte, *The Organization Man,* provide, of course, the most useful documentation of this philosophy in the suburbs they have examined, and make the schools the key institution of suburban life. John Keats in *Schools Without Scholars* (Boston, 1958) extends their findings. Donald Bestor, *Educational Wastelands* (Urbana, 1953) is another source.

189. The doctrine of the "unique function" of the schools is a universal one in U. S. education, by no means limited to suburbia. The resulting pattern of school government and politics is also general. But the special combination of quantitative and qualitative pressures is unique to suburbia — and therefore intensifies, in a special way, the general structure of school politics.

191. Professor Hunt's remarks were made in a seminar at the Graduate School of Public Administration, Harvard, April 14, 1957.

192. The problems of school doctrines are particularly emphasized in Seeley, *Crestwood Heights,* concluding chapter.

CHAPTER 6. *The Public Problems of Suburbia*

THE BURDENS OF THE WELFARE STATE

page
201. Statistics on governmental expenditures are taken from periodic reports of the Governments Division, U. S. Bureau of the Census and the American Assembly, *The Forty Eight States: Their Tasks as Policy Makers and Administrators* (New York, 1955), pp. 20–24. See also the Commission on Intergovernmental Relations, *A Report to the President,* 1955, Chapter IV, and William Anderson, *The Nation and the States, Rivals or Partners?* (Minneapolis,

1955), Chapter 11. Standard texts on state and local governments also provide similar descriptions of the current financial characteristics of local government.

202. The analysis of the expansion of urban functions refers to Detroit and is taken from Lent D. Lipson, *The Growth of a City Government,* Detroit Bureau of Government Research, 1942.

203. Walter Isard and P. E. Coughlin in *Municipal Costs and Revenues Resulting from Community Growth* (Boston, 1957) describe in some detail how local service standards can be developed and at times quantified. A good general discussion of the present expenditure pattern is found in Adrian, *Governing Urban America,* pp. 300–304. The increase in pensions for municipal employees is an important factor in the increases in local government expenditures generally. See also Solomon Fabricant, *The Trend of Governmental Activity in the United States Since 1900* (New York, 1952).

203. The figures on federal and state grants to local governments are cited from the American Assembly, *The Forty Eight States,* p. 20.

204. Suburban financial problems are emphasized in the *New York Times,* "Special Survey of Metropolitan Areas," January 27 to February 3, 1957, which gives several examples across the country. For the New York area, see the series "Where Is Bergen County Going?" by William E. Oriol, *Bergen Evening Record,* August 12–17, 1957. See also Thomas H. Reed, "Hope for 'Suburbanites,'" *The National Municipal Review,* December, 1950. The plight of some suburban governments was also described by H. Burton in his series, "Trouble in the Suburbs," *Saturday Evening Post,* September 17, 24, and October 1, 1955.

205. The proportion of local expenditures devoted to public safety, sewage disposal, water supply and streets is estimated by Adrian, *Governing Urban America,* p. 308.

205. The per capita figure of $67.59 is provided by Harold F. Alderfer, *American Local Government and Administration* (New York, 1956), p. 374.

THE SUPPLY OF RESOURCES

207. The figures on the degree of local government reliance on the property tax are taken from Roger A. Freeman, "What Ails the Property Tax," *National Municipal Review,* November, 1955, p. 508. For a good general summary of the deficiencies of the property tax see one presented in the New Jersey Commission on State Tax Policy's *The General Property Tax in New Jersey,* 1953.

208. The quotation "The nine billion dollars . . . " is from the Commission on Intergovernmental Relations, *A Report to the President*, p. 103.

209. Statistics on local nonproperty taxes are provided by Adelford, *American Local Government and Administration*, p. 382.

210. The analysis of comparative residential values between cities and suburbs is reported by George A. Duggar, "The Tax System and a Responsible Housing Program," unpublished Ph.D. Dissertation, Harvard University, 1956, Chapter II. I have relied heavily on this work in the discussion of the impact of the property tax on the suburb. A summary of Duggar's major thesis is found in his paper "A Framework for the Analysis of Urban Redevelopment Policy: Some Financial Factors in Local Programs and Some Implications," published in *The Papers and Proceedings of the Regional Science Association*, Vol. II, 1956.

211. The quotation "industries tend to locate . . ." is from the Tax Institute, *Financing Metropolitan Government*, p. 74.

211. The conclusion that poorer suburbs rely increasingly on a residential property base is emphasized by Duggar, "Analysis of Urban Redevelopment Policy," p. 217 (page citations are from published article).

212. For a further consideration of how economic and population trends may affect suburban resources see the author's "The New Metropolis: Grassroots, Greenbelts, or Gargantua," *American Political Science Review*, March, 1958.

THE SCRAMBLE FOR VALUES

213. Duggar's ratio concept of financial efficiency is a convenient analytical tool for handling the interplay between public resources and needs in a local government. A high ratio between tax revenue and service benefits expresses a favorable financial position; a low ratio a poor one. From a municipality's point of view, land use devoted largely to higher-value property increases the difference between revenue returns and service costs on a per unit or square foot basis, while a concentration of lower-value property reduces the differences so that costs calculated over the life of the property can actually exceed revenues received from the property. From the property owner's point of view, in both the extreme cases of high- and low-value property, tax burdens exceed benefits received from public services. For high-value property, however, this difference is offset by indirect benefits, which add to property value — in particular, by increments to site value that

accrue because there *are* services provided and increments which are derived from a location near other high-value property. For low-value property, the difference is not offset, because the site value is usually a much lower proportion of the total value of the property in comparison with the value of the house. Thus, the loss in value represented by taxes is (1) not compensated by an equal addition to value represented by the benefits, and (2) not compensated sufficiently by indirect values accruing to the site or by reason of neighborhood location. Without these additional compensations, the value of inexpensive homes therefore tends to fall (depending on how inexpensive and how high the taxes are), and the value of expensive homes (again depending on the exact cost and location) tends to rise, even though in each situation, tax revenues per unit exceed benefits received through services.

215. The quotation "a sort of mercantilist interplay . . ." is from Henry Fagin, "Financing Municipal Services in a Metropolitan Region," *Journal of the American Institute of Planners,* Fall, 1953.

216. Duggar, "Analysis of Urban Redevelopment Policy," p. 221, emphasizes the obstacles the property tax system places in the way of the development of an effective national housing program.

217. The quotation "the very cities that can . . ." is from Fagin, *Financing Municipal Services,* p. 217.

STRATEGY OF THE ANOINTED

218. In his article, "Analysis of Urban Redevelopment Policy," p. 223, Duggar lists the tactics suburbs employ to maintain property values. He examines them in considerable detail in his dissertation. E. C. Banfield and Morton Grodzins, "Housing Policy and the Government of Metropolitan Areas," also provides excellent examples of many of these practices, as does Fagin, *Financing Municipal Services.* The practices of the New Jersey suburbs are detailed by Fagin, *Municipal Services,* pp. 215–18.

219. The analysis of Wayne Township is found in Charles H. Haar, "Zoning for Minimum Standards: The Wayne Township Case," *Harvard Law Review,* April, 1953, pp. 1051–63. The references to other metropolitan areas are contained in Duggar, in Chapter IV of his dissertation. Duggar also emphasizes the effects of building regulations on low-cost housing development.

220. The quotation "three decisive services . . ." is from State and Local Government Institute, University of Pennsylvania, *Report to the Board of Supervisors,* Middletown Township, p 18. For general discussion see Austin F. MacDonald, *American City*

Government and Administration (6th ed., 1956), Chapter 20, and Adelford, *American Local Government and Administration*, p. 374 and following.

STRATEGY OF THE UNWASHED: (1) UP BY THE BOOTSTRAPS

221. The comparison between city and suburban per capita public costs is from Duggar, Chapter VI of the dissertation. The simple impossibility of some rapidly growing suburbs to provide public services on the basis of present valuations is stressed by Henderson, "Mass Produced Suburbs," p. 84.

222. The quotation "It is an interesting fact . . ." is from John Scott, "Are Suburbs Parasites?" *Public Management*, May, 1954. The amateur quality of many suburban governments is also described by Adrian, *Governing Urban America*, pp. 41–47.

223. The fact that many suburban school systems have serious deficiencies is reported by the *New York Times*, "Special Survey of Metropolitan Areas." There has been, of course, a considerable trend toward the consolidation of independent school districts in the United States. The trend is most pronounced in rural areas, however, and even where consolidation takes place in the suburbs, it is almost always limited in scope. See John C. Bollens, *Special District Governments*.

224. For an analysis of the continued reliance of local government on the property tax, see Adelford, *American Local Government and Administration*, p. 407. For a breakdown of the differences in the use of the tax among types of local government, see the American Assembly, *The Forty-Eight States*, p. 22. On the question of comparative inequalities between property and non-property taxes, Duggar, in Chapter II of his dissertation, has an extensive analysis.

STRATEGY OF THE UNWASHED: (2) THE NEW "NEW FEDERALISM"

225. The literature on federalism is sizable. Several of the important works include: Jane Perry Clark, *The Rise of the New Federalism* (New York, 1941); William Anderson, *The States and the Nation*, and *Reports of the Commission on Intergovernmental Relations* previously cited; *Federalism: Mature and Emergent*, Arthur MacMahon, ed. (New York, 1955); R. R. Bowie and C. J. Friedrich, *Studies in Federalism* (Boston, 1954), and Leonard White, *The States and the Nation* (Baton Rouge, 1953).

226. The figures on grants are from the American Assembly, *The Forty-Eight States*, p. 22.

226. The quotation "governments that spend money . . ." is from V. O. Key, *American State Politics,* p. 8.

227. The government functions now supported by grants are effectively summarized by Anderson, *Nation and the States,* Chapter 11.

228. With regard to the future of the grant program, it is instructive to consider the history of the Commission on Intergovernmental Relations itself. Established with a clear mandate to return money and functions to the states, its final report is a model defense of the present system. Note also the valiant, but ineffective, efforts of the National Conference on Federal-State Relations of the U. S. Chamber of Commerce, 1953, to reverse the trends toward larger grant programs.

229. The analysis of the economic effects of the grant program is based on James A. Maxwell, *The Fiscal Impact of Federalism* (Cambridge, 1946), concluding chapter. See also A. H. Birch, *Federalism, Finance and Social Legislation* (London, 1955), Chapter II, and Alvin H. Hansen and Harvey S. Perloff, *State and Local Finance in the National Economy* (New York, 1944).

230. The figures on state grant allocations by types of local governments are from the American Assembly, *The Forty-Eight States,* pp. 35–36.

230. With respect to educational grants, the establishment of the minimum foundation programs for school assistance in many states has been significant in post-World War II years. The publications of the Metropolitan School Council of Columbia Teachers College, provide good summaries of these formulas.

231. The quotation "in the eyes of state officials . . ." is from the American Assembly, *The Forty-Eight States,* p. 36.

232. As to the financial losses incurred on a per pupil basis by school districts after consolidation, see the calculations of the Florida Minimum Foundation Program for schools, according to size and enrollment of school districts, in Florida Legislative Reference Bureau, *Financing Florida's Education* (Tallahassee, 1950).

THE SEPARATION OF PURSE AND POWER

232. The quotation "left hollow shells . . ." is from Leonard White, *The States and the Nation,* p. 4.

233. The quotations as to the dangers of federal encroachment are from the *Proceedings of the National Conference on Federal-State Relations* and the 41st Annual Meeting of the U. S. Chamber of Commerce, 1953. See in particular the address of Senator Everett M. Dirksen, "Big Government — Road to Tyranny," April 29, 1953.

233. The reference to the intent of the Constitutional Convention and

subsequent court decisions is based on the analyses of Anderson, *Nation and the States,* Part I.

234. The defense of cooperative federalism on the grounds of its necessity in the modern world is well represented in Professor MacMahon's Introduction in *Federalism: Mature and Emergent.*

234. The essentials of the argument that localities continue to exercise substantial prerogatives are given in V. O. Key, *An Introduction to State Politics,* p. 7.

234. The quotation "have underwritten the continuance . . ." is from Rowland Eggers, "Nature Over Art: No More Local Finance," *American Political Science Review,* June, 1953, p. 463.

235. In considering the nature of federal supervision it should be remembered that the broad purposes of grant programs, especially in welfare, are, of course, set forth in federal legislation, and minimum service standards are nationally established. But except for occasional flurries in the welfare program on issues such as the secrecy of recipient rolls, it is difficult to establish a case of ideological conflict among the nation, the states, and localities. A real issue may exist between the grant-in-aid device and insurance principle in welfare legislation, as illustrated by proposals for compulsory health insurance, but in highways, education, and public health, fundamental objectives are rarely in debate.

236. A good example of local initiative and power is in the disaster assistance program authorized by Public Law 875. Here, federal standards of eligibility are vague, state and local prerogatives broad, and the entire history of the program can be read as one in which the federal government has been a reluctant partner in an activity initiated by local action. See, for example, the hearings before the Special Subcommittee on Rehabilitation of Flood Stricken Areas, 1952. An even more prominent illustration is the Rivers and Harbors work of the Corps of Engineers. A contemporary discussion of local influence here is Arthur A. Maass, *Muddy Waters* (Cambridge, 1951). V. O. Key's *The Administration of Federal Grants to States* (Chicago, 1937) is a thorough study of the grant programs in the 1930's, and a confirmation of the sensitivity of federal administrators to local interests. See also "The Battle of Blue Earth County" and "The National Cement Issue" in *Public Administration and Policy Development: A Case Book,* Harold Stein, ed. (New York, 1952), as representative examples, and John Gaus, *Reflections on Public Administration* (University of Alabama, 1946). Gaus describes in a comprehensive and persuasive manner how local autonomy continues in the environment of modern administration.

238. The sensitivity of Congressmen to the opinions of their local con-

stituencies is emphasized in almost every study of the Congress. A particularly good summary is found in Ernest S. Griffith, *Congress: Its Contemporary Role* (New York, 1951). The political orientation of governors toward the metropolitan area is discussed in some detail in the last chapter of "The Metropolitan Governor," the author's Ph.D. Dissertation.

239. David B. Truman provides an excellent analysis of the influence of federalism on the party structure in "Federalism and the Party System," *Federalism: Mature and Emergent*, pp. 115–136.

240. The quotation "are now more likely to be . . ." is from Rowland Eggers, "Nature over Art," p. 460.

SECURING THE SUBURBAN HABITAT

243. Luther Gulick, *Metro* (New York, 1957) pp. 18–19, stresses the present deficiencies in urban transportation. For a more extensive treatment see Wilfred Owen, *The Metropolitan Transportation Problem* (New York, 1956).

244. The discussion of the water problem in metropolitan areas is based generally on the President's Water Resources Policy Commission, *A Water Policy for the American People* (Washington, 1950), Chapters 12 and 13. The statistics referred to are from pp. 176–77 and 186.

245. Owen, *Metropolitan Transportation,* Chapter I, makes clear the essentiality of effective metropolitan transportation. For an indication of the contemporary importance attached to this problem, see the Arden House Conference on Metropolitan Area Problems *Report,* 1957.

246. The comparisons between times required to travel across Manhattan Island were supplied by the Regional Plan Association of New York.

247. The inadequacy of the present Federal Aid Program was reported in the Arden House Conference *Report.*

248. The statistics on the number of contractual arrangements between city and suburbs for the sale of water are from Adrian, *Governing Urban America.*

248. The quotation "In America we have deep-seated objections . . ." is from the *Milwaukee Journal,* December 16, 1956.

249. The figures on metropolitan Boston's water consumption are from the Metropolitan District Commission *Report,* 1956. The New Jersey waterworks pattern is described in the President's Water Resources Policy Commission, *Water Policy,* p. 178.

250. Bollen's views on the potentialities of the Authority's develop-

ment into a metropolitan government are found in his *The States and the Metropolitan Problem,* p. 91.

251. The summary of the activities of the New York Port Authority is taken from the Authority's *Annual Report,* 1957.

253. The quotation "the agitation for further integration continues . . ." is from Charles R. Cherington, "The Metropolitan District Commission," paper delivered before the Institute of State and Local Government, University of Pennsylvania, 1956.

CHAPTER 7. *The Miniature Re-examined*

DEFENDERS OF THE FAITH

page

259. The quotation "the Grassroots concept . . ." is from Roscoe Martin, *Grassroots Government* (University of Alabama, 1957), p. 5. Martin is particularly concerned with examining the democratic nature and effectiveness of rural government in the United States. But his searching criticism can be applied to all small government. His arguments and those in this chapter are to be contrasted to the defense of big government on the grounds of necessity. This "feasibility" argument has received substantial emphasis in the last generation. Arthur Schlesinger, Jr., chronicles its pre-New Deal origins in *The Crisis of the Old Order* (Boston, 1956). William Anderson, *Nation and the States,* presents the case with specific reference to state and local governments.

261. Plato's explicit statements concerning the small community are found in his *Laws,* 738d, 6-e, 8. The quotation "to the fulfillment of its work . . ." and following are from Aristotle, *Politics,* Book VII (IV), Chapter 4. In the discussion of the views of other political theorists, a classic analysis and defense of the small community and its government is found in Robert McIlwain's *The Growth of Political Thought in the West from the Greeks to the End of the Middle Ages* (New York, 1932), Chapter 1.

262. The quotation "We begin our public affections . . ." is from Edmund Burke, *Reflections on the French Revolution,* Everyman's Edition, ed. by Ernest Rhys (New York, 1943), p. 193.

263. The quotation "nothing less can be ultimately desirable . . ." is from John Stuart Mill, *Representative Government,* Everyman's Library, 1948, p. 217.

263. The quotation "tiny fountain-heads of democracy . . ." is from James Bryce, *Modern Democracies* (New York, 1921), Vol. I, p. 131.

263. The quotation "democracy must begin at home . . ." is from

John Dewey, *The Public and Its Problems* (New York, 1927), p. 215.

264. The quotation "the herd is regaining . . ." is from Learned Hand, *Memorial Address on Justice Brandeis before the Supreme Court,* 317 U. S. Reports.

264. The quotation "sense of personal competence . . ." is from Elkins and McKitrick, "A Meaning for Turner's Frontier," p. 325.

264. The quotation "people take what they can use . . ." is from Granville Hicks, *Small Town* (New York, 1946), p. 117.

264. For a general argument regarding the need for small communities in the modern world, see C. J. Friedrich, *Constitutional Government and Democracy* (Boston, 1950), Chapter XIII.

265. The quotation "held together *not* by the knowledge . . ." is from Louis Hartz, *The Liberal Tradition in America* (New York, 1955), p. 53.

THE LOGIC OF THE FAITH

266. Lane Lancaster, *Government in Rural America,* speaks movingly of the general benefits to be expected from small town life; see especially pp. 374–79. Selections from *Capitol, Courthouse and City Hall,* Robert L. Morlan, ed., 1954, presents similar recitals.

271. The quotation "the fruits of civilization . . ." is from Arthur E. Morgan, *The Small Community,* p. 16.

PROBING THE LINES

273. The quotation "the man who is as good . . ." is from Hartz, *Liberal Tradition,* p. 53.

273. For a systematic analysis of the Jacksonian concept of democracy, see Robert A. Dahl, *A Preface to Democratic Theory* (Chicago, 1956), Chapter 2.

273. The quotations "you have to go on living . . ." and "the test of a man's ability . . ." are from Sherwood Anderson, "Home Town," *The Sherwood Anderson Reader,* Paul Rosenfeld, ed. (Boston, 1947).

274. Contemporary examples of the anecdotal character of local government are found in L. H. Robbins, "Democracy, Town Meeting Style," *New York Times Magazine,* March 23, 1947, and George L. Seese, "Local Democracy Gets a Workout," *American City,* April, 1949.

275. The quotation "institutionalizes the neighborliness . . ." is from R. A. Woods, *The Neighborhood in Nation Building* (New York, 1923), p. 71.

276. The quotation "It is a case of love . . ." is from Anderson, *Reader*.

CHECKLIST OF OPERATIVE DEMOCRACY: (1) THE RULE
OF LAW

276. The "atomistic" assumptions of the American tradition are detailed in Hartz, *Liberal Tradition*, Chapter I.
277. For a systematic analysis of constitutionalism, see Friedrich, *Constitutional Government*, Chapter I.
278. The quotation "Not only does the teacher . . ." is from Lancaster, *Government in Rural America*, p. 295.
279. The quotation "every predatory pioneer instinct . . ." is from Hicks, *Small Town*, p. 132.
280. The quotation "in general, the American functionaries . . ." is from Tocqueville, *Democracy in America*, p. 266.

CHECKLIST OF OPERATIVE DEMOCRACY: (2) THE ROLE
OF CONTROVERSY

282. The quotation "one in which . . ." is from Dahl, *A Preface*, p. 145. The Madison quotation is from the *Federalist Papers*, No. 10.
284. Friedrich's views concerning direct participation are summarized in his *Constitutional Government*, p. 570.
284. The quotation "but expect to suffer . . ." is from Dahl, *A Preface*, p. 145.
285. The quotation "New England querulousness . . ." is from Lancaster, *Government in Rural America*, p. 7.

CHECKLIST OF OPERATIVE DEMOCRACY: (3) THE QUEST
FOR FREEDOM

285. The quotation "the local is the ultimate universal . . ." is from Dewey, *Public and Its Problems*, pp. 212–13.
286. The quotation "Energy, self reliance and independence . . ." is from Tocqueville, p. 336.
287. The quotation "the country village is made up . . ." is from R. A. Woods, *Neighborhood in Nation Building*, p. 73.
287. The quotation "spheres of free choice . . ." and following are from E. C. Banfield and Morton Grodzins, *Housing Policy and the Government of Metropolitan Areas*, Report for ACTION, 1956, I–15. The quotation "for the effective management . . ." is from II–28–30.

OTHER ROADS

291. So far as the greenbelts alternative is concerned, Keats' call for planned suburbia and Riesman's somewhat wistful plea for "prophets and planners" have much in common with this alternative. So does much of the philosophy of modern planning, though the profession has grown far more sophisticated in handling its political values lately. Planning and democratic government in the liberal tradition are certainly not incompatible, but as Friedrich, *Constitutional Government,* Chapter XXIII, has pointed out, the problem is far more complex than most planners suppose.

294. The quotation "sporadic outbursts of popular . . ." and following is from Lancaster, *Government in Rural America,* p. 5.

296. The quotation "New York blends the gift . . ." and following is from E. B. White, *Here Is New York,* pp. 13, 15, and 43.

PROBABILITY AND POTENTIALITY

299. The investigations of metropolitan leadership now being carried out in a number of areas today by the Government in Metropolitan Areas Project of the Edgar B. Stern Family Fund, Luther Gulick, Director, under the immediate supervision of Norton E. Long will provide much more information on the present status of metropolitan politics. The judgments made here, however, appear in line with Long's interim findings.

Index